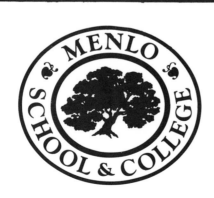

The Musée d'Orsay, Paris

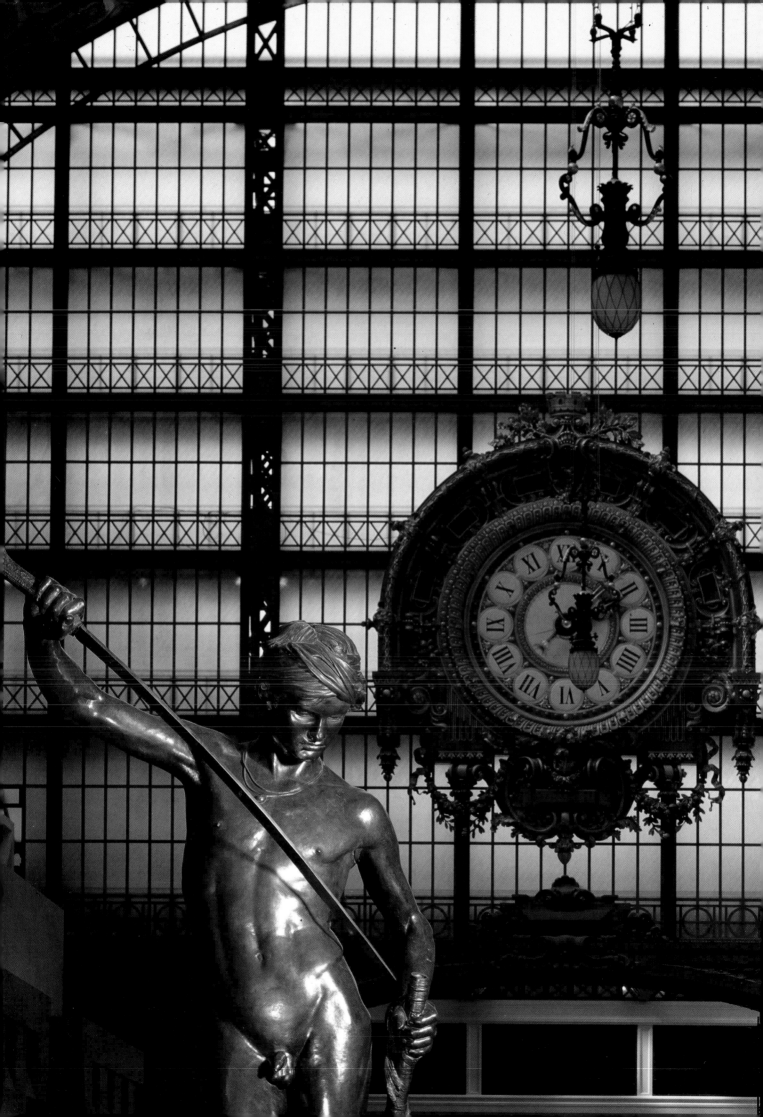

The Musée d'Orsay, Paris

Introduction by Michel Laclotte

Harry N. Abrams, Inc., Publishers, New York

Translated from the French by Jane Brenton

*Frontispiece: Mercié's David (ill. 15),
with the former station clock in the background*

Library of Congress Cataloging-in-Publication Data

Musée d'Orsay.
   The Musée d'Orsay, Paris.

   Translation of: Le Musée d'Orsay.
   1. Art, French—Catalogs.   2. Art, Modern—19th
century—France—Catalogs.   3. Art, Modern—20th century
—France—Catalogs.   4. Art—France—Paris—Catalogs.
5. Musée d'Orsay—Catalogs.   I. Laclotte, Michel.
II. Title.
N6847.M7913   1987   709′.44′07404361   87–1196
ISBN 0–8109–1446–8

Contents

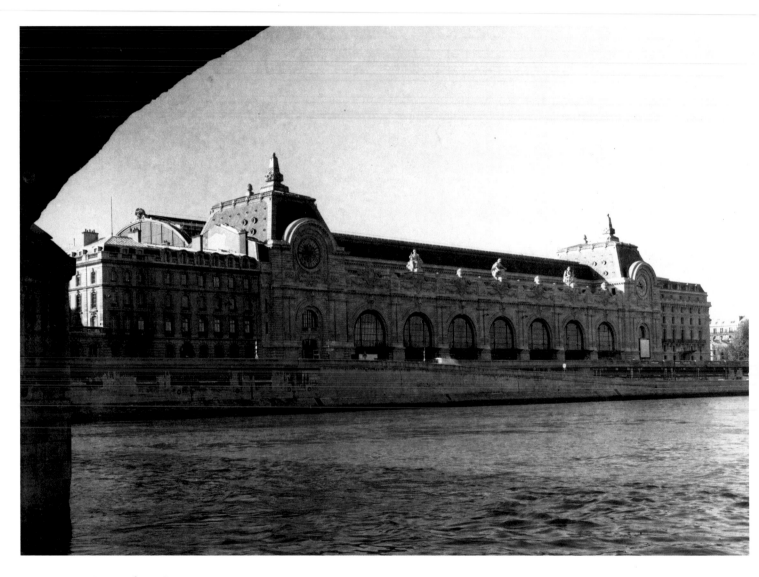

*The Musée d'Orsay from the
right bank of the Seine*

Introduction

Paris has acquired a new museum, the Musée d'Orsay, just across the river from the Louvre.

Inevitably the question will be asked, what possible need is there for another museum in a city already so richly endowed? What will it offer to the public that cannot be seen elsewhere? What will be different about it? How will its displays be presented? In attempting to answer these questions I shall touch briefly on the events that led up to the decision to found a new cultural centre, and explain the general purpose it is intended to serve, before moving on to a conducted tour of the museum galleries.

To anyone who has visited the Jeu de Paume in recent years it must be obvious that the building was far too small. Situated in the Tuileries gardens, with a beautifully light and open aspect, it was the ideal home for the Louvre's collections of Impressionist painting when it first opened in 1947. Thirty years later this was demonstrably no longer the case. The building could not do justice to a collection swollen by numerous bequests and acquisitions. Nor, given the universal appeal of Impressionism, could it safely accommodate the visitors who arrived each year in increasing numbers. It was clear that more space was urgently needed, the more so as the collection received a massive injection of new works in 1977 as a direct consequence of the transfer of the Musée National d'Art Moderne from the Palais de Tokyo to its new home in the Pompidou Centre. All the Post-Impressionist paintings belonging to the Musée National d'Art Moderne (the Pont-Aven School and the Neo-Impressionists), together with numerous late nineteenth-century works by French and foreign artists (largely Naturalist and Symbolist in character, and inherited for the most part from the former Musée du Luxembourg) at that time reverted effectively to the Louvre. This was in no way exceptional, since it had always been the practice, at periodic intervals, to remove paintings, sculptures and drawings that could no longer be regarded as representative of 'modern' art from the Luxembourg to the Louvre. Thus it was always envisaged that the Post-Impressionist works temporarily displayed at the Palais de Tokyo from 1978 onwards would one day be reunited with the Impressionists: it was obviously desirable for Signac and Cross to be seen with Seurat, and Bernard and Sérusier with their close associate, Gauguin.

One possible solution might have been to extend the Jeu de Paume itself. But that would still not have provided the necessary space, and especially not in the light of recent interpretative developments. In one of those radical shifts in perspective that from time to time breathe new life into the history of art and aesthetics, a 'new' nineteenth century has begun to emerge, one that is far less of an orderly linear progression than the doctrinaire critics of the past had contemplated. First came the memorable exhibition 'Sources du XXe siècle' (Paris, 1960), which established Art Nouveau fairly and squarely as one of the major movements that have enriched and altered the course of twentieth-century Western art. Then, in the ensuing years, there have been reappraisals of Symbolism in its various manifestations, of industrial and 'Beaux-Arts' architecture, of Second Empire eclecticism, of photography and even of 'academic' sculpture, for so long utterly dismissed and derided. In addition, certain schools of European and American painting, hitherto somewhat eclipsed in France by the brilliance of Paris, have now, happily, come to be viewed in a more impartial light.

Of course it would be foolish to deny that, in some respects, this new interpretation is still open to debate: there is a certain cultural snobbery and speculative self-interest attached to espousing the latest fashionable ideas, and we cannot be certain that all these newly regarded artists are in fact neglected geniuses. Nevertheless, over the last twenty years a persuasive case has been made, in a series of stimulating books, articles and exhibitions, for a radical reappraisal of nineteenth-century art history, and there is no possible way in which an enlarged Jeu de Paume could have given expression to that broader perspective.

The primary need was for space – and a lot of it. That space was found in the Gare d'Orsay, a vast and virtually disused railway station right in the heart of Paris, in the immediate vicinity of the Louvre and the Tuileries.

The idea of establishing a museum of late nineteenth-century art in the Gare d'Orsay building dates back to 1973, when a proposal put forward by the Direction des Musées de France was approved in principle by the government of President Georges Pompidou. The station was already threatened with demolition to make way for the construction of a vast hotel, and railway traffic had been reduced to a few suburban services. The immediate effect of the decision was that the building itself was rescued. Long regarded as a *fin-de-siècle* monstrosity, it profited from the revival of interest in the nineteenth century, an aesthetic about-turn that unfortunately came too late to save Louis-Pierre Baltard's central market buildings, Les Halles,

demolished in 1973. The Orsay plan was approved and set in motion by President Valéry Giscard d'Estaing, and a civil commission was formed in 1978 to supervise the scheme, to which his successor François Mitterrand pledged his full support in 1981. Thus the long and necessarily difficult enterprise of setting up a new museum was made possible by the active championship of three French presidents.

If the museum breaks new ground in terms of its contents – its intended scope, the collections themselves – so it does in terms of its context, the adaptation of an existing building (the station and its adjacent hotel) to a new function as a multi-disciplinary museum.

First, a few words about the contents. As a national museum, the Musée d'Orsay is the repository of the state collections of the art of the second half of the nineteenth century and the early years of the twentieth. It therefore stands between the Louvre, the home of the national collections for the years preceding 1850, and the Musée National d'Art Moderne, which has charge of works dating from after 1905–10 (those, with a few exceptions, of artists born after 1870).

It is perhaps worth mentioning at this point that the dates chosen – 1848–50 on the one hand, and 1905–10 on the other – were arrived at only after careful consideration and debate. Various other possibilities were discussed for the starting date: any earlier, moving back into the Romantic period, would have required a much bigger museum altogether; any later, say 1863–65, and the date would have had little meaning except in the narrow context of French painting. It was finally decided that the mid-point of the century most accurately corresponded to changes taking place over the whole spectrum of activity, and not only in the political or social sphere. The emergence of Courbet and Millet at the Salons of 1848 and 1850, the foundation of the Pre-Raphaelite Brotherhood in 1848, the erection of Joseph Paxton's Crystal Palace (1850–51) and of the new Louvre (started in 1852), were all in their different ways indications of a change in sensibility – as, at the other end of the scale, was the radical break marked by Picasso's *Les Demoiselles d'Avignon* of 1907.

Dealing with a period that is particularly rich and prolific, the museum aims to reflect that diversity by looking beyond painting, sculpture and the decorative and graphic arts (drawing, print-making and photography) to give an account of developments in the other visual arts: architecture, town-planning and film – a turn-of-the-century invention – as well as other processes for the dissemination of images: posters, the press, book illustrations. In addition, a number of small 'dossier' exhibitions on individual themes, as well as films and audio-visual displays, will bring out the relationships between the visual arts and other contemporary forms of artistic expression (such as literature and music, represented at the museum by a programme of concerts), and serve to situate developments across the spectrum in a historical context.

Adopting a multi-disciplinary approach, unlike the Louvre or the permanent installations of the Musée National d'Art Moderne, the museum faced certain problems from the outset. If such an ambitious scheme was to be translated into practice, if all the spheres of artistic activity and all the various techniques were to be properly represented, then clearly the existing resources of the national collections (the paintings, sculptures and rare *objets d'art* in the Louvre, the Jeu de Paume and the Palais de Tokyo) would not suffice. It was necessary to enlist the cooperation of other museums and organizations (Versailles, Fontainebleau, Compiègne; the Musée des Arts Décoratifs; the state furniture collection (Mobilier National); the Sèvres porcelain factory), which agreed to contribute a number of major items. Where possible, state-owned paintings and sculptures were recalled from provincial museums and other works were offered in exchange. Above all, herculean efforts were made to increase existing stocks. The Musée d'Orsay is indebted in this respect to its many benefactors, among them the newly formed Society of Friends of the Museum; it has also been the beneficiary of a number of major bequests, offset against payment of death duties; and it has itself pursued an active purchasing policy, with the aid of special grants. For the most part the need was to remedy the more glaring omissions in the existing collections, while that was still possible, but in some areas it was necessary to start from scratch, notably with *objets d'art*, furniture, architecture and photography. In respect of prints and engravings, however, it was decided not to establish new collections, but to represent the various print-making techniques (including poster art and book illustration) by borrowing on a regular basis from the Bibliothèque Nationale, the principal repository of the national collections in these branches of the graphic arts. Drawings (apart from pastels and architectural drawings housed in the Musée d'Orsay) would similarly remain in the nearby Cabinet des Dessins in the

Louvre, readily available for display in a changing series of exhibitions.

Can we therefore claim that the museum offers a comprehensive panorama of art in the second half of the nineteenth century? Indeed not. Many major artists will be missing, especially foreigners. There are entire movements, schools and techniques that are unrepresented, or dealt with inadequately. But, within those limitations, we have endeavoured to take into account the sheer versatility of creative expression within the period and to show how the different strands of activity are interwoven. We have not attempted to create an artificially balanced view. The accidents of the art market, the preferences of a particular collector or the generosity of a painter's descendants will sometimes have caused one artist to figure more prominently than another of equal importance. That is no bad thing. A museum should not be like an encyclopaedia that gives a strictly objective and impersonal account: it must inevitably reflect the tastes, the choices – and also the blind spots and oversights – of the collectors, connoisseurs and curators who over the years have built up the collections.

There will be plenty of time in the future for discussion of the image of the nineteenth century presented by the Musée d'Orsay, and for that image to be expanded and refined.

Let us now pass on to the building that provides the context for the exhibitions, the Gare d'Orsay and the adjoining Hôtel d'Orsay, designed by Victor Laloux and built on the site of the former Cour des Comptes, destroyed by fire in 1871. The whole structure was put up in under two years, and was opened on 14 July 1900 as part of the World Fair celebrations. It was a

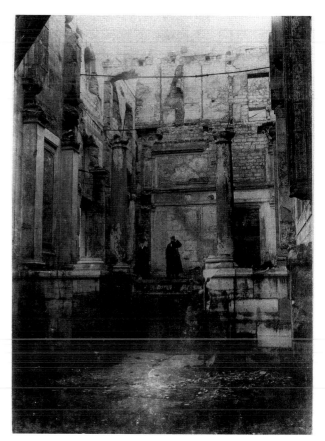

The ruins of the former Cour des Comptes (Palais d'Orsay), burnt down in 1871

supremely functional design, with the trains running on the lower level, while all the peripheral activities associated with ticket offices, waiting-rooms and left-luggage offices, etc., were grouped together on the upper level, beneath the monumental vaulted roof. The station was enclosed on two sides by the four

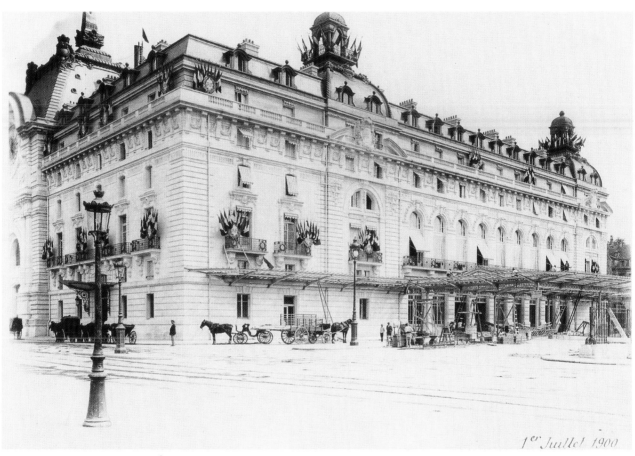

The Gare d'Orsay shortly before its opening in 1900

hundred bedrooms and reception rooms of a luxury hotel, its stone façades concealing the metal structures within and vying in grandeur with the great palaces that line the Seine.

There was much to be done to adapt this dinosaur of the railway age to its new function: within its volume, spaces had to be created that were capable of housing permanent displays and temporary exhibitions, as well as entrance halls, storerooms, workshops and rooms for the various services; the best possible lighting conditions had to be ensured for the different categories of exhibits, and an efficient system of access devised for visitors; at the same time the identity

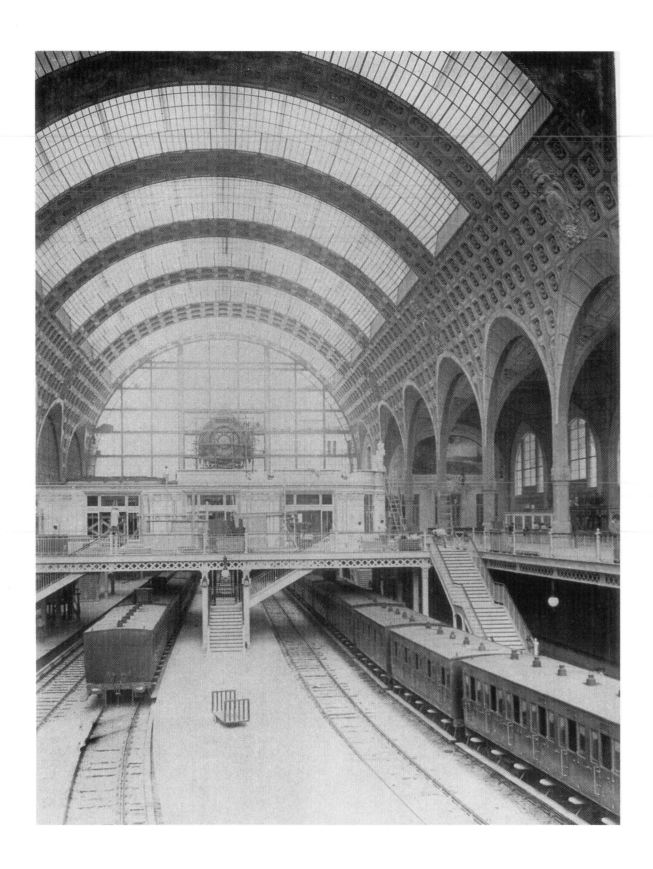

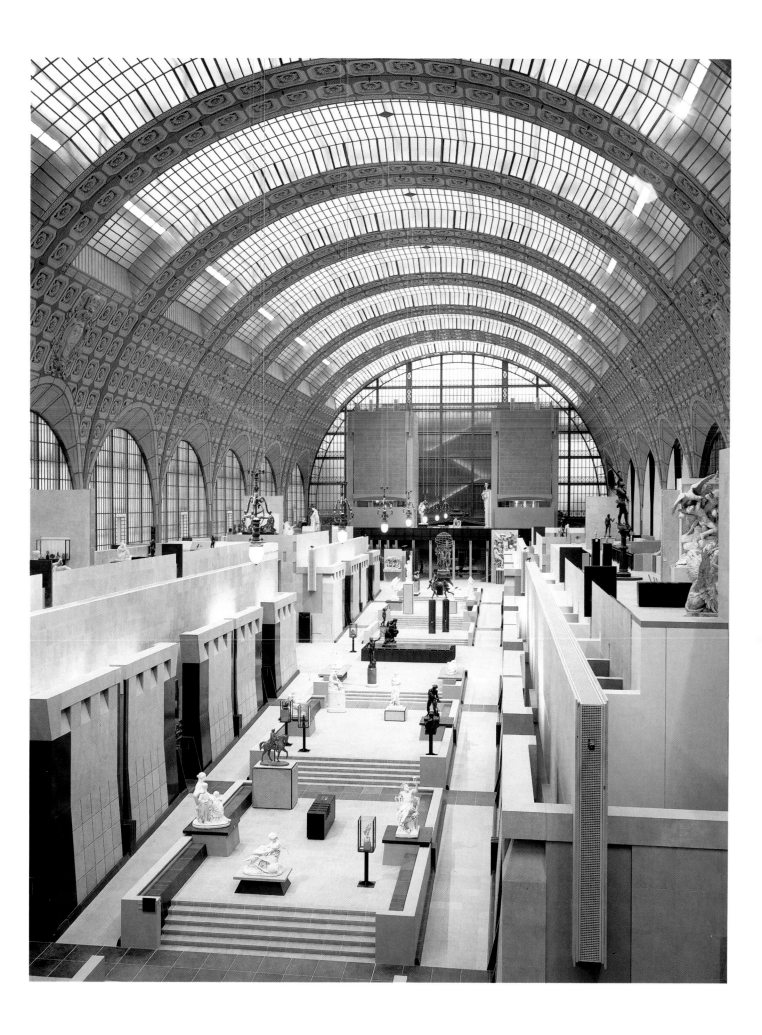

of Laloux's original building needed to be preserved. This was the challenge that confronted the architects who entered the competition held in 1979.

The winning design was submitted by ACT (R. Bardon, P. Colboc, J. P. Philippon), who were joined in 1980 by the Italian architect Gae Aulenti, winner of a second competition for the interior design and museum layout. The solution they have provided is bold and imaginative. The vaulted roof space of the 'Nave' is kept open and undisturbed; within it is a new structure consisting of a central avenue (following the alignment of the old railway lines) on either side of which are ranged exhibition rooms surmounted by terraces. These rooms and terraces communicate on two levels with rooms in the entrance hall suite, adjacent to the Nave and looking out over the Seine. In the roof space, at the top of the station and hotel, are a series of airy galleries with natural overhead lighting. The elaborately decorated reception rooms on the first floor of the hotel are integrated with the rest of the museum as exhibition areas, and the hotel dining-room becomes the museum restaurant.

Thus the exhibition space is divided into three main levels, linked by stairways and escalators situated at either end of the building.

As we have said, the design is bold and uncompromising. At no point is there any use of pastiche, nor has any attempt been made to create a stylistic harmony between the new structure and the old. Laloux's stucco décor has been respected; the cast-iron pillars and beams (including those in hitherto inaccessible parts of the station, in the roof space and on the upper levels) have been restored and given new prominence. The new architecture, while itself making a strong series of geometric statements in metal and stone, never masks the presence of the original building.

Internal coherence is supplied by the use of the same materials and colours throughout (Burgundy stone, light-coloured partitions, dark brown or blue metalwork, etc.). But within that overall unity the rooms are clearly differentiated, a variety of architectural solutions being employed to ensure the optimum conditions for the different types of display.

The design perfectly complements the range and diversity of the artefacts and activities to be accommodated within the museum. In planning the layout of the exhibition space, it was felt essential to create a number of distinctly demarcated areas, both for the sake of clarity and to reduce the displays to a manageable scale. On a purely practical level, it was important to keep separate the educational facilities ('dossiers' and theme exhibitions, reference rooms, audio-visual displays) and the galleries themselves, which needed an atmosphere of peace and quiet. Generally it was desirable to make a distinction between the different media and techniques, while taking care to avoid arbitrary groupings with no basis in historical truth. And, finally, the physical layout had to reflect the differences and antagonisms between opposing schools and aesthetic tendencies: thus it was decided to show in quite separate areas of the museum, on the one hand the development of Impressionism (after 1870) and of Post-Impressionism, and on the other the various alternative strands which evolved over the same period, and which in the past have been dismissed wholesale as the work of 'official hacks' or *pompiers*.

The Galerie Bellechasse

14

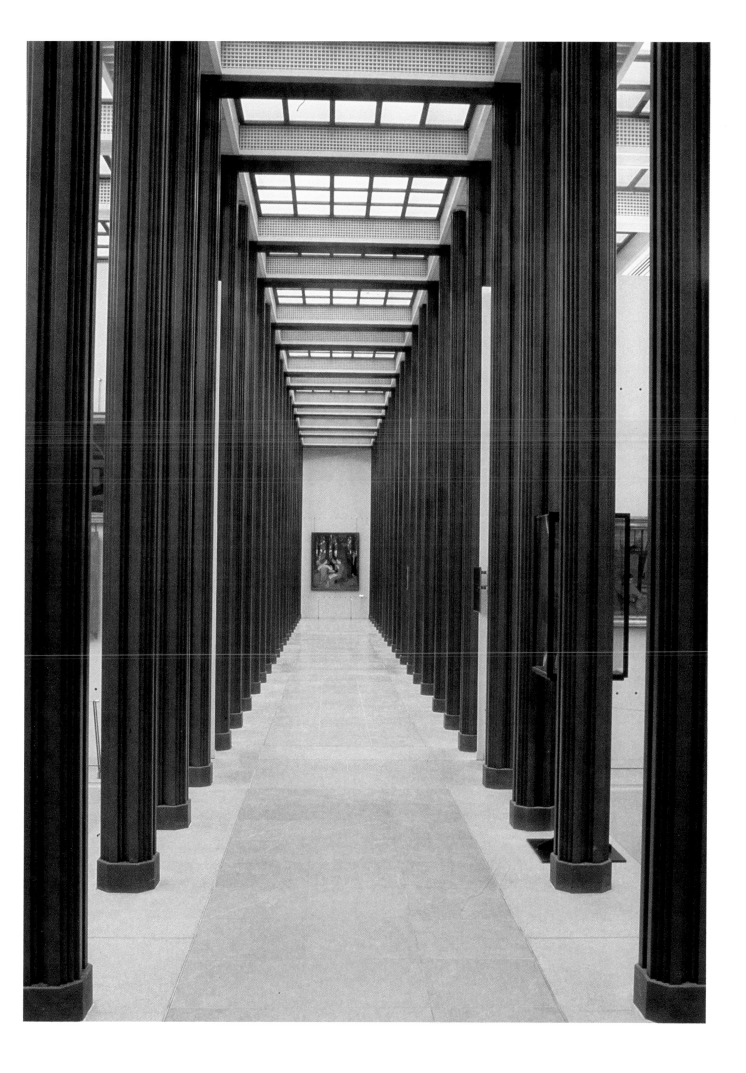

The collections, then, are displayed on three levels, in a series of 'sequences' clearly differentiated by their individual architectural settings and by their contents.

The visitor begins on the first level with a brief historical introduction (films and displays of objects designed to illustrate some aspect of history or society in the latter half of the nineteenth century), and thereafter the ground floor is devoted exclusively to the period 1848–75. The central avenue is lined with monumental sculpture from Rude to Carpeaux; the row of rooms on one side is devoted to a sequence on Realism up to the beginnings of Impressionism; that on the other side to the inheritance of Romanticism (Delacroix) and of Neoclassicism (Ingres), culminating in eclecticism and Symbolism. Eclecticism is most fully represented in the section on the decorative arts and finds its apotheosis in the Opéra room, which pays tribute both to Charles Garnier's great building and to the performances presented there. On the same level are a number of areas set aside for temporary exhibitions of drawings, engravings and photographs, and for 'dossiers', thematic displays relating to the period 1848–75.

To reach the second level, which is right at the top of the building, the visitor can either ascend via the escalators at the end of the central hall, or can make his or her way up through the exhibition rooms of the Pavillon Amont, the station's 'upstream' or western pavilion, devoted to permanent and temporary displays on the theme of architecture and town-planning.

This topmost level contains the longest sequence of works in the museum, being set aside exclusively for Impressionism after 1870 and the various movements that developed in its wake (Neo-Impressionism, the Pont-Aven School, the Nabis, etc). On the same level is a cafeteria and an audio-visual display area, as well as space for exhibitions of the graphic arts.

The route down from the second to the third level (situated on the middle floor) leads past a number of documentary exhibitions on the press, poster art and book illustration, and also the historical reference facilities in the Galerie des Dates.

The third and last stage of the tour begins in the former reception rooms of the hotel, which contain examples of official art and the large-scale decorative works of the Third Republic. The visitor then re-enters the open spaces of the Nave. The terraces set above the central avenue show the sculpture of the last third of the century, dominated by Rodin, and ending with Maillol and Bourdelle in the early years of the twentieth century. The first group of rooms opening off the terraces is devoted to Naturalism, Symbolism and academic art at the end of the century. There then follows the great sequence of Art Nouveau (France and Belgium), with an extension in two towers erected at the end of the central hall, and in adjacent rooms devoted to the architects and designers of

Glasgow, Vienna and Chicago. Space has been left for 'dossier' exhibitions for the period 1870–1910, and the history of painting is brought to a conclusion with a selection showing, on the one hand, the development afer 1900 of the former Nabis (Bonnard, Vuillard, etc.), and on the other, the new directions in painting of the years 1904–06 (Matisse, the Fauves), as an introduction to the art of the twentieth century. The visit ends with a final sequence – and here the word is particularly apt – on the invention of cinematography.

Michel Laclotte
Inspecteur Général des Musées

Note on the captions

Where no medium is given, the work is in oil on canvas.
Dimensions are given in centimetres and inches.
For paintings, height is given before width;
for sculpture, height only;
for *objets d'art*, height, width
and depth (height only for chairs).

The text of this book is the work of the following contributors:
Valérie Bajou, Marc Bascou, Françoise Cachin, Anne Distel,
Claire Frèches, Chantal Martinet, Françoise Heilbrun,
Geneviève Lacambre, Ségolène Le Men, Antoinette Le Normand Romain,
Henri Loyrette, Philippe Néagu, Jean-Michel Nectoux,
Sylvie Patin, Anne Pingeot, Nicole Savy,
Philippe Thiébaut, Georges Vigne.

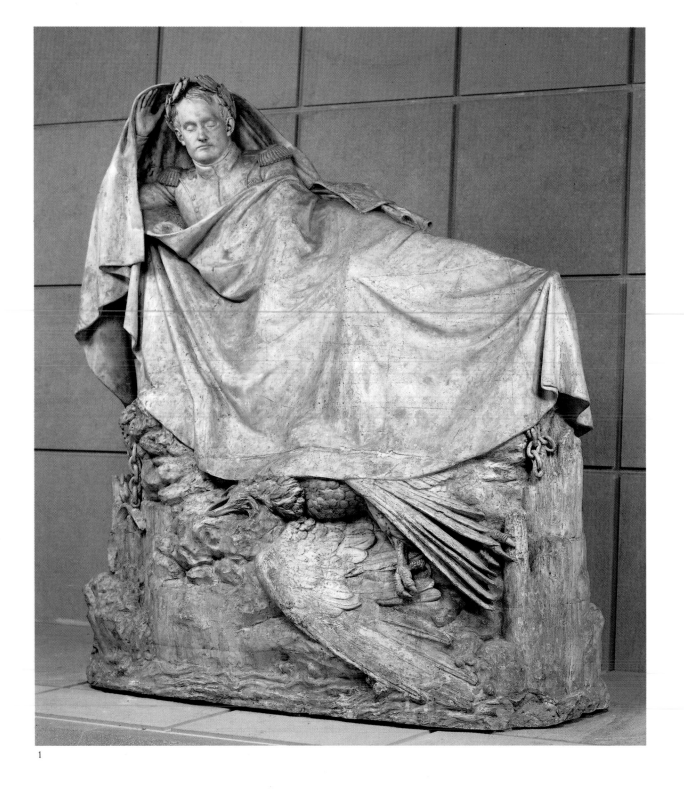

1

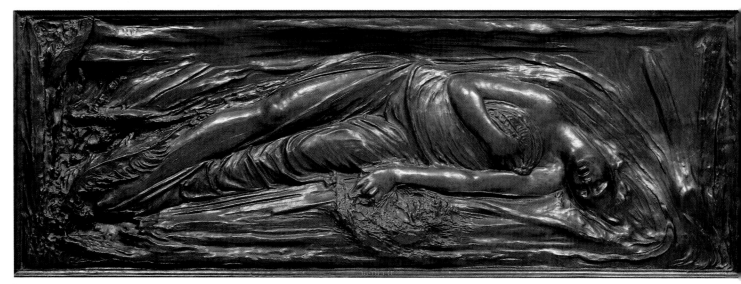

2

Sculpture:
the last Romantics

Although Romanticism began to influence painting in the 1820s, it was not until ten years later that the first Romantic sculptures appeared.

Taking their inspiration from Dante, Shakespeare or Chateaubriand, rather than from ancient history, they were intended to be both faithful copies of nature and eloquent expressions of feeling. Antoine Préault (1809–79) exaggerated forms, proportions and modelling. 'Shout louder' was François Rude's exhortation to his wife as she posed for his *Génie de la Patrie* (*Spirit of Patriotism*) – which was immediately christened 'the shrew in a rage'. Bitterly attacked by the academic critics, these artists found themselves gradually excluded from the Salons during the July Monarchy of King Louis-Philippe (1830–48). Without commissions they were hard put to survive, and had no means of bringing themselves to the public's attention except through publications and the press. In 1847, Rude (1784–1855) executed for a certain Captain Noisot a monument symbolizing that officer's affection and loyalty for his Emperor, whom he had served as Commander of the Grenadiers on the island of Elba, but it was not until the Second Empire that the state gave any sign of official approval. Préault's medallions of Dante and Vergil were acquired by Napoleon III in 1853. Jean-Baptiste Carpeaux (1827–75) found himself in serious trouble at the French school in Rome (the Villa Médicis) over his *Ugolin* (*Ugolino*), which represented all that the Institut de France in its role as guardian of the classical tradition most deplored; but state commissions were issued to Jean-Bernard Duseigneur (1809–66) in 1867 for a cast of *Roland furieux* (*Orlando Furioso*) and to Préault for a cast of his *Ophélie* (*Ophelia*) in 1876. It should however be noted that the plaster casts of these works dated from 1831 and 1842 respectively!

'I stand not for the finite, but for the infinite' was Préault's inscription on his medallion of Delacroix, now in the Louvre. It is a phrase that neatly encapsulates the spirit of the times, which was to find its fullest expression in the Symbolism of Auguste Rodin who, noted Camille Mauclair, was loved by the poets of his day 'because he makes the most finite of the arts suggest infinity'.

1 *F. Rude:* Napoléon s'éveillant à l'immortalité (Napoleon awakening to Immortality), *1846 Plaster. 225 (88.6). Acquired 1891. The bronze is at Fixin (Côte-d'Or)*

2 *A. Préault:* Ophélie (Ophelia) *Plaster executed in 1842. 75 × 200 (29.5 × 78.7). Acquired and cast in bronze 1876*

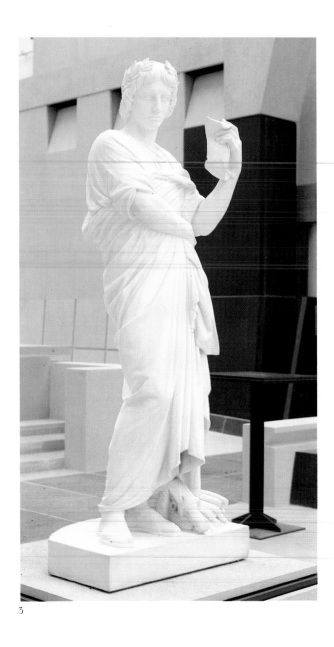

3

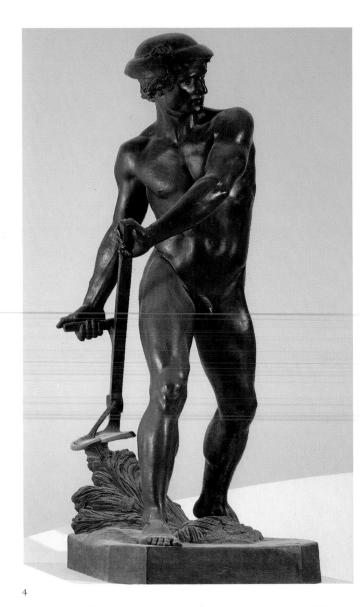

4

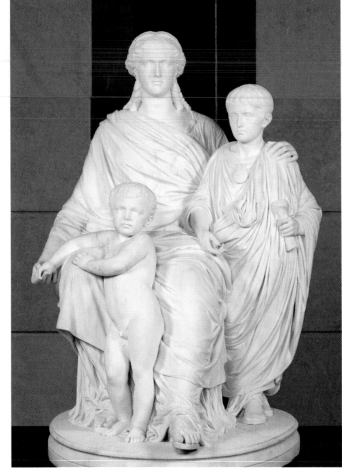

5

Painting: Ingres, Delacroix, Chassériau after 1850

At the beginning of the Second Empire (1852–70) the artistic scene was dominated by two great figures: Jean-Auguste-Dominique Ingres (1780–1867) and Eugène Delacroix (1798–1863). The former, the champion of classical art, won the Prix de Rome in 1801 and was elected a member of the Institut de France in 1825; the latter, the leading exponent of Romanticism, was obliged to wait until 1857 before finally being admitted to that august body. Both were appointed to the imperial commission responsible for the Paris World Fair of 1855, the only painters on the committee. This was the first such occasion to include an international retrospective of painting; this was housed in a Palais des Beaux-Arts, constructed especially on the avenue Montaigne. A vast temporary display of the art of the first fifty years of the century, it gave Ingres and Delacroix the ideal opportunity to show some of their best work. Ingres's *La Source* (*The Spring*), a reworking of an earlier study, was not completed until 1856, and was then exhibited in the artist's studio before being put on show by its new owner, Count Duchâtel, in a special room 'surrounded by large plants and aquatic flowers, so that the Nymph of the Spring will look even more like a real person'. This 'adolescent Eve', harking back to an 'incalculable antiquity' according to some observers, was to Gustave Moreau an '"academy" (in the antique style) ... executed by a marvellous scholar'. *La Source* is the most famous example of the fashion for smooth-textured painting, practised not only by the pupils of Ingres, such as Hippolyte Flandrin (1809–64) or Amaury-Duval (1808–85), but also by Léon Bénouville (1821–59) and other pupils of François Picot (1786–1868), and by students of Charles Gleyre (1806–74), such as Jean-Louis Gérôme (1824–1904). The latter, at the age of only twenty-two, painted a picture which attracted attention at the 1847 Salon and became famous under the title of *Un Combat de coqs* (*A Cockfight*), a free interpretation of a classical theme.

Delacroix's technique could hardly have provided a greater contrast. It was much admired by Charles Baudelaire, who called it 'a veritable explosion of colour'. This description of the ambitious canvas *La chasse aux lions* (*The Lion Hunt*), commissioned for the Musée de Bordeaux and

3 *G. J. Thomas:* Virgile (Vergil), *1859–61 Marble. 183 (72). Commissioned 1859, entered national collection 1874*

4 *E. Guillaume:* Le faucheur (The Reaper), *1849–55 Bronze. 168 (66.1). Acquired 1855*

5 *E. Cavelier:* Cornélie, mère des Gracques (Cornelia, Mother of the Gracchi), *1861 Marble. 171 (67.3). Acquired 1861*

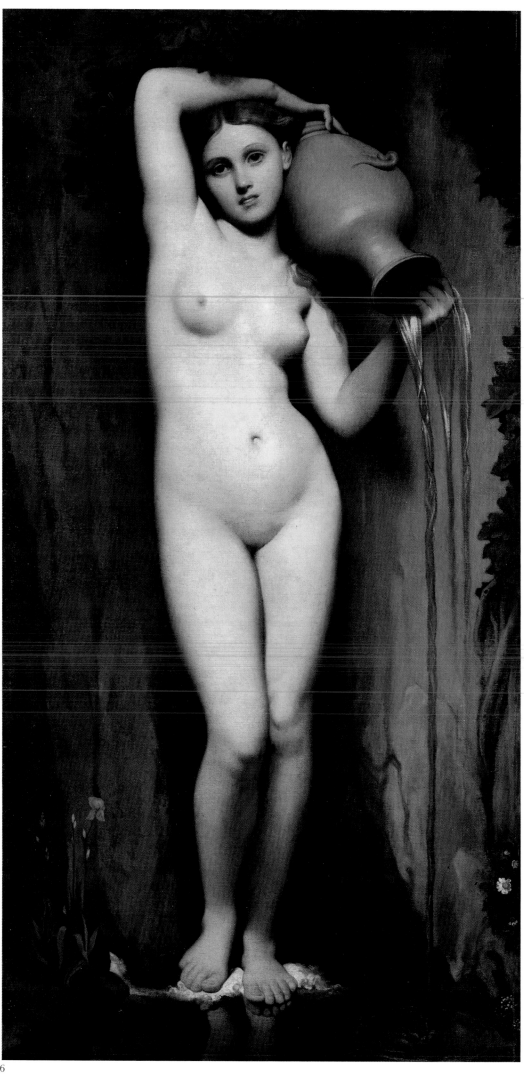

6 *J. A. D. Ingres:* La Source
(The Spring)
*163 × 80 (64.2 × 31.5). Started
in Florence c. 1820, completed
in Paris 1856 with the aid of
Paul Balze and Alexandre
Desgoffe. Bequest of Comtesse
Duchâtel, 1878*

7 *E. Delacroix:* La chasse aux
lions (The Lion Hunt), *1854
86 × 115 (33.9 × 45.3). Sketch
for the painting commissioned
by Musée de Bordeaux and
shown at Paris World Fair
1855. Acquired 1984*

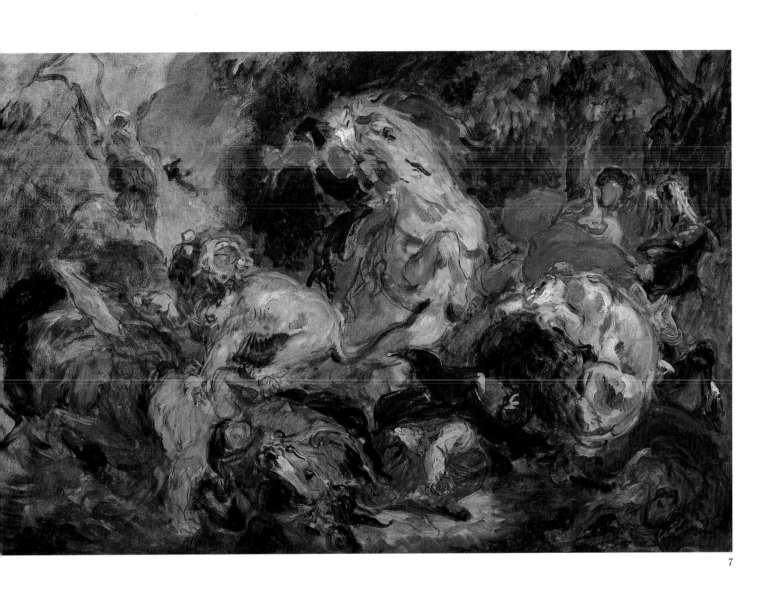

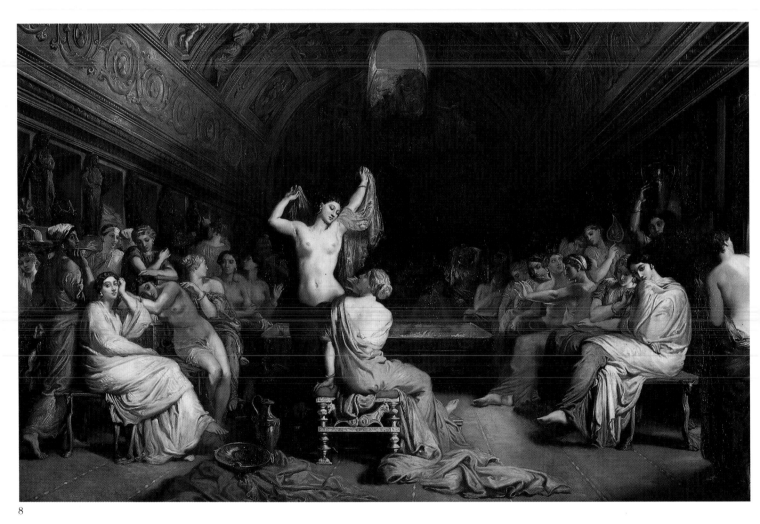

8

8 *T. Chassériau:*
Tépidarium; salle où les
femmes de Pompéi venaient
se reposer et se sécher en
sortant du bain (Tepidarium:
Room where the Women of
Pompeii Rested and Dried
Themselves on Leaving the
Bath)
*171 × 258 (67.3 × 101.6). Salon
of 1853. Acquired 1853*

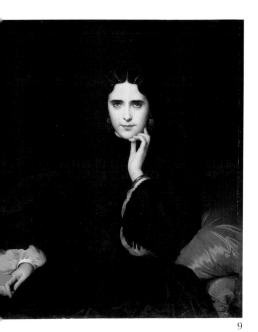

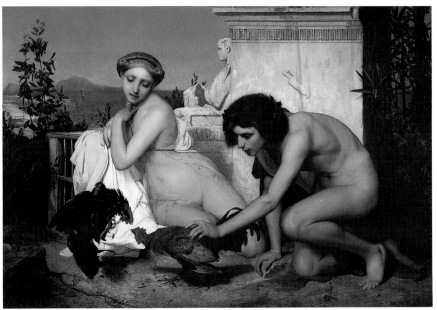

9   10

exhibited in 1855, applies even more aptly to the large, impassioned sketch for it in the Musée d'Orsay, referred to in Delacroix's diary for 3 May 1854: 'In the morning, fired with enthusiasm, went on with the sketch for *The Lion Hunt*.' Featured in all the Delacroix retrospectives, including the posthumous exhibition of 1874, this sketch must inevitably have had an influence on painters like Manet, Renoir, Signac and Matisse.

In his lifetime, too, Delacroix had his adherents, among them Théodore Chassériau (1819–56), formerly a pupil of Ingres. He was a portraitist and also a painter of goddesses and nymphs, biblical and oriental scenes, and decorative works for churches and public buildings. In the course of his brief career – he was only thirty-seven when he died – he won praise from critics and public alike, because he seemed to bring together 'the two rival schools of drawing and of colour'. The *Tépidarium*, acclaimed at the Salon of 1853, is a case in point: the setting is carefully modelled on Pompeian antiquity, but Chassériau brings his women to life, their languorous poses reminiscent of Delacroix's exotic harem scenes. The half-size figures place Chassériau outside the monumentalist traditions of history painting. The *Tépidarium* was in fact one of the first examples of the historical *genre* painting which achieved dominance under the Second Empire.

Although the tour of the Musée d'Orsay opens with a tribute to Ingres and Delacroix, showing how their late paintings relate to the works of subsequent painters, it is perhaps worth reiterating that – like Corot, who is also represented in the Musée d'Orsay – they were born in the eighteenth century: the main body of their work remains in the Louvre.

9 *Amaury-Duval:* Madame de Loynes *(1837–1908), 1862 100 × 83 (39.4 × 32.7). Bequest of Jules Lemaître, 1914*

10 *J. L. Gérôme:* Jeunes grecs faisant battre des coqs *ou* Un combat de coqs (Young Greeks Holding a Cock Fight), *1846 143 × 204 (56.3 × 80.3). Salon of 1847. Acquired 1873*

Sculpture: eclecticism

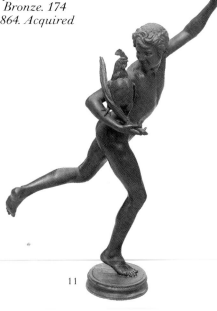

11

French society was transformed by the industrial revolution
that took place during the Second Empire. Fortunes changed
hands, and the newly affluent bourgeosie set about creating
its own style. Needing confirmation of their status, its
members tended to look to the past to provide models.
Historical subjects were the fashion in the nineteenth
century; writers, and later artists, scoured earlier civilizations
for themes they could adapt to their own purposes. Such
evidence of culture and good taste was warmly received by
their new patrons.

The Hellenistic bronzes of Pompeii, and Giovanni da
Bologna's *Mercury*, were the inspiration to Alexandre
Falguière (1831–1900) and Hippolyte Moulin (1832–84) for
their figures of athletic young men, exhibited at the Salon of
1864. Together with Paul Dubois and Antonin Mercié, these
two sculptors formed a group known as Les Florentins, in
acknowledgment of their debt to Tuscany. Many of the
drawings of Dubois (1829–1905) were based on works by
Benozzo Gozzoli. Dubois' *Petit chanteur du XVème siècle*
(*Florentine Singer*) won the gold medal at the Salon of 1865,
arousing such enthusiasm that a quarrel broke out between
the Emperor's cousin Princess Mathilde and the Director of

12 *P. Dubois:* Chanteur
florentin (Florentine Singer),
*1865. Silvered bronze. 155 (61).
Commissioned 1865 and
shown at Paris World Fair
1867*

13 *A. E. Carrier-Belleuse:*
Hébé (Hebe), *1869. Marble.
207 (81.5). Entered national
collection 1869*

14 *H. Moulin:* Trouvaille à
Pompéi (A Find at Pompeii),
*1863. Bronze. 187 (73.6).
Acquired 1864*

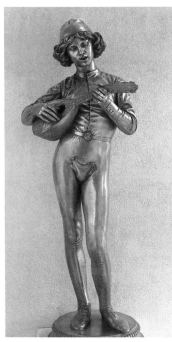

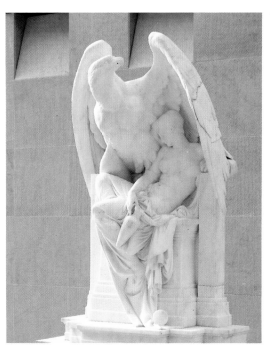

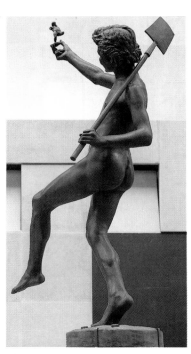

12

13

14

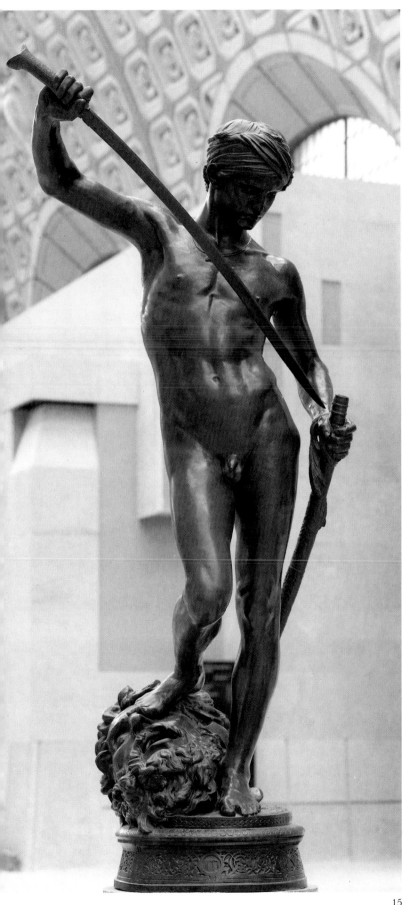

15

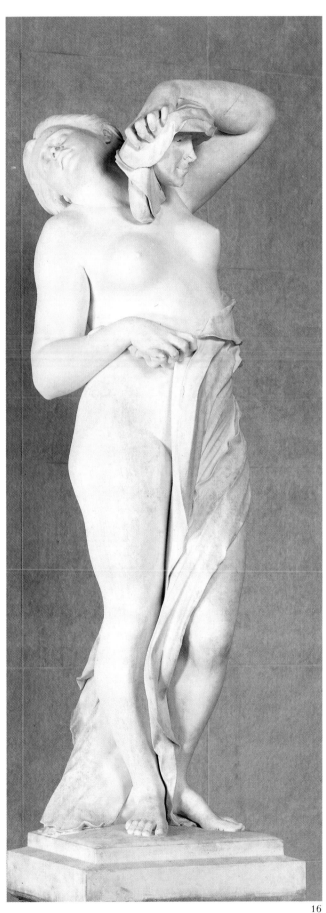

16

15 *A. Mercié:* David, *1872–73*
Bronze. 184 (72.4). Assigned to
national collection 1874

16 *E. Christophe:* La
Comédie humaine *ou* Le
masque (The Human
Comedy *or* The Mask),
1857–76
Marble. 245 (96.5). Acquired
1876

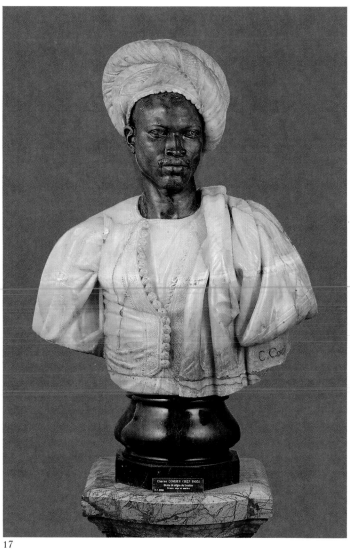

17

the Beaux-Arts, Count Nieuwerkerke, as to who should have
the first cast; it was the Princess who emerged victorious.
Small replicas of the figure were produced both in bronze
(Barbedienne) and in unglazed porcelain (Sèvres). Mercié
(1845–1916), while still technically a student in residence at
the Villa Médicis in Rome, was awarded the Légion
d'Honneur for his second-year work, a *David* sheathing his
sword, a superbly flowing and developed human figure.

Albert-Ernest Carrier-Belleuse (1824–87) also used a
classical model for his finest relief, *Hébé et l'aigle* (*Hebe and
the Eagle*). *The Comédie humaine* (*The Human Comedy*) by
Ernest Christophe (1827–92) inspired Baudelaire's thoughts
on the 'correspondences' between poetry and sculpture, in
Chant XXI of *Les Fleurs du mal* of 1857.

Love of history in this period was matched by a taste for
far-off places. Charles Cordier (1827–1905) obtained funding
for a series of expeditions, the most tangible result of which
was the lavish use, in his sculpture, of onyx mined in the
newly opened Algerian quarries. The employment of rich,
coloured stone in statuary was then much in vogue, reflecting
the affluence of the age.

Painting: eclecticism

The huge canvas by Thomas Couture (1815–79), *Romains de la décadence* (*Romans of the Decadence*), commissioned in 1846 and exhibited at the Salon of 1847, is based on a quotation from one of Juvenal's satires: 'More cruel than war, vice battened on Rome and avenged the conquered world.' The composition draws on established formal models, and there are clear references to Tiepolo, Rubens, Poussin and, in particular, Veronese. However, it is interesting that Couture had no hesitation in showing his figures in unheroic poses. This was in marked contrast to the idealism of those artists who exactly conformed to what they were taught at the Ecole des Beaux-Arts, where the ultimate reward, for winners of the Prix de Rome, was a period of residence in Italy at the Villa Médicis. Among such prize-winners were Alexandre Cabanel (1823–89), honoured in 1845; William Bouguereau (1825–1905) and Paul Baudry (1826–86), in 1850; Elie Delaunay (1821–91), in 1856; and Henri Regnault

18 *T. Couture:* Romains de la décadence (Romans of the Decadence)
466 × 775 (183.5 × 305.1).
Salon of 1847. Acquired 1847

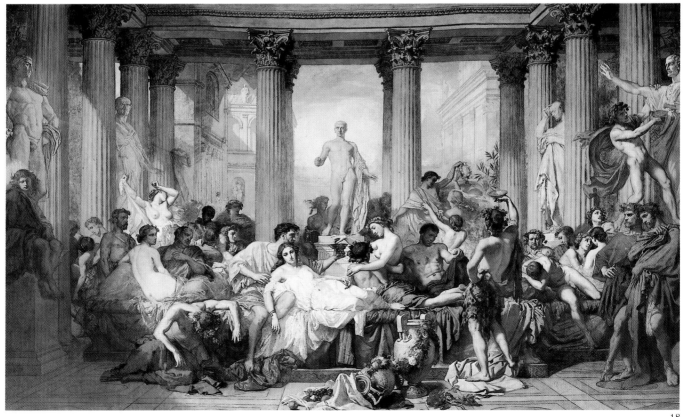

19 *A. Cabanel:* Naissance de
Vénus (Birth of Venus)
*130 × 225 (51.2 × 88.6). Salon
of 1863. Acquired by Napoleon
III 1863, assigned to national
collection 1879*

(1843–71), in 1866. Success at this early stage was the guarantee of a brilliant career. Thus in 1863, already the recipient of a Salon medal, Cabanel was elected to the Institut de France and made a professor at the Ecole des Beaux-Arts. In the same year he had enormous success at the Salon with his *Naissance de Vénus* (*Birth of Venus*), which was immediately bought by Napoleon III for his private collection.

Cabanel's pupil, Regnault, was unusual in that he spent only two years in Italy before moving on to Spain. All official residents of the Villa Médicis were obliged to make regular submissions of their work. Regnault sent his fourth-year work from Tangiers: *Exécution sans jugement sous les rois maures de Grenade* (*Summary Execution under the Moorish Kings of Granada*). Such was the youthful painter's fame that his death in battle at Buzenval in 1871 shocked the artistic world.

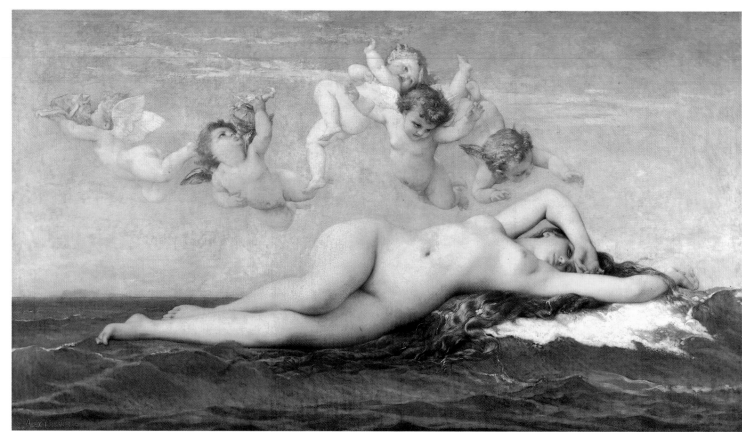

20 *H. Regnault:* Exécution
sans jugement sous les rois
maures de Grenade
(Summary Execution under
the Moorish Kings of
Granada), *1870*
302 × 146 (118.9 × 57.5).
Acquired 1872

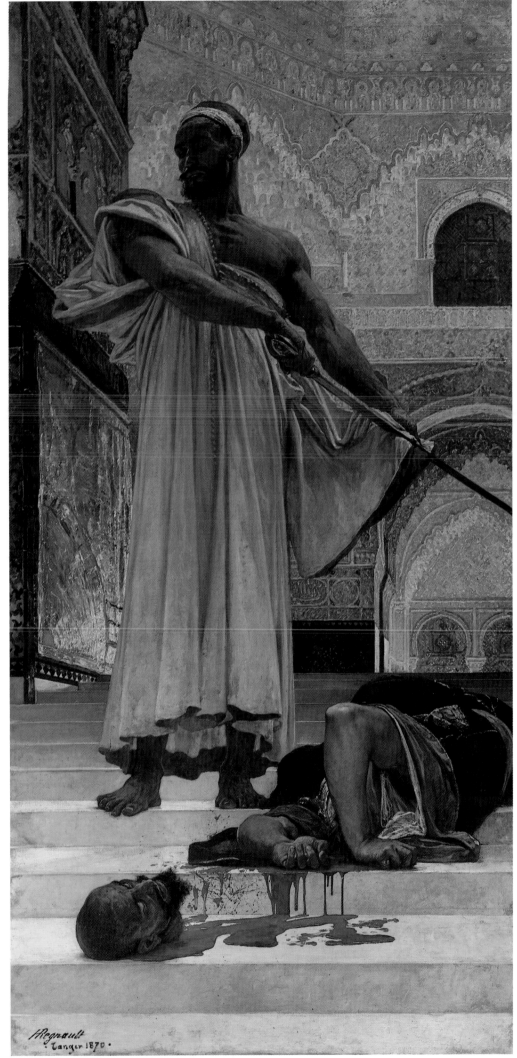

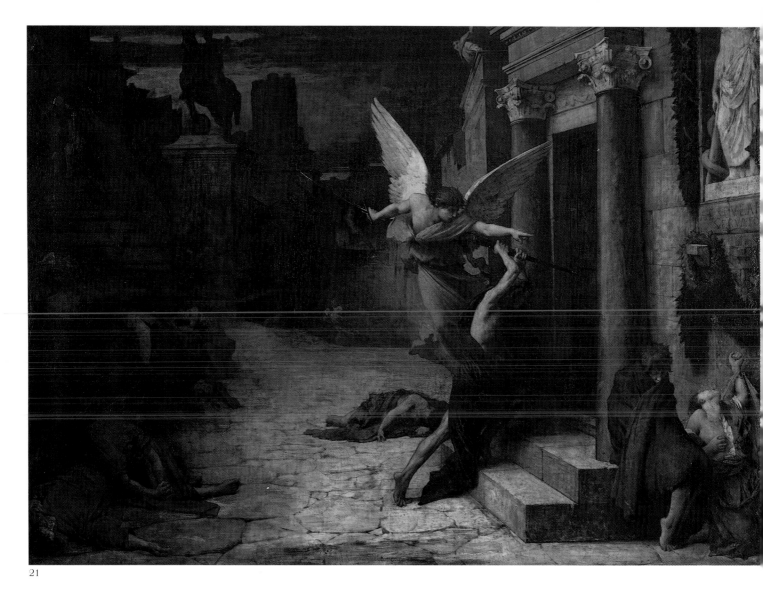

21

21 *E. Delaunay:* Peste à
Rome (Plague in Rome)
131 × 176.5 (51.6 × 69.5).
Based on the legend of St
Sebastian in the Golden
Legend *of Jacobus de*
Voragine. Salon of 1869.
Acquired 1869

One of the finest examples of Second Empire history
painting is Delaunay's *Peste à Rome (Plague in Rome)*,
exhibited at the Salon of 1869. The canvas was the
culmination of many years of work. Life drawings were made
for every single figure, and there are numerous smaller
versions and preparatory studies which reveal how the
composition developed in dramatic intensity, moving towards the isolation of the central group of exterminating
angels.

Decorative arts: eclecticism

Eclecticism embodies the belief that all styles are equal. This was an emergent trend in the mid nineteenth century, and corresponded to the aspirations of a rising bourgeoisie, who looked to the past or to the colonial experience for their models. As industry and commerce boomed, so the stylistic blend gained an international currency. The World Fairs, with their exhibitions of artefacts from many different countries, prompted a realization of the dire consequences of over-rapid industrialization, and a number of ventures were started which aimed to reconcile Utility with Beauty. Design schools, societies for the promotion of design, and museums of applied arts were established; competitions and special exhibitions were held, and reviews and pattern-books were published. Eclecticism was a source of creative regeneration, since it encouraged designers to measure themselves against the geniuses of antiquity, to take as their standard the very best that history and the contemporary world could offer: it also fostered a revival of interest in nature. Hence commercial designers show a variety of stylistic emphases within a framework of Naturalism: Sevin (Neoclassical); Avisseau and Frullini (Neo-Renaissance); Schilt and Cremer (Neo-Rococo); Deck (Islamic); Braquemond and Rousseau (Japanese), to name but a few.

The big industrial firms hired the best designers – architects, sculptors, painters and above all ornamentalists – whose industrial work was exhibited and won awards. What these artists had in common, in spite of their apparent diversity of style, was a desire to think on a large scale, a concern for quality, a superb audacity in the way they juxtaposed motifs or used unusual combinations of materials and colours, and an enthusiasm for new scientific ideas. As well as one-off pieces commissioned by individual patrons or destined for international exhibitions, there began to appear works designed with mass-production in mind, quickly produced and available to a wider public. At the other end of the spectrum, the traditions of craftsmanship were maintained by a small number of producers who rejected mechanization and the division of labour.

22 *A. L. Barye, sculptor:*
Clock with Chariot of Apollo
Bronze with green patina, red marble. 85 × 94 × 36 (33.5 × 37 × 14.2). From a mantelpiece garniture originally including two candelabra, commissioned by Isaac Pereire for the Château d'Armainvilliers in 1858. Loaned by Ministère des Affaires étrangères

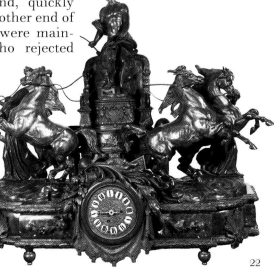

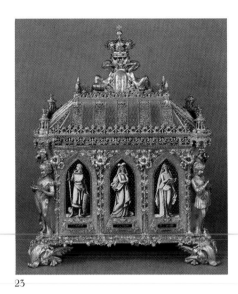

23

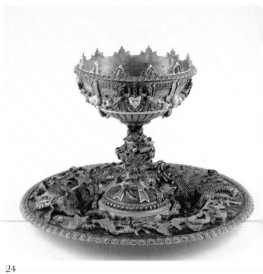

24

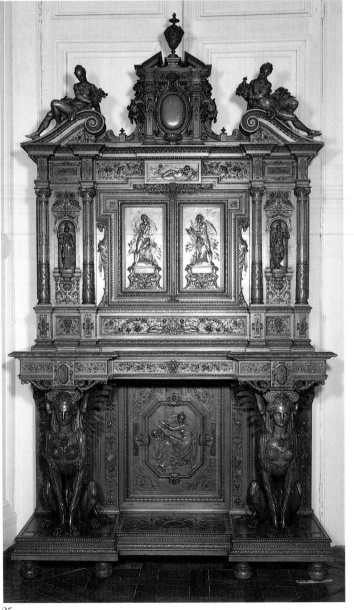

25

23 F. D. Froment-Meurice, goldsmith; J. F. Duban, architect; A. V. Geoffroy-Dechaume, sculptor; J. J. Feuchère, sculptor; M. Liénard, ornamentalist: Jewel casket, one of a pair Silver, parcel-gilt, painted enamel, emeralds and garnets. 42.6 × 35.8 × 27.5 (16.8 × 14.1 × 10.8). Exposition nationale des produits de l'Industrie, Paris, 1849. From a dressing-table set commissioned for the wedding of the Duchess of Parma, grand-daughter of Charles X, in November 1845, completed only in 1851. Acquired 1981

24 C. J. Avisseau, ceramicist; O. Guillaume de Rochebrune, designer and engraver: Cup and stand Faïence with coloured relief and inlaid decoration. Cup 34.5, d. 26.5 (13.6, d. 10.4). Stand 8, d. 51.5 (3.1, d. 20.3). World Fair, Paris, 1855. In reaction against the rise of industrially produced ceramics, Avisseau revived pottery as an art form, inspired by the work of Bernard Palissy. Acquired 1983

25 Fourdinois, company founded by Alexandre Georges Fourdinois in 1835 and managed from 1867 by Henri-Auguste Fourdinois: Neo-Renaissance cabinet Carved walnut, jasper and lapis-lazuli. 253 × 143 × 60 (99.6 × 56.3 × 23.6). World Fair, Paris 1867. Musée des Arts Décoratifs

26 C. G. Diehl, cabinet-maker; E. Brandely, designer; E. Fremiet, sculptor: Medal cabinet Cedar, walnut, ebony and ivory, with silvered bronze and (galvanized?) copper. 238 × 151 × 60 (93.7 × 59.4 × 23.6). World Fairs, Paris 1867 and Vienna 1873. Acquired 1973. Fremiet's plaster for the central relief, Entrée triomphale de Mérovée à Châlons-sur-Marne (The Triumphal Entry of Merovaeus into Châlons-sur-Marne), was given by Madame René Martin in 1973

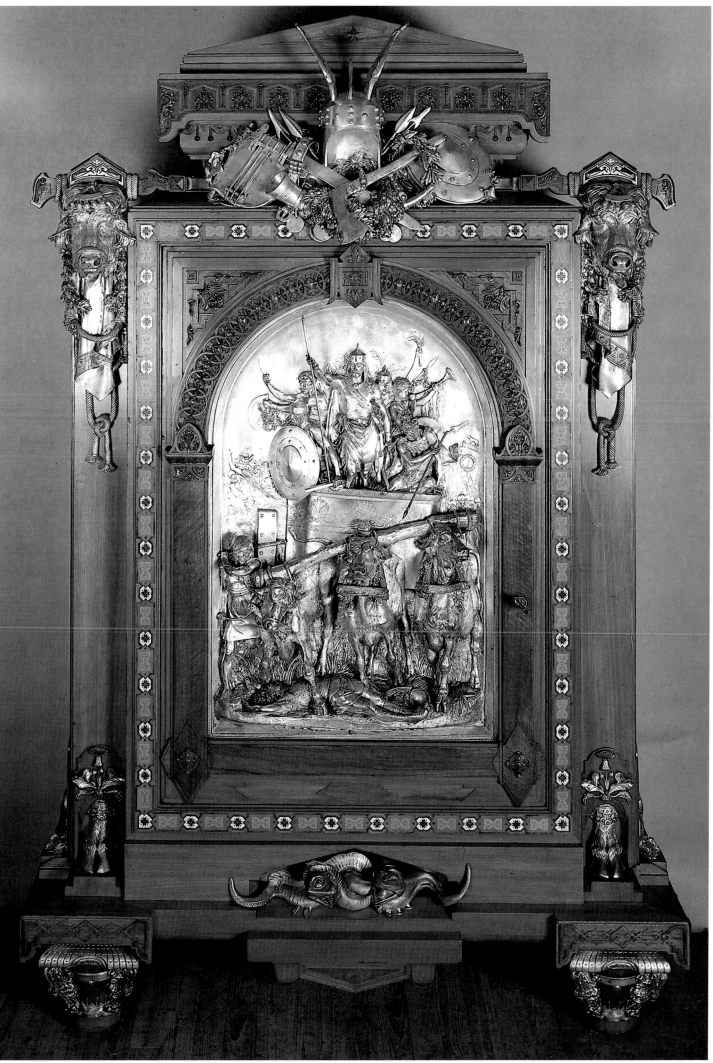

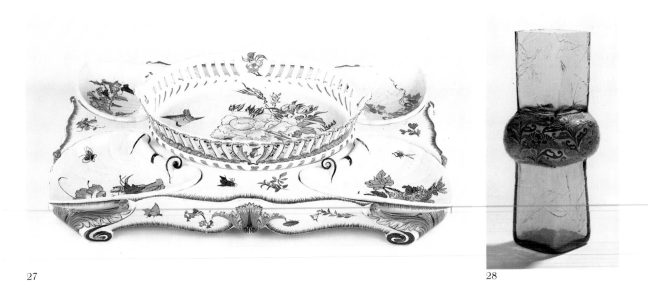

27

28

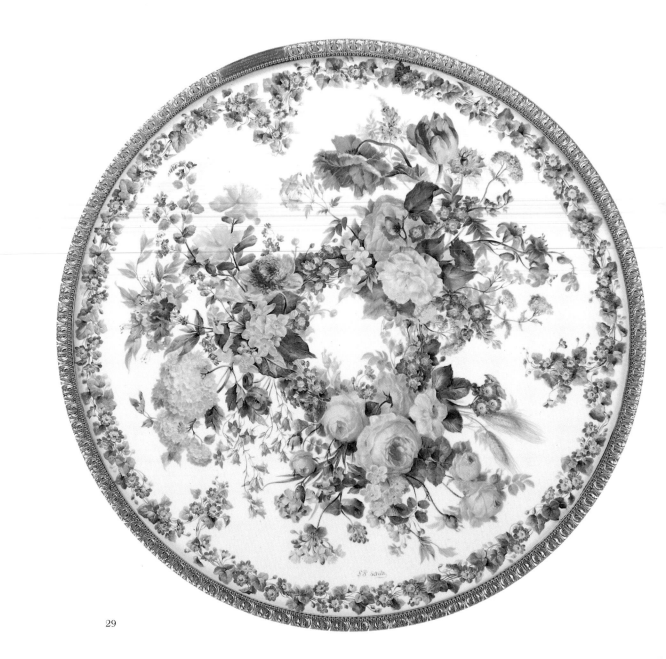

29

27 *Manufacture de Creil et Montereau: F. Bracquemond, painter and engraver; E. Rousseau, ceramicist and glassmaker:* Table centrepiece Faïence with printed and painted underglaze decoration. 15 × 62 × 42 (5.9 × 24.4 × 16.5). *World Fair, Paris 1867. Part of the 'Japanese' dinner service commissioned from Bracquemond by Rousseau in 1866, manufactured by Leveille up to 1903. Acquired 1984*

28 *E. Rousseau, ceramicist and glassmaker:* Vase bambou. Bamboo vase. *Engraved and enamelled glass. 28 (11). World Fair, Paris 1878. Acquired 1984*

29 *Sèvres, Manufacture Impériale de Céramique:* Guéridon (Tray), *1850–53 Porcelain with painted decoration, incised and gilded bronze. D. 87 (34.3). Presented to Duchess of Hamilton by Empress Eugénie, 1853. Acquired 1982.*

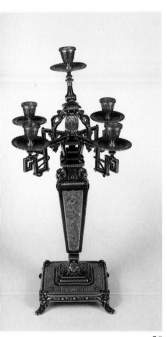

30

30 *Christofle et Cie, company managed by H. Bouilhet and P. Christofle; A. E. Reiber, designer:* Candelabrum, one of a pair Patinated and gilt bronze, cloisonné enamel. 56 (22). *Part of a set originally including a flower-stand, executed for the Vienna World Fair, 1873. Acquired 1982*

31 *E. Lièvre, designer; E. Detaille, painter:* Cupboard on supporting table Rosewood, gilt bronze, engraved ironwork. 211 × 111 × 57 (83.1 × 43.7 × 22.4). *Probably manufactured by L'Escalier de Cristal, as was a similar piece decorated with a painting of a Japanese woman by Clairin (Hermitage Museum, Leningrad). Acquired 1981*

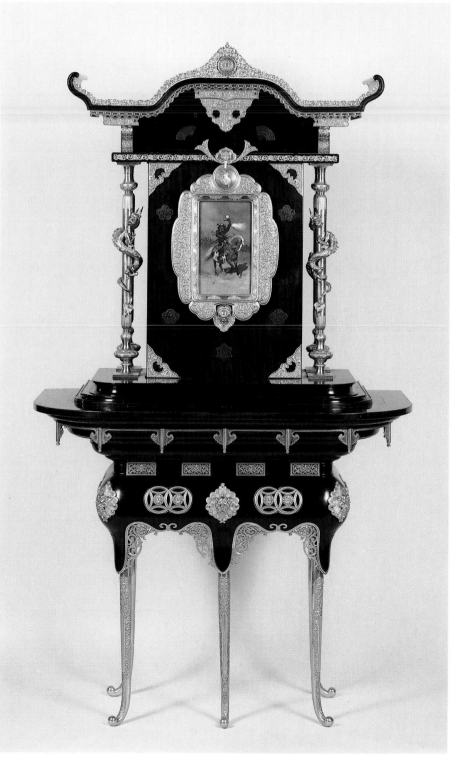

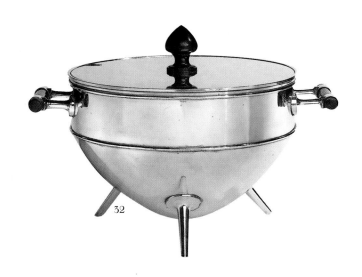

Arts and Crafts

*32 J. W. Hukin & J. T. Heath,
London and Birmingham;
C. Dresser, designer:* Soup
tureen
*Silvered metal and ebony.
21 × 31, d. 23.5 (8.3 × 12.2, d.
9.3). Patented 1880. Acquired
1985*

*33 Morris, Marshall,
Faulkner & Co., London;
P. Webb, architect and
designer:* Table
*Polished oak, brass.
73 × 167 × 61
(28.7 × 65.7 × 24). Philip
Webb was a partner in
Morris's firm from 1861,
designing most of the furniture
in the early years of the firm.
Acquired 1979*

A. W. N. Pugin (1812–52), whose principles of honest, functional architecture were derived from a study of Gothic art, sowed the seeds for the Arts and Crafts Movement that grew up in England from the 1860s onwards as a reaction against the dehumanizing effects of mechanization. Thomas Carlyle and John Ruskin, while condemning the way men were being taken over by machines, did not allow their moral indignation to sway their essentially reactionary view of society. Others such as Robert Owen (the father of English Socialism), Henry Cole (organizer of the first World Fair, the Great Exhibition of 1851, and one of the pioneers of industrial design) and, above all, William Morris, adopted a more pragmatic approach.

It is to Morris (1834–96) that the credit goes for translating theory into practice. In 1861 he set up his own firm and devised a system of production that integrated craftwork with mechanization, making it possible to produce both everyday household articles and luxury goods. Morris attracted many imitators and disciples: some, such as Arthur Heygate Mackmurdo (founder of the Century Guild, 1882), Walter Crane (Art Workers' Guild, 1884), Charles Robert

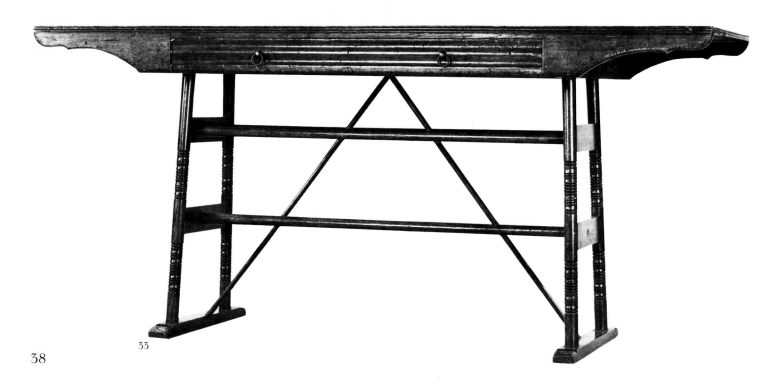

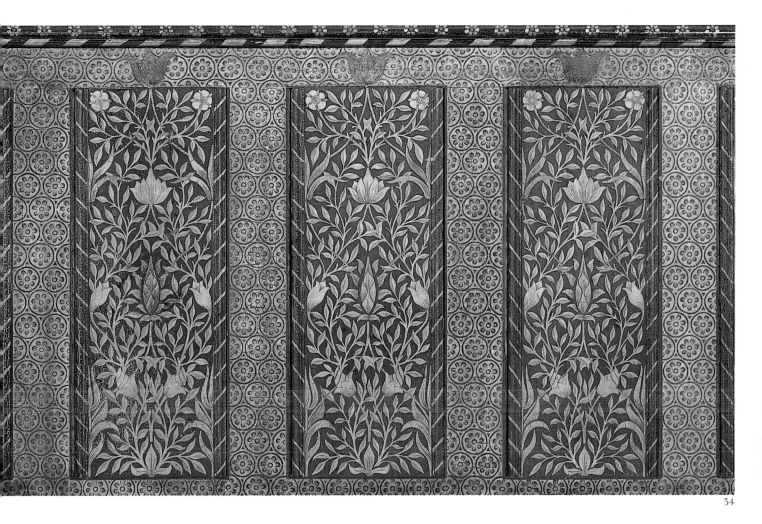

Ashbee (Guild of Handicraft, 1888) and Ernest Gimson (Kenton and Co., 1890), ultimately foundered on the contradictions inherent in the Arts and Crafts Movement, which tended to create luxury craft items beyond the pockets of all but the prosperous few.

Others, among them Edward William Godwin (1833–86) and Christopher Dresser (1834–1904), chose to work in association with industrial concerns; strongly influenced by Japanese design, they developed a stripped-down Anglo-Japanese style that was ideally suited to mass-production.

Almost all these designers had a background in architecture, and in some instances practical experience of the profession; it was this as much as anything that gave them their vision of a harmonious art of living that would be available, theoretically at least, to all.

34 *Morris & Co., London; W. Morris, painter and designer:* Painted wood panelling, detail *100 × 1200 (39.4 × 472.4) overall. From the home of the Earl of Carlisle, Palace Green, London. The decor of the dining-room also included paintings by Burne-Jones:* Cupid and Psyche *(City Art Gallery, Birmingham). Acquired 1979*

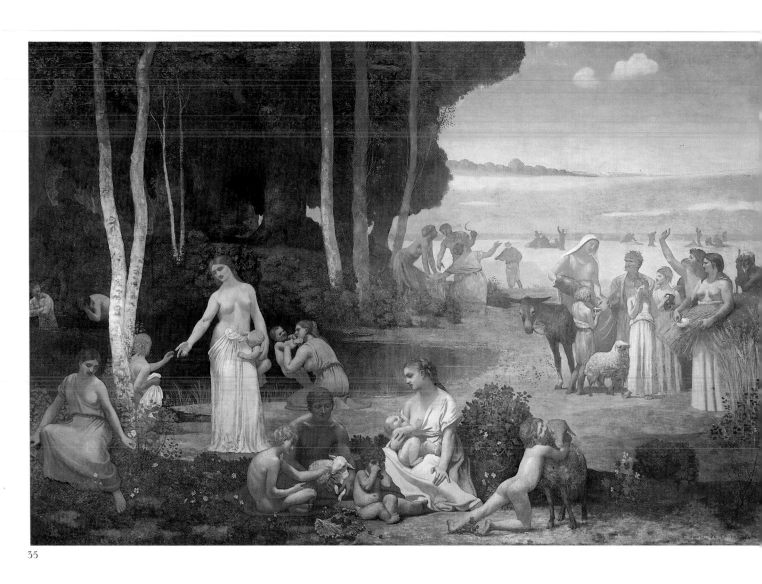

35

Puvis de Chavannes, Moreau, Degas

Pierre Puvis de Chavannes and Gustave Moreau were both admirers, as young men, of the vast decorative works executed by Chassériau between 1844 and 1848 for the stairway of the Cour des Comptes. (These suffered war-damage in 1871 and were removed in 1898, shortly before the building was demolished to make way for the Gare d'Orsay; today they are in the Louvre.)

Decoration is a strong element in the work of Puvis de Chavannes (1824–98), whether or not a painting was conceived with a particular location in mind. His *Eté* (*Summer*) could not be described as a naturalistic depiction of agricultural activity, nor is it precisely an allegory. In the words of the critic Georges Lafenestre, who saw the picture exhibited at the Salon of 1873, where it was acquired for the nation: 'This is not summer in Beauce or Brie. It is summer in an eternal land which the artist's soul inhabits; feelings there are no less intense, but they are more generalized.'

It is precisely this quality of timelessness, allied to a rejection of chiaroscuro in favour of pale, clear colours and flattened, simplified design, that made his work so attractive to the Symbolist painters of the latter years of the century, and in particular to Gauguin, Maillol and the Nabis. *Le pauvre pêcheur* (*The Poor Fisherman*), of 1881, was initially greeted with mild puzzlement, before being hailed as the 'ultimate emblem of poverty' (*synthèse de la misère*) when it entered the Musée du Luxembourg in 1887.

Like Puvis de Chavannes, Edgar Degas (1834–1917) abandoned his law studies in order to concentrate on painting and, also like him, travelled in Italy, where some of his relations lived. It was during a visit to Florence, in 1858, to see his aunt Laure Bellelli (née De Gas – it was the painter himself who adopted the form Degas) that he started *La famille Bellelli* (*The Bellelli Family*). This ambitious composition draws on the tradition of the posed family photograph. Even more strikingly, it echoes the style of Ingres, for whom Degas had a profound admiration. The final canvas was preceded by numerous sketches, drawn and painted, both of details and of the whole picture. The work was discovered in the artist's studio after his death and was acquired for the

35 P. Puvis de Chavannes: L'Eté (Summer) 305 × 507 (120 × 199.6). Salon of 1873. Acquired 1873 for Musée de Chartres and assigned to national collection 1986

36 *P. Puvis de Chavannes:* Le
pauvre pêcheur (The Poor
Fisherman), *1881*
*155 × 192.5 (61 × 75.8). Salon
of 1881. Acquired 1887*

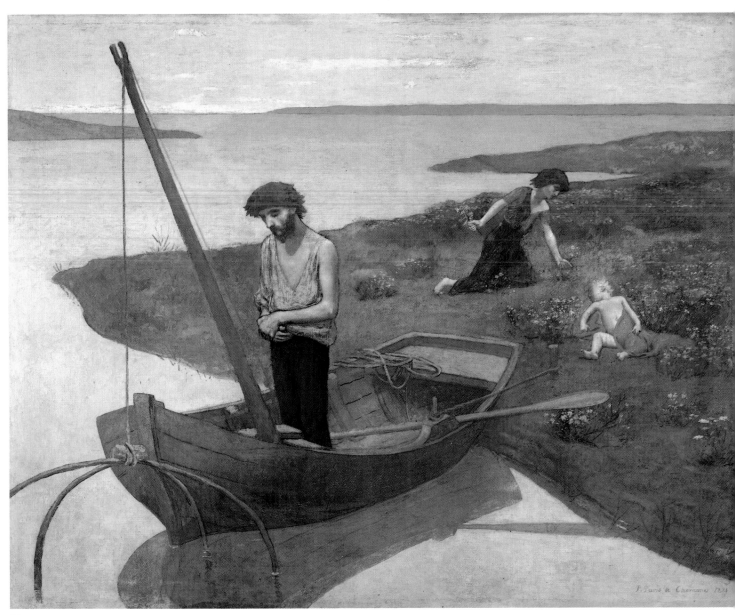

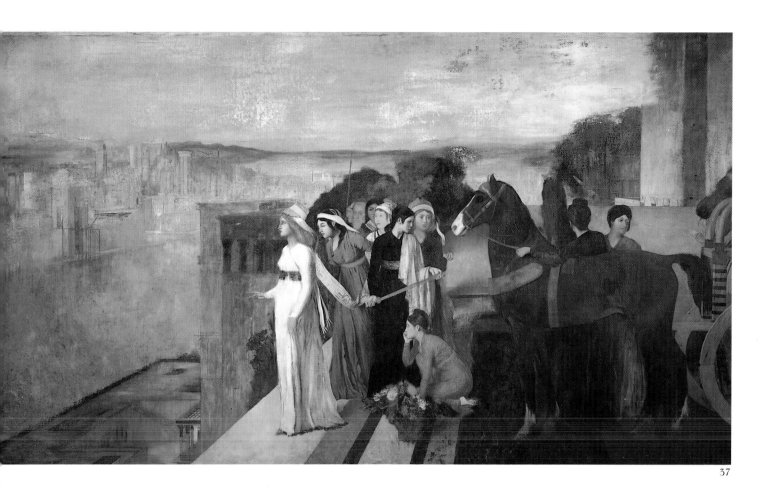

national museums when the contents were put up for auction. The painting demonstrates Degas' consummate skill in portraiture, as alert to details of contemporary life as to the psychology of his sitters. A number of other portraits of his family and friends are also to be seen in the Musée d'Orsay.

In the early years of his career Degas aspired to the status of a history painter, as witness his *Sémiramis construisant Babylone* (*Semiramis Building Babylon*) of 1861; although this particular canvas was not exhibited at the Salon, it is typical of the series of history compositions exhibited by the young painter in the 1860s.

The Degas of these early years has many points of similarity with Gustave Moreau (1826–98), with whom he became friendly in 1859. Moreau was a pupil of Picot and knew Chassériau well. From 1864 onwards he was hugely successful at the Salon: the Musée d'Orsay has in its possession his *Jason*, from the Salon of 1865, and the *Orphée* (*Orpheus*) shown there in 1866. The latter was selected for permanent exhibition in the Musée du Luxembourg, and was regarded at the time as a masterpiece worthy of the Renaissance. The iconographic invention of the young Thracian girl reverently bearing the head and lyre of the bard slain by the Maenads marks one of the first appearances of a theme used widely by the Symbolists in the second half of the nineteenth century, to represent the artist (Orpheus or John the Baptist) whose ideas and creations live on beyond his death.

37 *E. Degas:* Sémiramis contruisant Babylone (Semiramis Building Babylon), *1861*
151 × 258 (59.4 × 101.6).
Acquired 1918

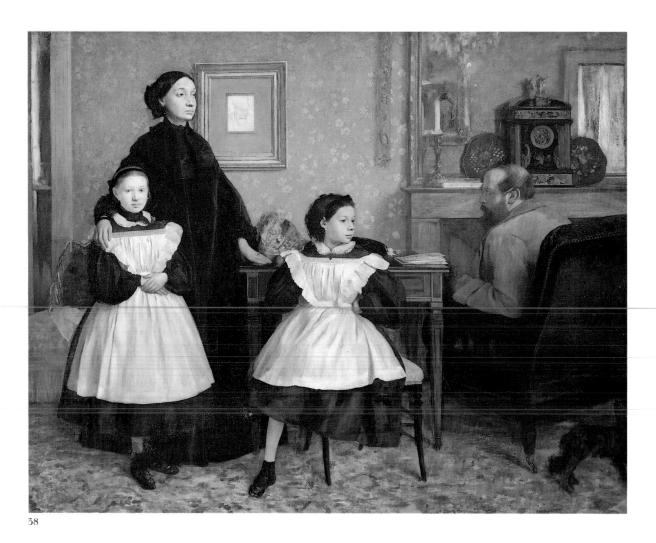

38

38 *E. Degas:* Portrait de
famille; la famille Bellelli
(The Bellelli Family). *Baron
G. Bellelli, his wife, née Laure
De Gas, the artist's aunt, and
their daughters*
*200 × 250 (78.7 × 98.4). Started
in Florence, 1858, and perhaps
exhibited at the Salon of 1867.
Acquired 1918, with assistance
from Comte and Comtesse de
Fels, by kind agreement of
René De Gas*

39 *G. Moreau:* Orphée
(Orpheus), *1866*
*154 × 99.5 (60.6 × 39.2). Salon
of 1866. Acquired 1866*

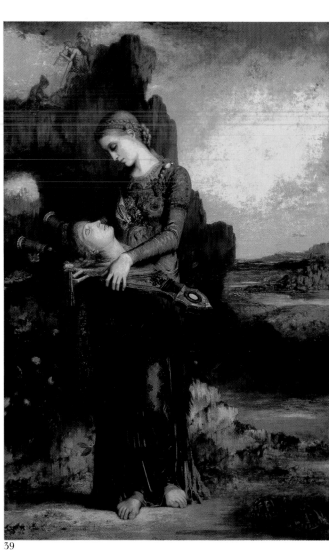

44

39

Aspects of painting outside France

Until the very end of the nineteenth century, few serious efforts were made to secure works by foreign painters for the contemporary collection of the Musée du Luxembourg (one of the exceptions being Oswald Achenbach, during the Second Empire). If non-French painters were represented, it was usually because they were resident in France. No one thought to take advantage of the unique opportunity presented by the World Fairs, with their international art exhibitions, and when the idea surfaced in 1900 it was already too late to do much about it.

In 1915, Edmund Davis donated his collection of English painting, and an annexe was opened at the Jeu de Paume, in 1922, specifically for foreign works. Even so, the museum had

40 *A. Böcklin:* La chasse de Diane (Diana the Huntress), *1896*
100 × 200 (39.4 × 78.7).
Acquired 1977

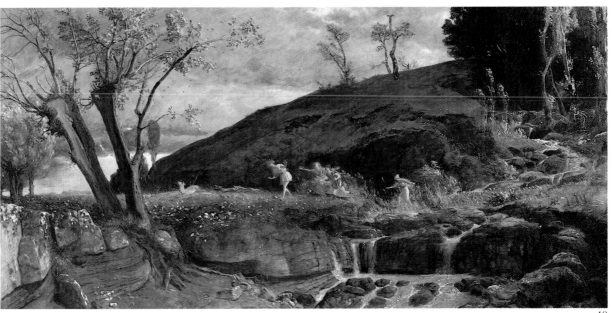

40

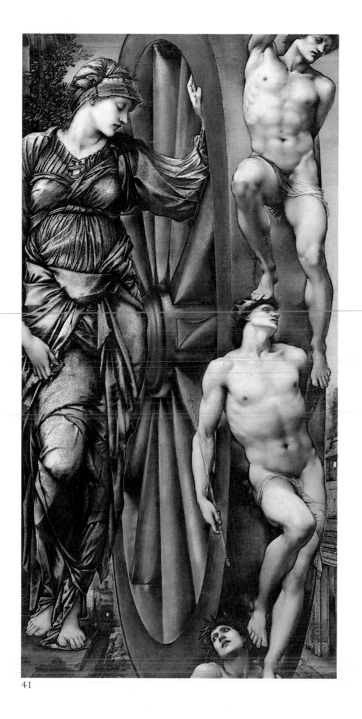

41

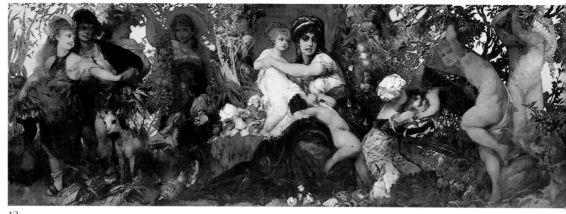

42

no major painting by Sir Edward Burne-Jones (1833–98) until that deficiency was remedied recently by the acquisition of *The Wheel of Fortune* – which was, in fact, one of the artist's own favourite works: Puvis de Chavannes had tried unsuccessfully to have it included in one of the first Salons of the Société Nationale des Beaux-Arts, of which he was then President. Burne-Jones, associated with the second 'romantic' phase of Pre-Raphaelitism, reveals in this picture a debt to Michelangelo, Mantegna and Botticelli, whose works he studied in the course of his last trips to Italy, in 1871 and 1873, and who were to have a profound influence on the paintings of his maturity.

Hans Makart (1840–84) was a highly respected painter in his native Austria, and his reputation spread to France at the time of the World Fair of 1878. His vast compositions attempt to make history painting into something immediate and enthralling; exuberant swirls of Baroque forms, they are full of echoes of Rubens. Makart was also well known as a decorator, and his two large compositions of *Abundantia* were originally destined to grace the dining-room of the Palais Hoyos in Vienna.

The Swiss painter Arnold Böcklin (1827–1901) had little contact with France, preferring to travel in German-speaking countries and visiting Italy on several occasions. Elements of Symbolism begin to appear in his work from around 1870 onwards. His landscapes, whether calm or stormy, have a peculiar atmospheric quality that suggests the forces of nature at work; the mythological figures he introduces are no more than a confirmation of the stated theme. *La chasse de Diane* (*Diana the Huntress*) is a reworking of a theme treated thirty years before, and still betrays its original classical influences.

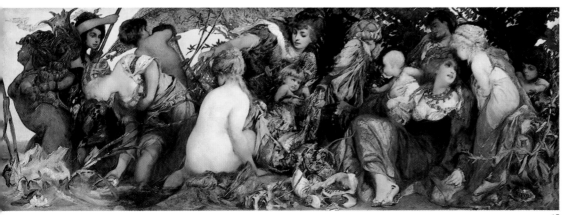

43

Carpeaux

'A statue conceived by the poet of the *Divine Comedy* and created by the begetter of Moses: that would indeed be a masterpiece of the human spirit', wrote Jean-Baptiste Carpeaux (1827–75) in 1854, the year in which he won the Prix de Rome at his tenth attempt. Carpeaux is of course referring to Dante and Michelangelo, who were revered by the sculptors of the latter half of the nineteenth century and were the direct inspiration for his own *Ugolin* (*Ugolino*). This piece was originally conceived as Carpeaux's official submission in his final year of residence at the Villa Médicis, and, although it did not conform to the rules laid down by the Académie de France in Rome, was recognized as a masterpiece by Count Nieuwerkerke, himself a sculptor. Through him, Carpeaux was introduced to the Imperial court, and though not the official portraitist (a post held by Jean-Auguste Barre) he produced a number of vivid terracottas of Napoleon III and the Empress. His sole official commission was for a full-length marble statue of the Prince Imperial with his dog. The three figures shown here give an indication of Carpeaux's talents – qualities of observation and lively expression – which are equally apparent in his paintings.

Naturally enough, the major public commissions were reserved for winners of the Prix de Rome – and there was no lack of new façades to decorate in the Second Empire. Carpeaux sculpted the allegorical figure of *La France impériale protégeant l'Agriculture et les Sciences* (*Imperial France protecting Agriculture and the Sciences*) to crown the

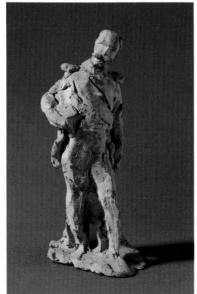

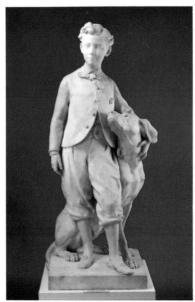

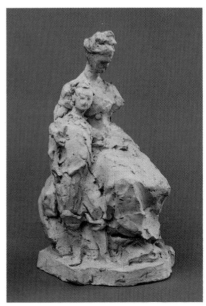

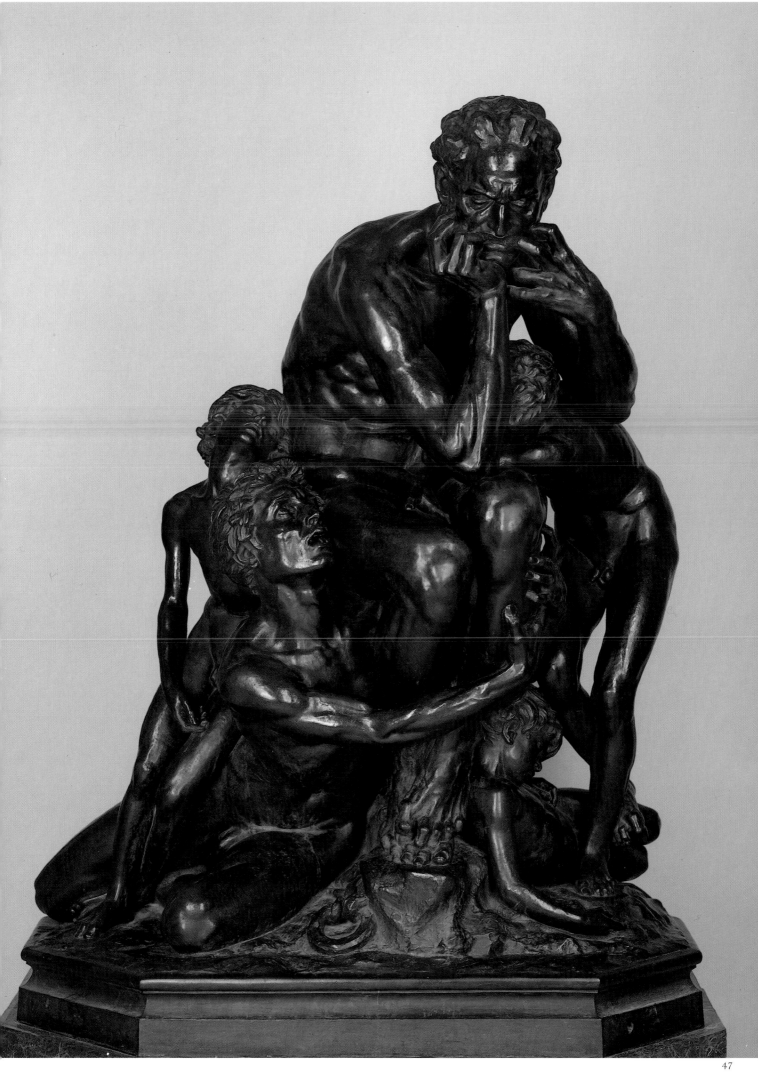

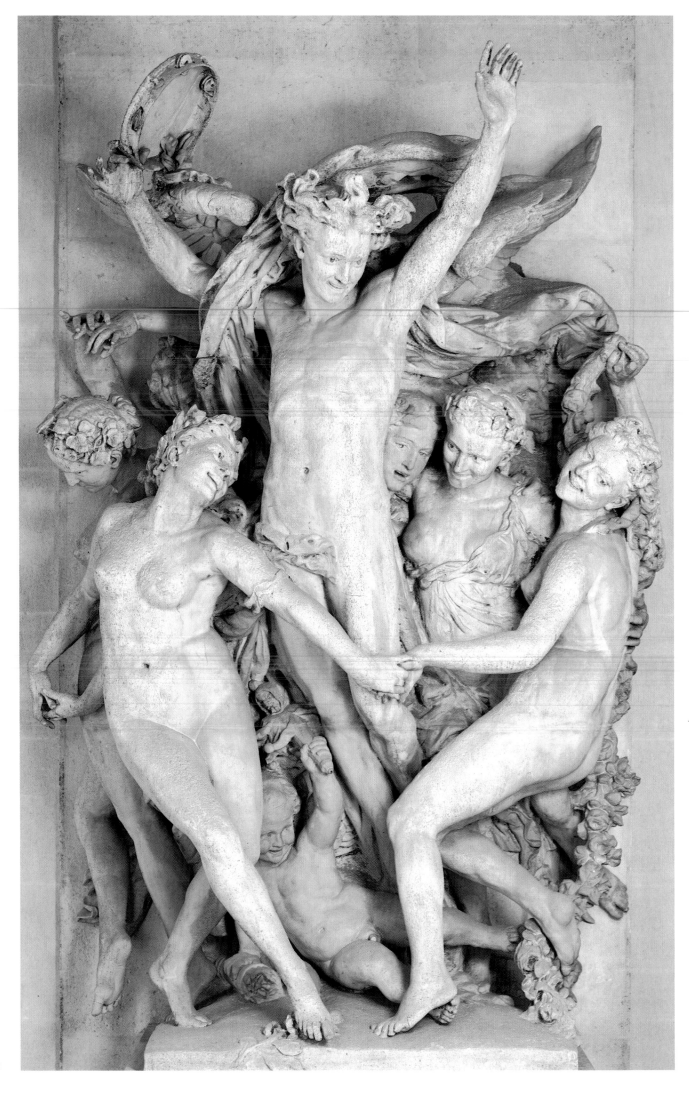

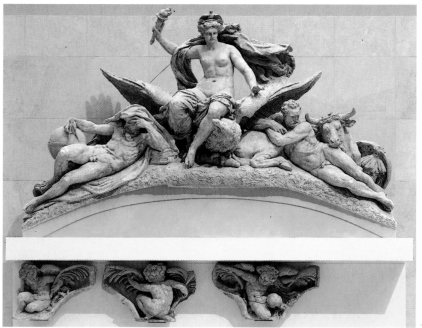

south front of the new Pavillon de Flore of the Louvre, designed by Hector Lefuel. Here too his admiration for Michelangelo was evident: the oculi were encircled by children bearing palms, and, beneath them, the relief of Flora was a splendid tribute to Rubens, a celebration of fleshly form and life. The theme of Flora surrounded by a ring of children was taken up as the central motif of *La danse* (*The Dance*). Commissioned for the new Opéra by his old student friend Charles Garnier in 1863 (although the official commission for a 'group of three figures' was not issued until 1865), the relief is full of movement and dynamism, reflecting the detailed work Carpeaux put into his many preparatory sketches and maquettes. The group's animation and verve could not have provided a greater contrast with the contributions from François Jouffroy, Claude Guillaume and Jean Perraud, the Academicians commissioned to decorate the other three piers. When the work was unveiled in 1869 there was a popular outcry. The prudes joined forces with the opponents of the regime and demanded action. Garnier himself, apparently, was 'lost in admiration for the vivid composition, the life-like modelling, and said, "Well, if the monument suffers a little from the exuberance of my sculptor, that will be a small price to pay, but the price would be huge if I stuck rigidly to my ideas and deprived France of a work that will certainly be a masterpiece."'

In the end, Garnier was obliged to bow to pressure from above, and another group was commissioned from the sculptor Charles Gumery. The war of 1870 and the death of Carpeaux, at the age of forty-seven, meant that the substitution was never effected. Gumery's group was placed in the Musée d'Angers. In 1964, threatened by pollution, Carpeaux's original was removed to the Louvre and replaced by a copy.

48 *J. B. Carpeaux:* La danse (The Dance), *1869 Stone. 420 (165.4). Commissioned 1865, unveiled 1869; removed from the Opéra to the Louvre, 1964, and to the Musée d'Orsay, 1986*

49 *J. B. Carpeaux:* La France impériale protégeant l'Agriculture et les Sciences (Imperial France Protecting Agriculture and Science) *Plaster. 268 (105.5). Commissioned 1863. Salon of 1866. Acquired 1892*

The new Opéra

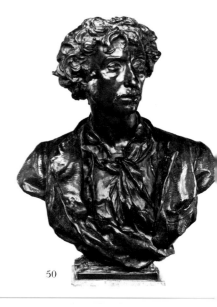

50

50 *J. B. Carpeaux:* Charles Garnier *(1825–98), architect of the new Opéra, Paris, 1869* Bronze. 67 (26.4). *Bequest of Madame Charles Garnier, 1921*

51 *A. Crépinet:* Design for the new Opéra, Paris, *1861* Pencil and watercolour. *50.6 × 68.9 (19.9 × 27.1). Runner-up in competition to Garnier's scheme. Acquired 1983*

52 *Atelier Rémy Munier:* Model of the Opéra quarter, scale 1:100, detail, *1984–86*

53 *J. E. Lenepveu:* Modello for the Opéra ceiling *D. 150 (59). Loaned by Musée de l'Opéra and Bibliothèque de l'Opéra*

On 29 December 1860 Napoleon III decreed the construction of a new Paris opera house as a matter of 'public interest'. The decision came not before time: the cramped building in the rue Le Peletier had never been regarded as anything more than a temporary base, and a number of abortive schemes had been drawn up over the past century for moves to a variety of locations. The winning design in the competition launched in December 1860 was submitted by an unknown young architect, Charles Garnier. The scale model of the Opéra area shows the problems he faced with the massed, uniform façades of Baron Haussmann's rebuilt Paris. The great achievement of Garnier's Opéra is that, although standing in the heart of an area that is a monument to the efficiency of Second Empire town-planning, it triumphantly sets itself apart from every other building in Paris, rejecting straight lines in favour of flowing curves, austerity in favour of ornamental exuberance, regularity in favour of the picturesque, grey in favour of sumptuous polychromatic effects. In the interior, Garnier transforms the spectator's experience, as he walks from the entrance to his seat, into a piece of French grand opera, conceived in architectural terms: extravagant dramatic effects, contrasts of light and shade, alternation of intimate passages with grandiose tableaux.

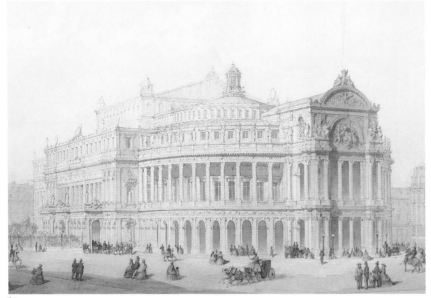

51

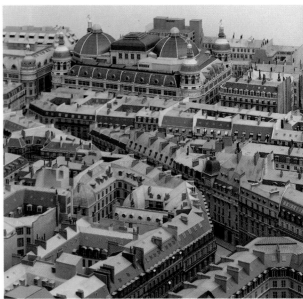

52

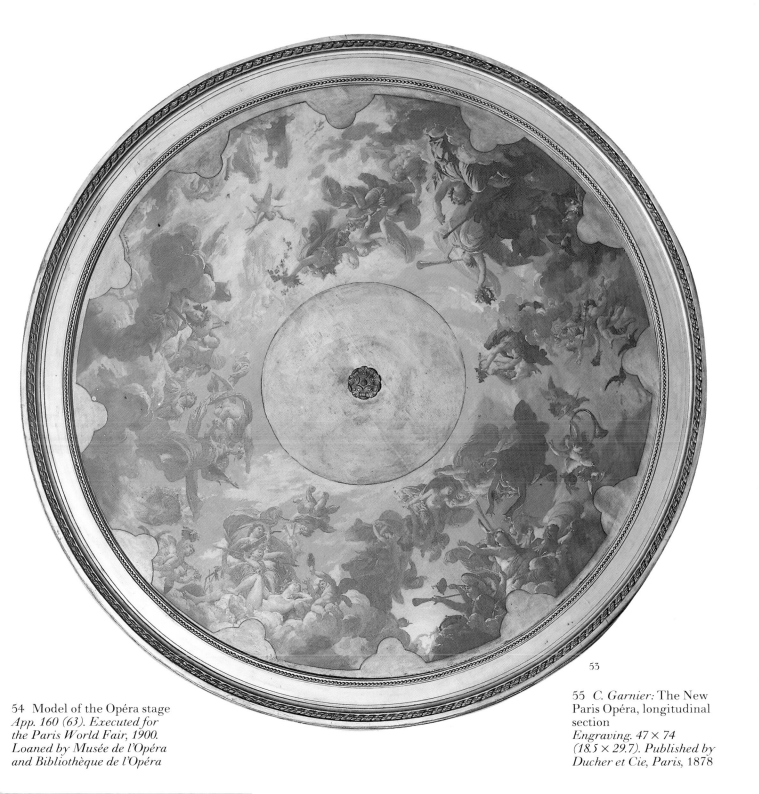

54 Model of the Opéra stage
*App. 160 (63). Executed for
the Paris World Fair, 1900.
Loaned by Musée de l'Opéra
and Bibliothèque de l'Opéra*

55 *C. Garnier:* The New
Paris Opéra, longitudinal
section
*Engraving. 47 × 74
(18.5 × 29.7). Published by
Ducher et Cie, Paris, 1878*

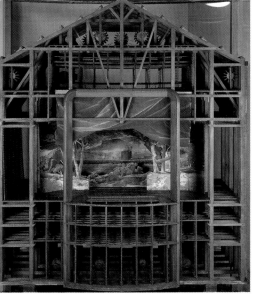

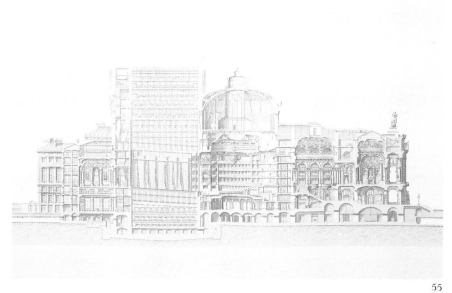

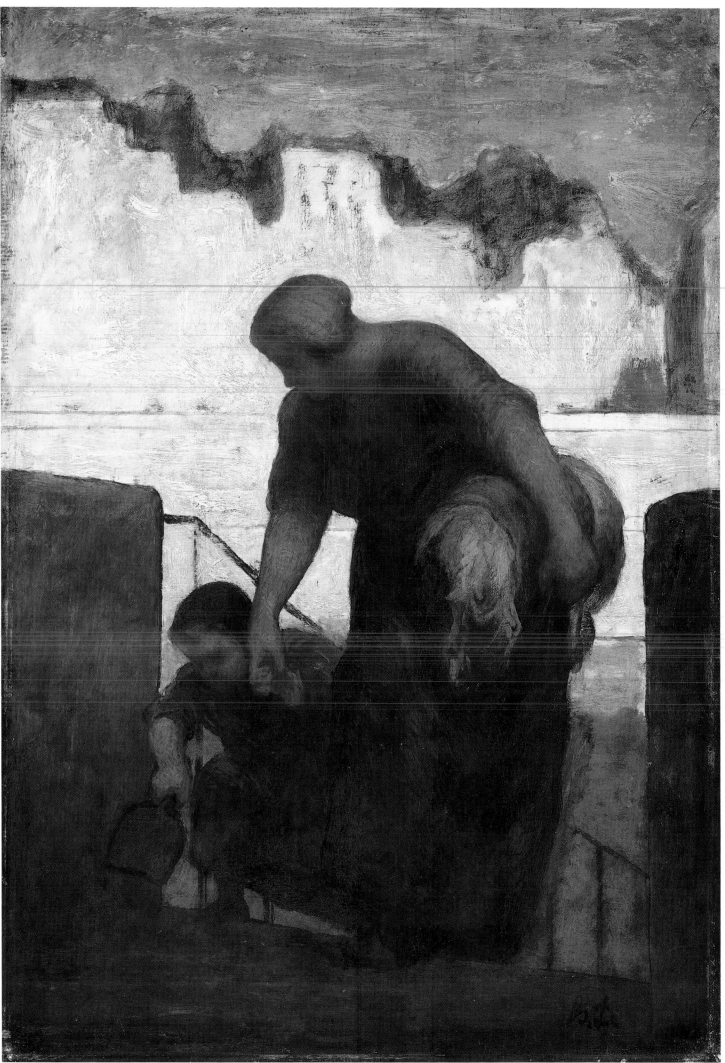

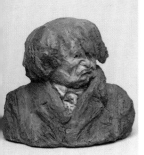

57

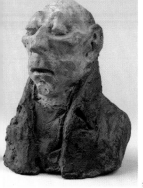

58

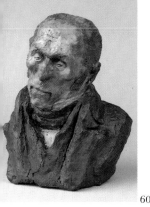

59

Daumier

Although during his lifetime Honoré Daumier (1808–79) was renowned chiefly for his caricatures and lithographs, the twentieth-century public is equally appreciative of the paintings and sculptures that he often used as points of departure. The Musée d'Orsay is fortunate in possessing virtually all Daumier's major sculptures. The *Emigrants* and *Ratapoil* have long been in the state collections, and thanks to the generosity of Monsieur Michel David-Weill, these were joined in 1980 by the original series of thirty-six painted clay busts of *Parlementaires* (*Parliamentarians*). Begun in 1832, these caricature-portraits of prominent political figures show how Daumier made use of the general vogue for caricature and turned it into a political weapon. He did not rely on anecdote but on piercingly exact observation and wonderfully expressive draughtsmanship and modelling. His bold distortions seem to reveal the inner nature of his subjects, at the same time distinguishing them as clearly identifiable human types. It is this very modern aspect of his work that sets him apart from the Romantics of his generation and justifies the decision to show his sculpture at the Musée d'Orsay rather than in the Louvre.

57–60 *H. Daumier:* Dr C. Prunelle *(1774–1863), parliamentarian (57);* Ch. Philipon *(1800–62), journalist (58);* J. C. Fulchiron *(1774–1859), poet and parliamentarian (59);* F. Guizot *(1787–1874), interior minister (60) Coloured unfired clay. 31 (12.2); 16 (6.3); 17 (6.7); 22 (8.7). Commissioned by Philipon as models for lithographs published 1832–35 in his periodicals* Le Charivari *and* La Caricature. *Acquired 1980 with assistance from Michel David-Weill and the Lutèce Foundation*

61 *H. Daumier:* Les émigrants (The Emigrants), *first version, c. 1848–50 Plaster. 31 × 67.5 (12.2 × 26.6). Acquired 1960*

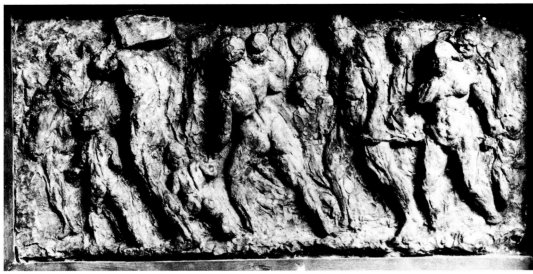

60

56 *H. Daumier:* La blanchisseuse (The Washerwoman) *49 × 33.5 (19.3 × 13.2). Acquired 1927 with assistance from D. David-Weill*

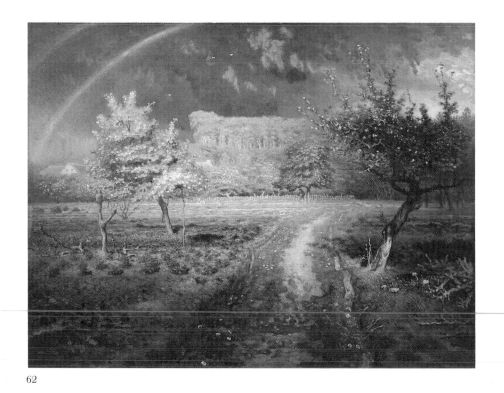

62

62 *J. F. Millet:* Le printemps
(Spring), *1868–73. 86 × 111
(33.9 × 43.7). Gift of Madame
Frédéric Hartmann, 1887*

63 *J. F. Millet:* L'Angélus
(The Angelus), *1857–59
55.5 × 66 (22 × 26). Bequest of
Alfred Chauchard, 1909*

64 *J. F. Millet:* Des glaneuses
(Gleaners)
*85 × 111 (35.5 × 43.7). Salon of
1857. Gift of Madame
Pommery, 1890*

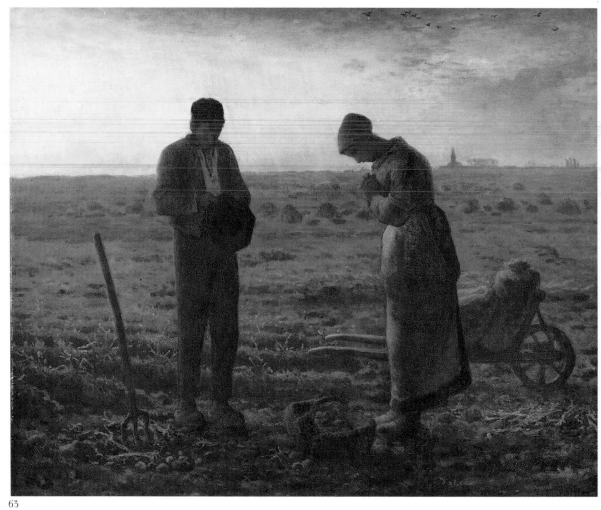

63

Millet

The scenes of peasant life that made Jean-François Millet (1814–75) famous in the 1880s were regarded in his lifetime as subversive. Under the Second Empire not a single one of his canvases was acquired for the Musée du Luxembourg, although two paintings were purchased shortly after Millet's death – *L'église de Gréville* (*The Church at Gréville*) and a small early picture of *Baigneuses* (*Bathers*). However, largely thanks to the generosity of individual collectors, the Louvre has been able to build up over the years a remarkable collection of his work. His *Le printemps* (*Spring*) was donated in 1887 by the widow of Frédéric Hartmann, who com-

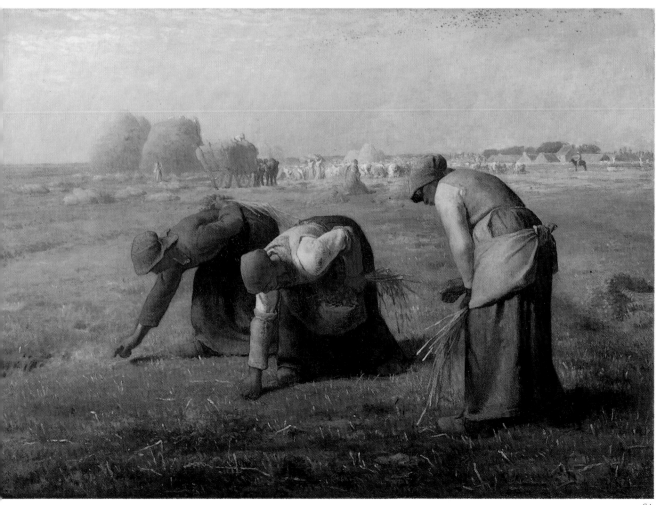

missioned from Millet a set of *Four Seasons* – never in fact completed. The canvas is a fine example of the painter's late manner. Beautifully lit and with wonderfully clear colours, it is not so much a landscape as the expression of a dialogue between nature, shaped by man, and man himself, a tiny figure under a menacing sky; the symbolism of the season is reinforced by the choice of a morning setting.

Millet's characteristic brand of Naturalism consists in this ability to evoke a precise instant while yet investing it with a universal significance. The most famous example of his work is *L'Angélus* (*The Angelus*), which came to the Louvre as part of a major bequest by Alfred Chauchard in 1909. He acquired it in 1890 from the American Art Association, which had taken the picture on a triumphant tour of the American cities after buying it, only a year before, at the Secretan sale of 1 July 1889.

Des glaneuses (*Gleaners*) passed to the Louvre in 1890. This major work had attracted bitter criticism when first exhibited at the Salon of 1857. In an age when it was believed that poverty had been eradicated, the painting seemed to conjure up the spectre of revolution. Paul de Saint-Victor wrote in *La Presse*: 'While Monsieur Courbet is tidying up and adjusting his style, Monsieur Millet is becoming more entrenched in his. His three *Gleaners* have immoderate pretensions; they pose like the Three Fates of Pauperism. They are scarecrows in rags.' Millet's cause was, however, taken up by one critic, Jules Castagnary, who sensed the emergence of a new style that would replace the exhausted genre of history painting. Castagnary chose therefore to find a parallel with the classical past, describing the canvas as 'one of those great and true passages such as Homer and Vergil lighted upon'. The comparison is not inapt: the gleaners recall the sculptures of the Parthenon. Their massive weight is an essential part of their power of expression.

The Barbizon School; late Corot

Millet went to live at Barbizon in 1849, and continued to paint scenes of peasant life, looking to the village itself or the Chailly plain for his subject matter rather than the nearby forest of Fontainebleau itself. That great area of woodland had for some twenty years been a favourite spot for artists, who arrived in their numbers to paint and draw from nature. One of these was Millet's friend Théodore Rousseau (1812–67), who had suffered many rejections at the hands of the academic jury under Louis-Philippe, and began to receive official recognition only after 1848, in the Second Republic. A perfectionist, he reworked his paintings obsessively and made it a rule to paint always from the motif – as for example in the forest landscape pierced by a vertical shaft of sunlight, exhibited at the Salon of 1849 as *Une avenue* (*An avenue*), which he painted in the spring of 1846 while staying with the landscapist Jules Dupré at L'Isle-Adam.

Narcisse Diaz de la Peña (1807–76) started out as a painter of amorous interludes and fantasies in a Romantic spirit, and by 1860 was successful enough to enjoy an extravagant lifestyle. After meeting Théodore Rousseau in 1837, he returned regularly to Fontainebleau and became perhaps the most skilled of all the group at conveying the effects of light on the trees and undergrowth. The critic Thoré noted that Diaz's supremacy lay in 'the quality of the colour, which is

65 *T. Rousseau:* Une avenue, forêt de L'Isle-Adam (An Avenue in the Forest of L'Isle-Adam) *101 × 82 (39.8 × 32.3). Salon of 1849. Bequest of Alfred Chauchard, 1909*

66 *N. Diaz de la Peña:* Les hauteurs du Jean de Paris (forêt de Fontainebleau) (The Jean de Paris Heights, Forest of Fontainebleau), *1867 84 × 106 (33.1 × 41.7). Bequest of Alfred Chauchard, 1909*

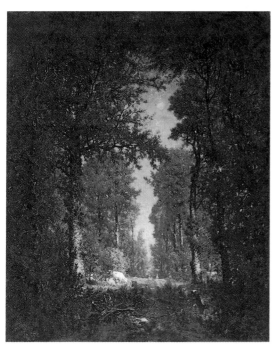

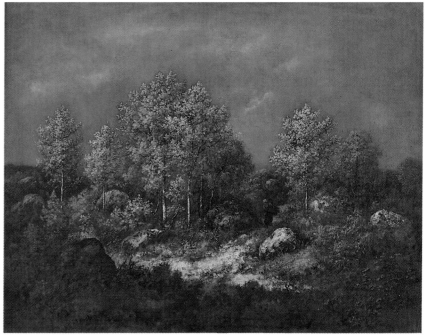

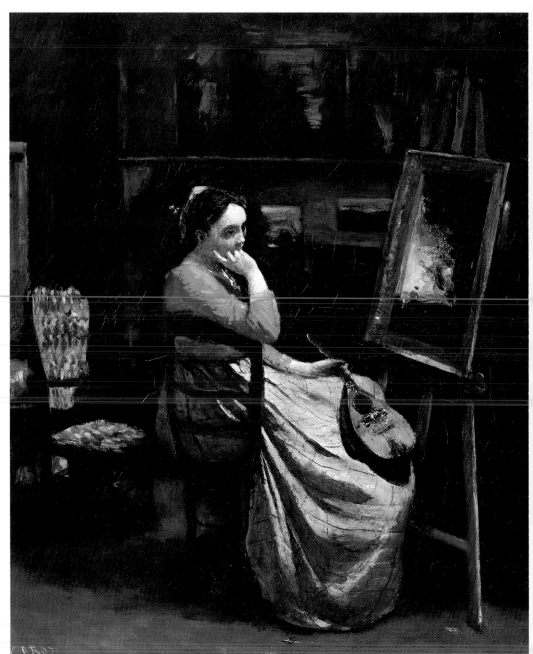

67 *J. B. C. Corot:* L'atelier de Corot. Jeune femme à la mandoline (Corot's Studio. Young Woman with Mandolin), c. *1865–70 56 × 46 (22 × 18.1). Acquired 1933*

68 *J. B. C. Corot:* Une matinée. La danse des nymphes (Morning. The Dance of the Nymphs) *98 × 131 (38.6 × 51.6). Salon of 1850–51. Acquired 1851*

67

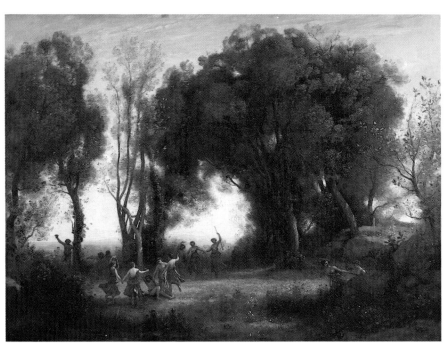

68

always determined by the light', and that 'his pictures resemble a mound of precious stones'. His technique almost certainly influenced Monticelli and Renoir, to whom he gave advice and encouragement.

Rousseau and Diaz have close ties with Romanticism and, like Delacroix, are represented in the Musée d'Orsay only by a few works of particular significance (notably those from the Chauchard collection; see p. 65). The rest of their work is to be seen in the Louvre.

Another major painter whose works are mainly in the Louvre, but who is represented in the Musée d'Orsay collections, is Jean-Baptiste Camille Corot (1796–1875), born in the eighteenth century but active well into the nineteenth. His career was unsensational, but he was greatly esteemed by the younger painters and by the more perspicacious of the critics, among them Charles Baudelaire who admired his technique and 'unfailingly strict harmonies'.

Corot travelled in Italy, stayed at Barbizon, and ranged the length and breadth of France, from Brittany to Dauphiné. To make his work acceptable to the academic Salon jury, he felt obliged to introduce historical and mythological figures into landscapes that otherwise would have been rejected as little more than sketches. It was the increasing respectability of Naturalism in the Second Empire that presented him with the freedom to pursue his own inclinations, encouraged too, no doubt, by the expansion in demand from private patrons.

At about this time his manner became more lyrical and he began to paint misty evocations of nature (well represented in the Chauchard collection). *La danse des nymphes* (*The Dance of the Nymphs*) is typical; it was exhibited at the Salon of 1850–51 and purchased by the state for the Musée du Luxembourg, where it was put on show in 1854 – the only painting by Corot to be given that official stamp of approval during his lifetime.

Less well-known, and largely dismissed by his contemporaries, is Corot's painting of individual figures, posed either outdoors or in studio interiors, and dressed in exotic disguises or theatrical costumes. Corot treated these works as exercises in pure painting, anticipating Cezanne's fundamental explorations of technique. Although he also painted portraits of friends and relatives, for studies of this type Corot preferred to employ professional models, not wishing to be distracted by individual personality. The melancholy of the attitude of the pensive young woman in *L'atelier* (*The Studio*) is tempered by the play of light on her dress and face, and on the tapestry of the chair to the left; there is a discreet symbolism in the objects about her, the landscape on the easel making a reference to painting and the mandolin suggesting a tune left unfinished.

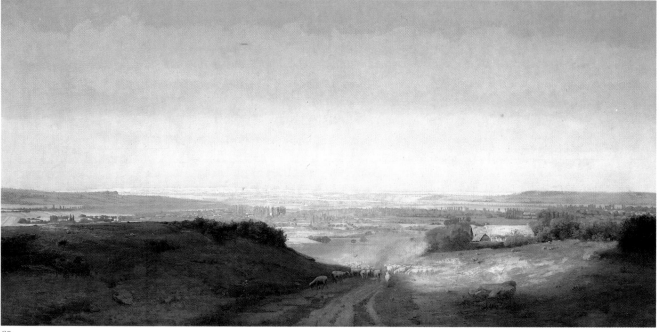

Daubigny and Chintreuil

Charles-François Daubigny (1817–78) belonged to the generation of Millet and Courbet. Both engraver and painter, he had a traditional education and went to Italy before devoting himself to observation of the French landscape. By 1848 his success was established, and as a member of the Salon jury under the Second Empire he was able to put in a word for younger artists such as Cézanne, Renoir and Pissarro. He worked all over France, and in 1860 was among the first of many painters to move to Auvers-sur-Oise, where his visitors included Daumier and Corot. Daubigny loved effects of light on water, and sailed the rivers of the Ile-de-France in his studio-boat *Botin*. His *Moisson* (*Harvest*) of 1851 is set in an open landscape; the bold use of colour on the horizon shows how far he had moved from official art as practised, say, by Rosa Bonheur. Antoine Chintreuil (1814–73) was much influenced by Corot and regarded himself as his pupil. He acquired some reputation under the Second Republic, showing at the juryless Salon of 1848, but in 1863 was relegated to the Salon des Refusés. His fame was largely posthumous, although at the 1869 Salon *L'espace* (*Space*), a delicate composition of greens and blues, was praised for 'a fine appreciation of light' and bought for the Luxembourg.

69 *A. Chintreuil:* L'espace (Space)
102 × 202 (40.2 × 79.5). Salon of 1869. Acquired 1869

70 *C. Daubigny:* Moisson (Harvest), *1851*
135 × 196 (53.1 × 77.2). Salon of 1852. Acquired 1853

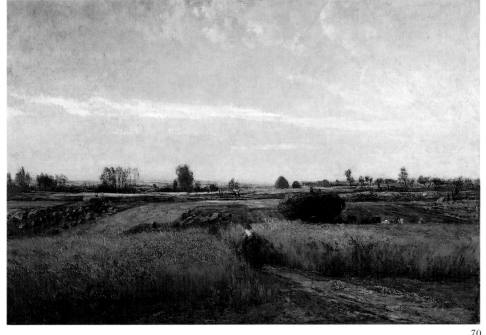

70

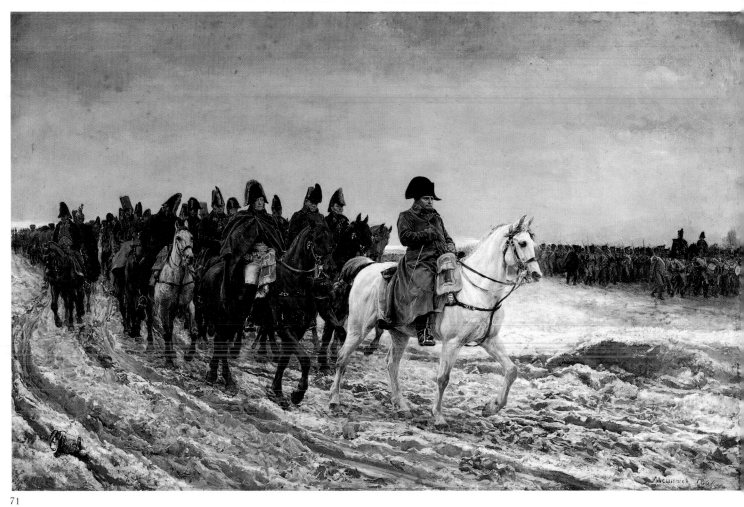

71

71 *E. Meissonier:* Campagne
de France, 1814 (The
Campaign in France, 1814)
*51.5 × 76.5 (20.3 × 30.1). Salon
of 1864. Bequest of Alfred
Chauchard, 1909*

Meissonier and the Chauchard collection

Realism of a totally different order from that of the landscape painters characterizes the work of Ernest Meissonier (1815–91), a painter of historical scenes, who dressed his models in authentic costume and exhaustively researched every aspect of period detail. His genre pictures, often minute in size, attracted high prices from collectors, and many are in the fine collection assembled at the end of the nineteenth century by Alfred Chauchard and bequeathed by him to the Louvre in 1909. A project that occupied Meissonier throughout most of his career was a series of five paintings in commemoration of the epic career of Napoleon. One of these is *Campagne de France 1814* (*The Campaign in France, 1814*), which was exhibited at the Salon of 1864. Together with Millet's *Angelus*, this is one of the gems of the Chauchard Collection, in which sumptuously framed landscapes and Naturalist scenes are mingled with tiny genre paintings, among which, interestingly, are a few Romantic works such as *Marchand turc fumant dans sa boutique* (*Turkish Merchant Smoking in his Shop*) by Alexandre Decamps (1803–60).

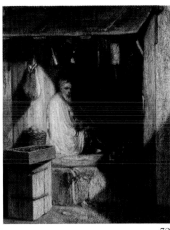

72

72 *A. Decamps:* Marchand turc fumant dans sa boutique (Turkish Merchant Smoking in his Shop), *1844* *36 × 28 (14.2 × 11). Bequest of Alfred Chauchard, 1909*

73 *E. Meissonier:* Le voyageur (The Traveller) *Coloured wax and fabric. 52 (20.5). Gift of Jean Du Pasquier, 1984, in memory of his mother, the artist's granddaughter*

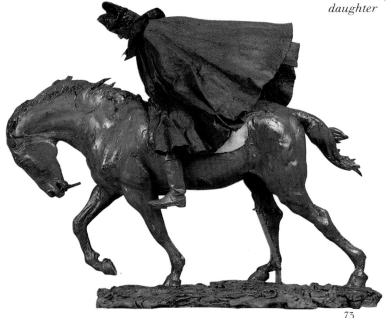

73

Courbet

Gustave Courbet (1819–77) experienced years of struggle in the early part of his career, in the reign of Louis-Philippe: only three of the twenty-four canvases he submitted to the Salon in the period 1841–47 were accepted by the jury and exhibited. The situation changed dramatically when he showed ten canvases at the juryless Salon of 1848 and went on to win a medal in 1849 – which meant that he could in future bypass the jury procedure. His fame was assured, but the critics were divided into two camps at the Salon of 1850–51 by the controversial *Un enterrement à Ornans* (*Burial at Ornans*), a vast composition for which Courbet used people from his home town of Ornans as models. When the selection jury for the World Fair of 1855 turned down the work, along with his recent manifesto-painting *L'atelier du peintre* (*The Painter in his Studio*), Courbet determined to hold a show of his own in competition with the officially blessed international restrospective – although in fact eleven of his

74 *G. Courbet:* Un enterrement à Ornans (A Burial at Ornans), *1849–50 315 × 668 (124 × 263). Salon of 1850–51. Gift of Juliette Courbet, the artist's sister, 1881*

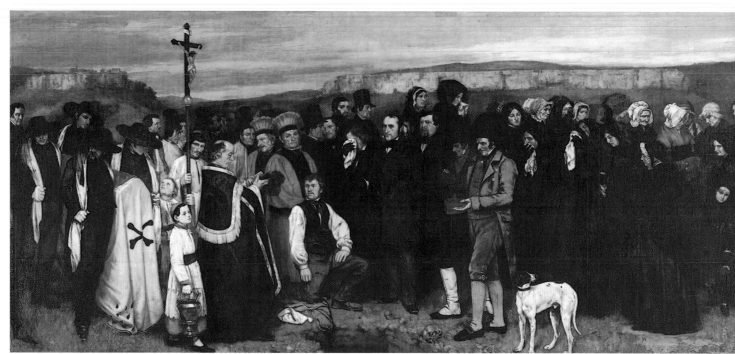

74

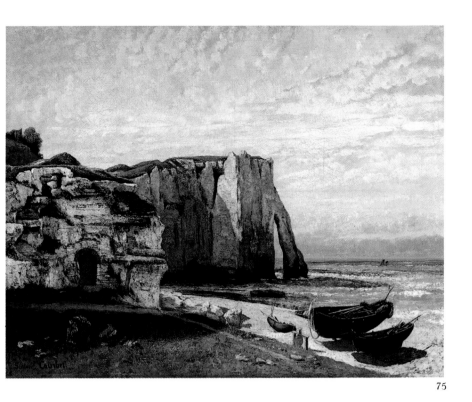

75

canvases had been included. In the event the Pavillon du
Réalisme, with an exhibition of forty of his paintings, was not
a success; only his friends praised the venture, among them
the critic Champfleury, generous enough to overlook the
portrait of himself in *The Painter in his Studio*, which he
disliked intensely.

Courbet's two major compositions did not enter the
national collections until many years later: the *Burial at
Ornans* was presented to the Louvre to coincide with an
exhibition held at the Ecole des Beaux-Arts in 1882,
'Exposition des oeuvres de G. Courbet', marking the artist's
long-delayed official recognition, and the *Studio* remained in
private hands until 1920.

Apart from these paintings, which shocked the Second
Empire public and were satirized by the cartoonists of the
day, Courbet also produced many far more accessible works
that appealed to collectors and yet remained honest expressions of his robust style. Count Nieuwerkerke, Director of
the Beaux-Arts in the Second Empire, purchased with funds
from the Emperor's civil list a landscape called *Le ruisseau
couvert* (*The Shaded Stream*), painted in 1865, which then
passed to the national collections. *La vague* (*The Wave*) was
acquired for the Musée du Luxembourg shortly after the
painter's death. *La falaise d'Etretat après l'orage* (*The Cliff at
Etretat after the Storm*), of the Salon of 1870, is a fine example
of Courbet's qualities as a landscape artist; like *The Wave*, it
was painted in 1869, while Courbet was staying at Etretat, a
small town on the Normandy coast which had been a
favourite spot for painters since the early years of the century.

76 *G. Courbet.* L'atelier du peintre. Allégorie réelle déterminant une phase de sept années de ma vie artistique (The Studio of the Painter. A Real Allegory Defining a Seven-year Phase in my Artistic Life) *359 × 598 (141.3 × 235.4). Shown at Pavillon du Réalisme, place de l'Alma, Paris 1855. Acquired 1920 with the aid of a public subscription and of the Société des Amis du Louvre*

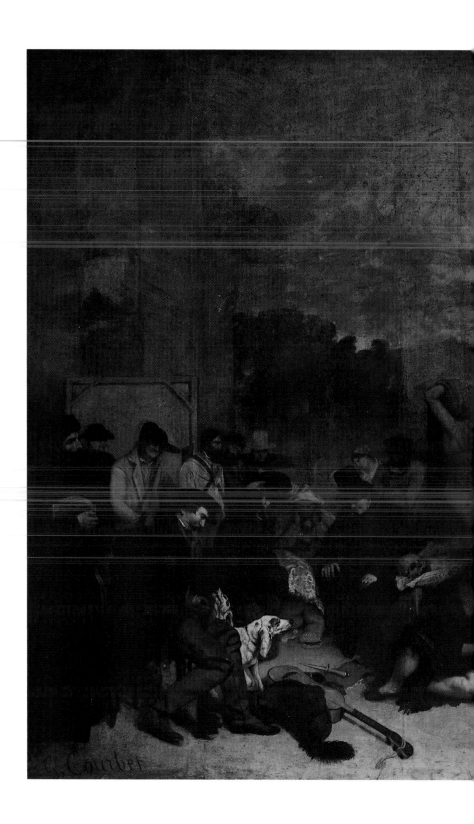

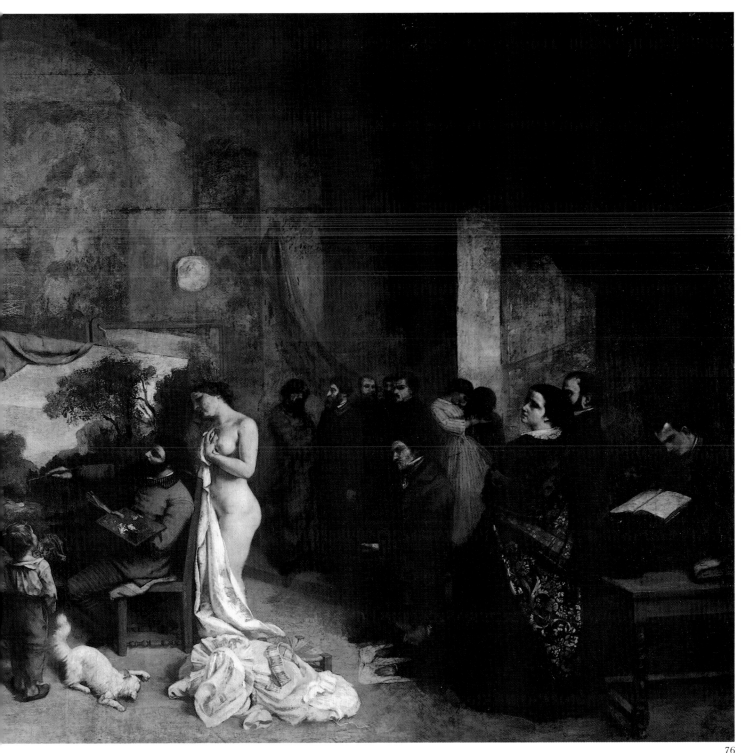

Peasant Realism

Jules Breton (1827–1906), educated in Antwerp and Paris, experimented from 1849–50 onwards with large-scale Realist compositions in the style of Courbet or Alexandre Antigna. He later concentrated on studies of agricultural workers in the fields around his native village of Courrières, in Artois (near Calais). His paintings of peasants are more anecdotal than those by Millet, and he won popular acclaim in the Second Empire for such pictures as *Le rappel des glaneuses* (*Calling the Gleaners Home*). Regarded practically as the official painter of peasant life, he was elected a member of the Institut de France in 1886, at a time when Naturalism was no longer controversial.

The mid-century pioneers of this agricultural genre were Constant Troyon (1810–65) and Rosa Bonheur (1822–99); Bonheur's *Labourage nivernais, le sombrage* (*Ploughing in the Nivernais Region*), commissioned by the state in 1848, has for succeeding generations evoked the world of George Sand's novels.

Ernest Hébert (1817–1908) is in a slightly different category. After winning the Prix de Rome in 1839 he made several trips to Italy, and there abandoned history painting to concentrate instead on scenes of popular life, following the example set by Léopold Robert and Victor Schnetz; his masterpiece, *La Mal'aria* (*Malaria*), in the Salon of 1850–51, reflected the prevailing Realist vein. His later compositions, however, are tinged with the sentimentality that brought him numerous commissions and great success as a painter of female portraits.

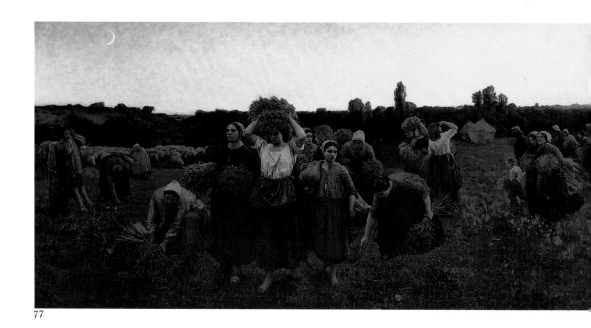

77

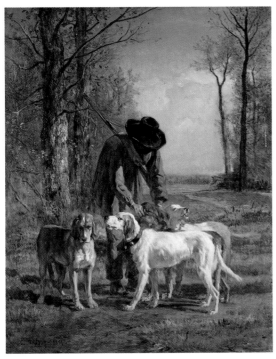

78

78 *C. Troyon:* Garde-chasse
arrêté près de ses chiens
(Gamekeeper Standing with
his Dogs), *1854*
*117 × 90 (46.1 × 35.4). Bequest
of Alfred Chauchard, 1909*

79 *R. Bonheur:* Labourage
nivernais (Ploughing in the
Nivernais Region)
*134 × 260 (52.8 × 102.4).
Commissioned 1848. Salon of
1849*

80 *E. Hébert:* La Mal'aria
(Malaria), *1848–49*
*135 × 193 (53.1 × 76). Salon of
1850–51. Acquired 1851*

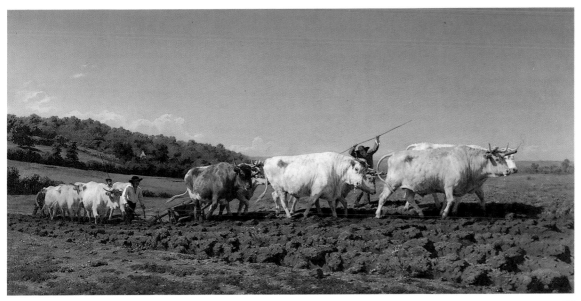

79

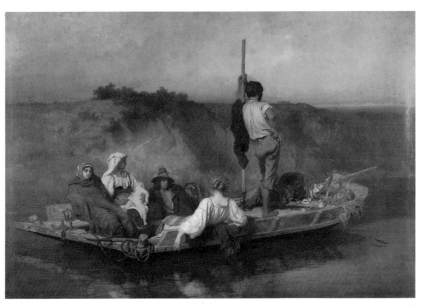

80

71

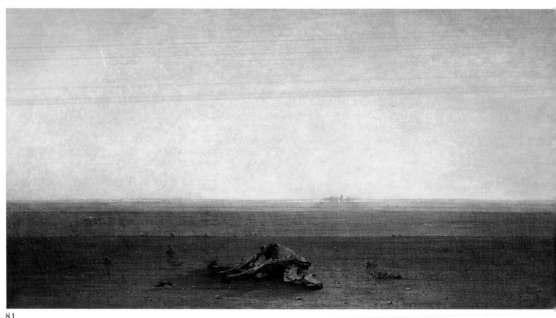

81

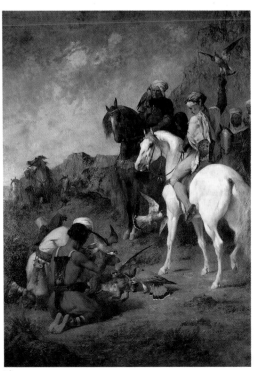

81 *G. Guillaumet:* Le Sahara
ou Le désert (The Sahara, or
The Desert), *1867*
*110 × 200 (43.3 × 78.7). Salon
of 1868. Gift of the artist's
family, 1888*

82 *E. Fromentin:* Chasse au
faucon en Algérie; la curée
(Falconry in Algeria;
Distributing the Quarry)
*162.5 × 118 (64 × 46.5). Salon
of 1863. Acquired 1863*

82

Orientalism

The Orient, as seen from nineteenth-century France, consisted of the Muslim countries of the Mediterranean, either as they existed in the imagination – for example in Ingres' *Odalisques* – or as they were actually experienced at first hand: the Holy Land and Eastern Turkey, painted by Charles Tournemine (1812–72); Egypt, in the works of Léon Belly (1827–77), among them the impressive *Pélerins allant à la Mecque* (*Pilgrims Travelling to Mecca*) of the Salon of 1861; and above all North Africa, which Delacroix had described after a visit in 1832 as a place where the ancient civilizations lived on. Apart from the obvious attraction of new subject matter, with its glimpses of a lost Eden, there was also the dazzling quality of the light, which spurred the painters to transform their palettes. The Romanticism of Delacroix, Decamps, Chassériau and, later in the day, Henri Regnault, gave way during the Second Empire to an increasing Naturalism, a trend noted in 1861 by the brothers Jules and Edmond de Goncourt in their novel *Manette Salomon*.

Eugène Fromentin (1820–76) visited Algeria on several occasions between 1846 and 1853, and in 1857 and 1859 published two accounts of his travels, *Un été dans le Sahara* and *Une année dans le Sahel*. These trips were to furnish him with subject matter for the rest of his life, and, drawing on his memories, he painted numerous imaginary scenes and picturesque reconstructions such as *Chasse au faucon en Algérie: la curée* (*Falconry in Algeria: Distributing the Quarry*) acquired for the Musée du Luxembourg at the Salon of 1863, a brilliantly coloured canvas with drawing of an almost Ingres-like perfection.

More obviously in the Naturalist spirit is the painting of Gustave Guillaumet (1840–87), who renounced the traditional study period in Rome and went instead to North Africa, making some ten trips in all.

Photographers, too, played their part in the discovery of the Orient. One of the first to visit Egypt was Maxime Du Camp, who went there in 1849 with his friend Gustave Flaubert and afterwards wrote about his experiences in a book with photographic illustrations, reproduced in association with the printer Blanquart-Evrard. Published in 1852, it was the first publication of its type and became the model for a whole generation of photographers well represented in the Musée d'Orsay, including J. B. Greene, F. Teynard, T. Devéria and A. Salzmann.

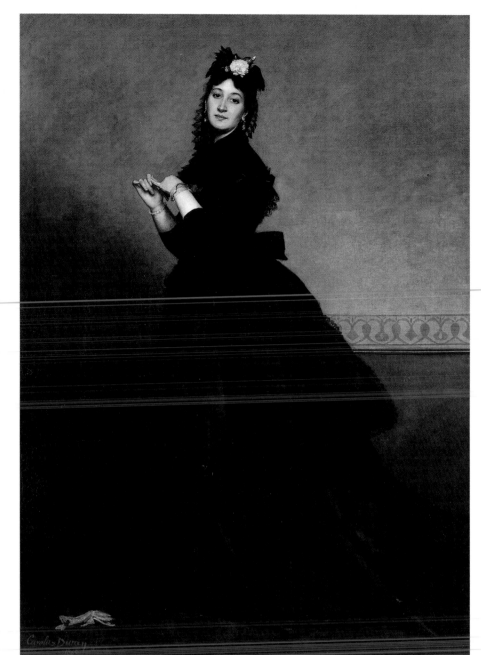

83 *Carolus-Duran:* La dame
au gant (Lady with a Glove),
1869
228 × 164 (89.8 × 64.6).
Madame Carolus-Duran, née
*Pauline Croizette
(1839–1912), painter. Salon of
1869. Acquired 1875*

84 *J. J. Tissot:* Portrait de
Mademoiselle L. L., ou Jeune
femme en veste rouge
(Young Woman in a Red
Jacket), *1864*
*124 × 99 (48.8 × 39). Salon of
1864. Acquired 1907*

85 *A. Stevens:* Ce qu'on
appelle le vagabondage, ou
Les chasseurs de Vincennes
(What People Call Vagrancy,
or The Hunters of
Vincennes), c. *1854*
*132 × 162 (52 × 63.8). World
Fair, Paris, 1855. Bequest of
the painter Léon Lhermitte,
1925*

83

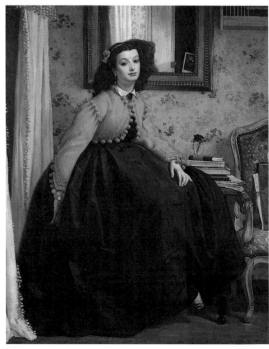

84

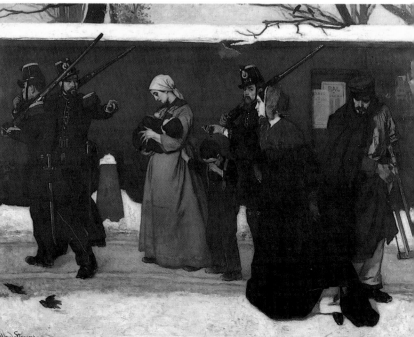

85

Further aspects of Realism; Fantin-Latour

Other painters allied themselves with Realism in their choice of modern themes, but retained a meticulous traditional technique. This official Realism, always in the best of taste, is represented by Alfred Stevens (1823–1906), James Tissot (1836–1902) and Carolus-Duran (1838–1910). The modernity of these fashionable painters consisted in an idealized image of an elegant and charming bourgeoisie.

Stevens studied in Brussels under a pupil of Jacques-Louis David and then moved to Paris, where he made his Salon début with paintings on humanitarian themes, such as *Ce qu'on appelle le vagabondage* (*What Is Called Vagrancy*). The picture is a powerful, frieze-like composition with flattened perspective and simplified forms, but the mood is one of melodramatic pathos. A friend of Manet, Stevens did on occasion paint Naturalist scenes such as *La baignoire* (*The Bath*), also in the Musée d'Orsay, but his fame depended on his evocations of the affluent bourgeois world.

Attention to detail in the setting, and meticulous rendering of costumes, characterize the work of Tissot, who started out as a painter of historical genre scenes, represented in the Musée d'Orsay by his sparkling *Faust et Marguerite* (*Faust and Gretchen*). Patronized by the rich and famous, Tissot

86 *T. Ribot:* Saint Sébastien, martyr (St Sebastian)
97 × 130 (38.2 × 51.2). Salon of 1865. Acquired 1865

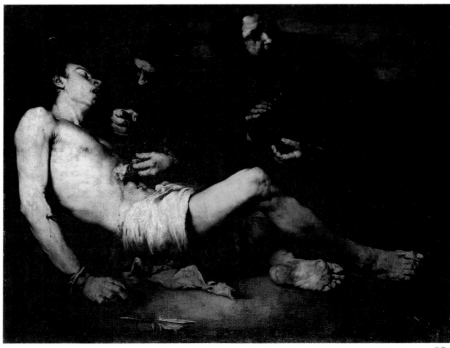

86

breathed new life into the traditionally static form of the society portrait, a fine example being his portrait of an unknown *Young Woman*, identified as *L.L.* (1864).

La dame au gant (*Lady with a Glove*) is typical of Carolus-Duran's portraiture; the dark colours and the spirited handling reflect the artist's admiration for Spanish painting. The anecdotal detail of the dropped glove is a reminder that the society portrait is really a genre scene, and that bourgeois Realism is an undemanding option.

Théodule Ribot (1823–91) received a traditional training as a pupil of Auguste Glaize. He specialized mostly in domestic interiors, often introducing everyday objects and members of his family as in *La ravaudeuse* (*Woman Darning*), in the Musée d'Orsay. His *Saint Sébastien* (*St Sebastian*) was acquired for the nation at the Salon of 1865. His predilection for religious subjects sets him apart from the other Realists, although it indicates not so much intensity of feeling as admiration for seventeenth-century Spanish art, and for José Ribera in particular.

Henri Fantin-Latour (1836–1904) studied under Horace Lecoq de Boisbaudran, learning from him the importance of visual memory in drawing. He formed his artistic allegiances as the result of copying paintings in the Louvre, and his first major composition was *Hommage à Delacroix* (*Homage to Delacroix*), inspired by the Dutch group-portraits of the seventeenth century. Fantin-Latour was a friend of Manet and the future Impressionists, who appear in *Un atelier aux Batignolles* (*A Studio in the Batignolles Quarter*), of 1870. He shared with them a taste for modern life and a dislike of anecdotal painting. His *Un Coin de table* (*Corner of a Table*) of 1872, takes liberties with conventional perspective in order to make the figures of Verlaine and Rimbaud the central feature of the composition. This is the only known portrait of the latter.

In the latter half of his career Fantin-Latour painted numerous still-lifes, which show meticulous observation and an interest in light effects. His rather austere portraits focus all the attention on the face, the simplicity of the presentation emphasizing the character of the sitter. But the paintings in which he took the greatest pleasure were poetic compositions, transpositions into visual terms of his response to literature or to the music of Wagner, Berlioz or Schumann.

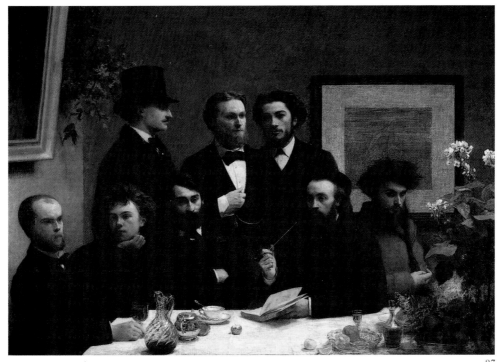

87

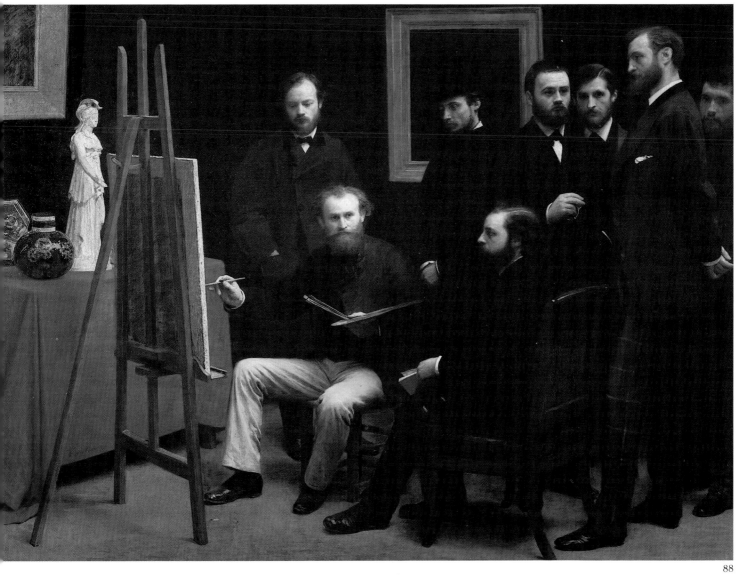

88

Whistler

89 *J. A. McN. Whistler:*
Arrangement en gris et noir,
portrait de la mère de l'artiste
(Arrangement in Grey and
Black; Portrait of the Artist's
Mother), *1871*
*144 × 162.5 (56.7 × 64). Salon
of 1883. Acquired 1891*

James Abbott McNeill Whistler (1834–1903) was barely
more than twenty when he left the United States and went
to study painting in France. Thenceforth he was to divide
his life between Paris and London. A friend of Courbet and of
Fantin-Latour – who painted him alongside Baudelaire,
Manet and others in his *Homage to Delacroix* – Whistler was
from the outset inclined towards Realism, and his work
therefore received a frosty reception in official circles. He
was, too, a fervent admirer of Far Eastern art, and in
particular Japanese prints, whose introduction to the West
had such a profound influence on so many European
artists.

This love of decorative simplicity was reflected in the
extreme delicacy of his palette, founded in exquisite harmonies of finely graduated, understated colour. Famous for
his views of the Thames, painted in a quivering haze
reminiscent of some of the effects achieved by Monet at a
certain period, Whistler was also a successful portraitist. His
Arrangement en gris et noir, portrait de la mère de l'artiste
(*Arrangement in Grey and Black, Portrait of the Artist's
Mother*), of 1871, entered the French national collections in
1891 thanks to the efforts of his friend the poet Stéphane
Mallarmé and of the critic Théodore Duret, who knew Manet
and the Impressionists and admired Whistler's work. This
rather austere painting has become the artist's best-known
work.

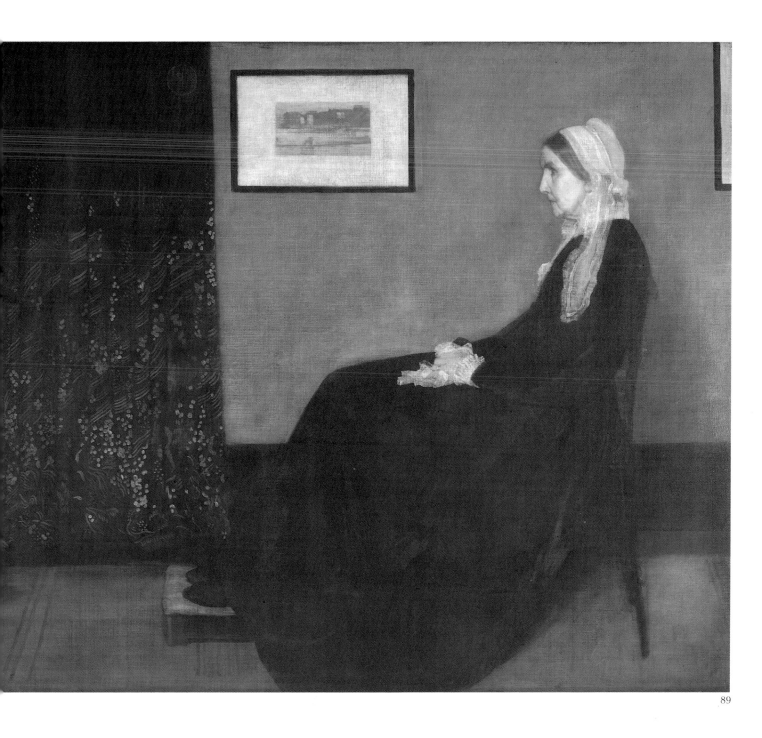

Aspects of
provincial painting

In the second half of the nineteenth century Paris was the centre of artistic life in France. Nevertheless, there were certain figures of powerful originality, a little apart from the mainstream, who lived and worked in relative isolation in the provinces. They in turn attracted admirers and imitators, and so founded regional schools of painting. The most obvious example is F. A. Ravier (1814–95), who, although initially a pupil of Corot, belongs to the School of Lyon. His free handling of skyscapes reflects the influence of Turner. Another outsider was Adolphe Monticelli (1824–86), who studied in Marseille and continued to work in the South of France even after he became nominally resident in Paris. His admiration for Delacroix and for the virtuosity of Diaz led him to develop a brilliant technique using heavy impasto, which came as a revelation to the young Vincent van Gogh. Also a southerner, Monticelli's friend Paul Guigou (1833–71) was a great admirer of Courbet. He was chiefly interested in the effects produced by the strong sunlight of Provence, and his studies on that theme are somewhat reminiscent of those by his young contemporary Fréderic Bazille.

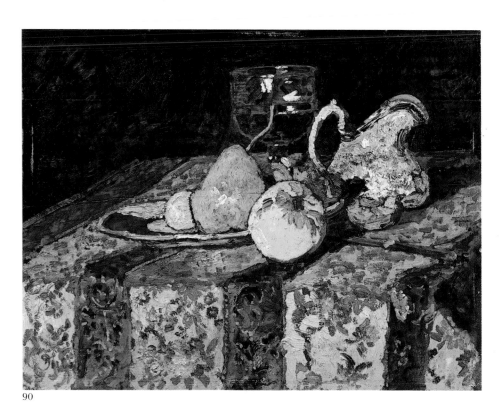

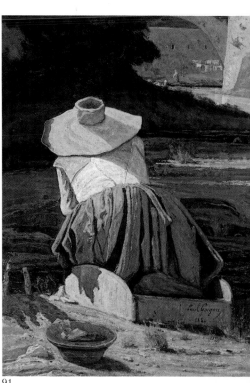

Plein-air landscape painting

In the first half of the nineteenth century there were numerous landscape painters who insisted on the need to observe nature faithfully and to set down at speed, working in the open air (*en plein-air*) and with the motif before them, the ephemeral character of the scene that presented itself to their eyes. In England there were, most notably, John Constable, J. M. W. Turner and Richard Bonington, and in France a line from Paul-Henri de Valenciennes through to Corot and the Barbizon School. Their heirs, in the middle years of the century, were J. B. Jongkind and Eugène Boudin, who developed these principles in the 1850s, each in his own distinctive manner. Jongkind (1819–91) was Dutch but lived and worked in France. He evolved a very free and spirited technique, which, combined with his Realist inclinations, was enough to ensure his presence – alongside Manet – at the Salon des Refusés of 1863; the picture by which he was represented was a landscape, *Ruines du château de Rosemont* (*The Ruined Château at Rosemont*). He was a watercolourist of exceptional talent and produced many striking landscapes of Holland, the Ile-de-France, Paris and Montmartre, the

92 *E. Boudin:* La plage de Trouville (The Beach at Trouville), *1864*
26 × 48 (10.2 × 18.9). Gift of Dr Eduardo Mollard, 1961

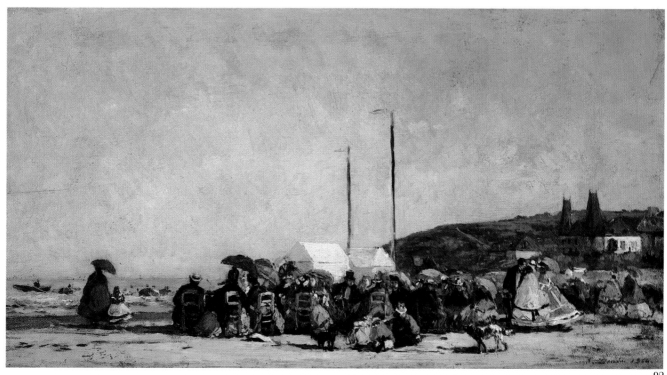

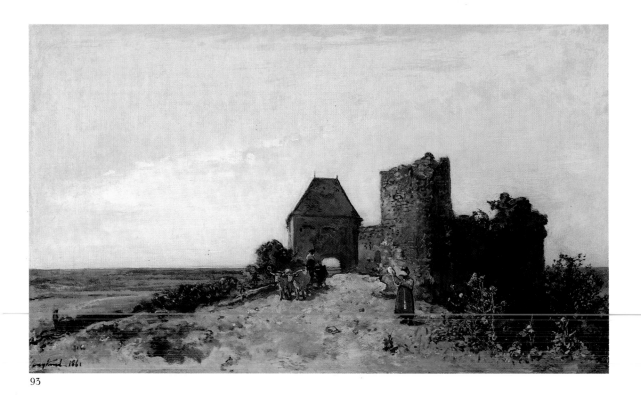

93

93 *J. B. Jongkind:* Ruines du
château de Rosemont (The
Ruined Château at
Rosemont), *1861*
34 × 56.5 (13.4 × 22.2). Salon
des Refusés, 1863. Gift of
Etienne Moreau-Nélaton,
1906

Normandy coast and the Isère. The French national
museums are fortunate to have in their possession a superb
series of his watercolours, thanks to the generosity of the
collector Etienne Moreau-Nélaton.

Eugène Boudin (1824–98) studied for a brief period in
Paris and was advised by Isabey and Troyon. Corot and
Courbet were the painters whose example he admired, but it
was above all his friend Jongkind who influenced him in the
course he would follow. Boudin was born in Honfleur and
died in Deauville: his painting is rooted in that area of the
Normandy coast where he spent so much of his life. Later,
when he was famous and could afford to travel, he painted
also in Brittany, around Bordeaux, in the South of France,
Venice and Holland. It was in 1862 that he began to paint
scenes showing the crowds of elegant summer visitors on the
beaches of Deauville and Trouville – a theme that verged
almost on genre painting. Yet the apparent superficiality of
the subject seemed to release his powers of expression. These
bright paintings, pulsating with light, were to make a deep
impression on the young Claude Monet, whose family lived
in Le Havre. 'If I have become a painter, I owe it to Eugène
Boudin,' he wrote, underlining the importance of the role
Boudin played in the genesis of Impressionism. Monet also
knew Jongkind well, and stayed with Bazille at the Ferme
Saint-Siméon near Honfleur. This simple farmhouse became
famous for the numbers of artists who stayed there in the
nineteenth century, among them Diaz, Troyon, Daubigny,
Corot and Courbet. There are major works by these painters,
sometimes called the Pre-Impressionists, in the Eduardo
Mollard collection, which, in accordance with the
benefactor's wishes, is kept together in the Musée d'Orsay.

Manet

When Edouard Manet (1832–83), a friend of the notorious poet Baudelaire, sent in to the 1863 Salon jury his *Déjeuner sur l'herbe*, then known as *Le bain* (*Bathing*), he was already, in the eyes of the younger artists and critics, a leader of what we would now term the avant-garde (although he had received official approval in 1861 for a daringly free exercise in the 'Spanish vein'). *Le bain* was rejected; and indeed the jury turned down so many paintings that year that Napoleon III himself opened a supplementary Salon. This was the famous Salon des Refusés, and there *Le bain* was an overnight sensation.

The picture was regarded as shocking both because it was painted with the freedom of a sketch and because of its subject – never mind that it was derived from an engraving by Raphael, the very painter most revered by the Ecole des

94 *E. Manet:* Le déjeuner sur l'herbe (Luncheon on the Grass), *1863*
208 × 264.5 (81.9 × 104.1).
Salon des Refusés, 1863. Gift of Etienne Moreau-Nélaton, 1906

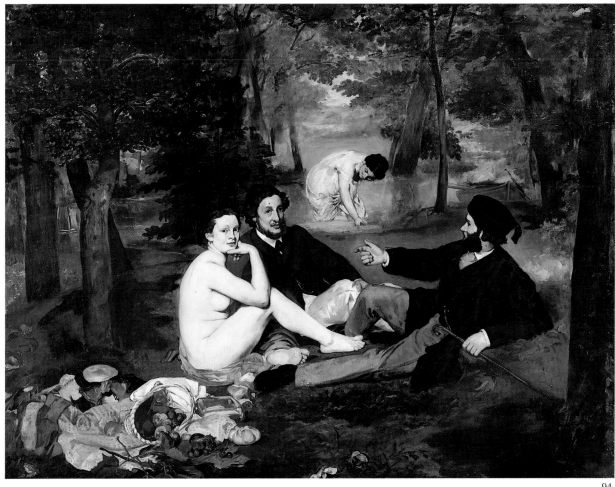

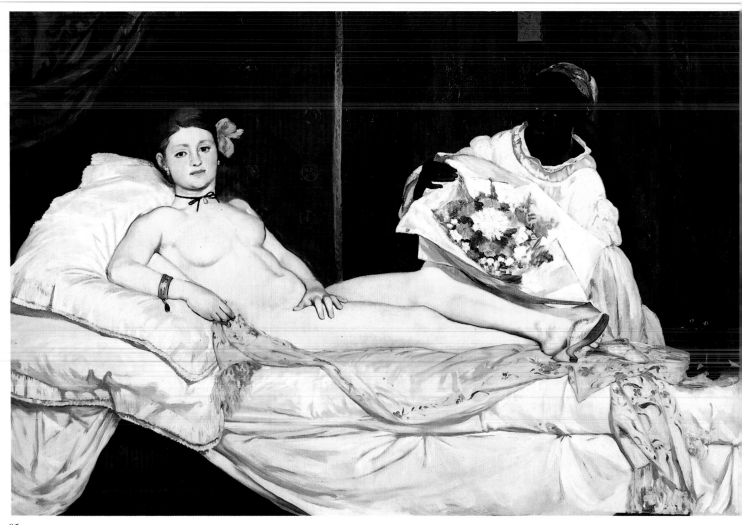

95

95 *E. Manet:* Olympia, *1863*
130.5 × 190 (51.4 × 74.8). Salon
of 1865. Presented to the
nation as the result of a public
subscription raised by Claude
Monet, 1890

Beaux-Arts. Certainly the subject was provocative: a naked woman posing unconcernedly in the company of two well-dressed young men who looked like students. 'Monsieur Manet seeks to make his name by shocking the bourgeoisie ... his taste is corrupted by a love of the bizarre,' wrote a critic of the day, failing to understand what Manet was trying to do – which was to transpose into a modern setting a traditional theme of Renaissance Italy, to create a contemporary version of the 'pastoral interlude' or *concert champêtre*.

An even greater scandal was sparked off by *Olympia* (1863) at the Salon of 1865. Once again Manet had transformed an idealized nude – Titian's *Venus of Urbino* – into a provocative and quasi-photographic image that showed a hidden side of life in the Second Empire: a naked prostitute with a challenging gaze, lying on her bed. Today we can still respond to the provoking fascination of this nude, but the 'immorality' of the context has lost its force. The painting is above all an extraordinary *tour de force*, both for its technique and its subject matter, a masterpiece of sensual expression that links the great classical art of the past with modern painting. The female figure who in her own day was seen as a 'redhead of out-and-out ugliness', a 'yellow-bellied odalisque', a 'Queen of Spades', looks now – because of the handling and the dazzling use of colour, the contradictions and the humour, even because of that brazen stare – like a Mona Lisa of the modern age.

As a young man Emile Zola was an astute and far-sighted critic. Manet painted his portrait as a gesture of gratitude for the impassioned defence of his work issued by the twenty-eight-year-old writer. In this portrait Zola is surrounded by

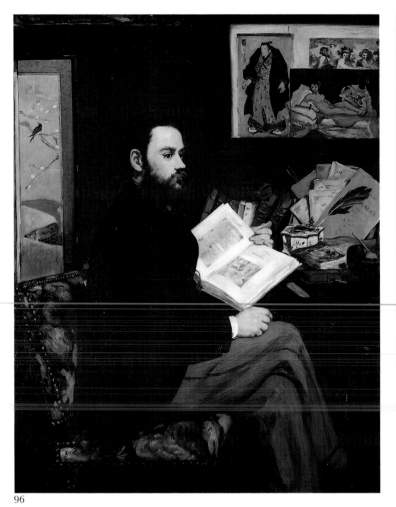

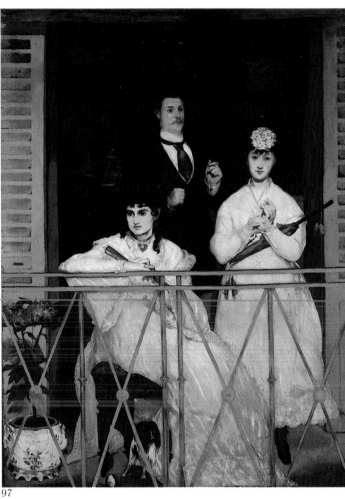

96

97

96 *E. Manet:* Emile Zola
(1840–1902), writer, 1868
146 × 114 (57.5 × 44.9). Salon
of 1868. Gift of Madame
Emile Zola, but retained by
her for her lifetime, 1918;
entered national collection
1925

97 *E. Manet:* Le balcon (The
Balcony), *1868–69*
170 × 124.5 (66.9 × 49). Seated:
Berthe Morisot, painter, the
artist's sister-in-law. Standing:
Fanny Claus, violinist;
Antoine Guillemet, landscape
painter. Salon of 1869. Bequest
of Gustave Caillebotte, 1894

objects reflecting his tastes and concerns: Japanese prints, engravings by Manet, Naturalist novels and, lying under his pen, the little blue book in which he wrote his defence of Manet.

At the next Salon, of 1869, Manet exhibited *Le balcon* (*The Balcony*), a contemporary treatment of a theme used by Goya. Seated in the foreground, in front of the painter Antoine Guillemet and the young violinist Fanny Claus, is one of Manet's favourite models, the beautiful Berthe Morisot, soon to join the Impressionist ranks as a painter in her own right.

Spurned by the authorities in the painter's lifetime, Manet's work came to be represented in the state museums only as the result of generous donations by private individuals and friends. In 1890 Claude Monet organized a campaign to purchase *Olympia* for the nation from Manet's widow. *The Balcony* entered the national collections as part of the controversial Gustave Caillebotte bequest, followed by *Le déjeuner sur l'herbe* in the Etienne Moreau-Nélaton gift of 1906, and *Le fifre* (*The Fifer*) in the collection of Count Isaac de Camondo, left to the state in 1911. These and other gifts and acquisitions have ensured that the museum now possesses an outstanding selection of Manet's works, including some of his finest pastels.

The Impressionists
before 1870

In the early 1860s the private studio class run by Charles Gleyre, a painter of Swiss origin, became the focus of activity for a number of young painters. Auguste Renoir enrolled in 1861, to be joined shortly afterwards by Frédéric Bazille, newly arrived from Montpellier, and later Claude Monet and Alfred Sisley. These painters formed a group united by common ideals, in particular a hostility towards academic art and an inclination towards Realism. Renoir (1841–1919), with no family money behind him, managed to keep his head above water by painting portraits, among them one of his friend Sisley's father, accepted for the Salon of 1865. Renoir was from the outset attracted to the human figure, whether the model was his companion Lise Tréhot – who must have posed for the small *Femme demi-nue couchée* (*Reclining Nude*) in the Musée d'Orsay – or his friend Bazille, who gave him shelter on more than one occasion during these difficult years. He admired Courbet and Delacroix, but he was also influenced by Manet and Monet. Bazille (1841–70), who died young in battle in the Franco-Prussian War, was another figure painter. *Réunion de famille* (*Family Gathering*), one of his most accomplished pictures, was executed in 1867 and exhibited at the Salon of 1868. It shows members of his family posing on the terrace of a house near Montpellier. A strong debt to Manet is apparent in the brilliance of the colouring, the bold presentation of human forms and the intensity of the light exaggerating the contrasts, but there is also an affinity with Monet, whom Bazille frequently accompanied on painting expeditions. Of all the group, Monet (1840–1926) was regarded as the most 'advanced'. As a young man in Le Havre he was decisively influenced by Boudin and Jongkind, who encouraged him to paint out of doors, and his early landscapes – which also owe much to Daubigny – have a freshness and confidence that did not escape the notice of the critics. Responding to Manet's picture of the same title, Monet painted his own large-scale composition *Le déjeuner sur l'herbe* (1865), two sections of which survive in the Musée d'Orsay, and then *Femmes au jardin* (*Women in the Garden*), rejected by the Salon of 1867, which includes a portrait of his future wife, Camille. This large and ambitious composition was started *in situ* as a *plein-*

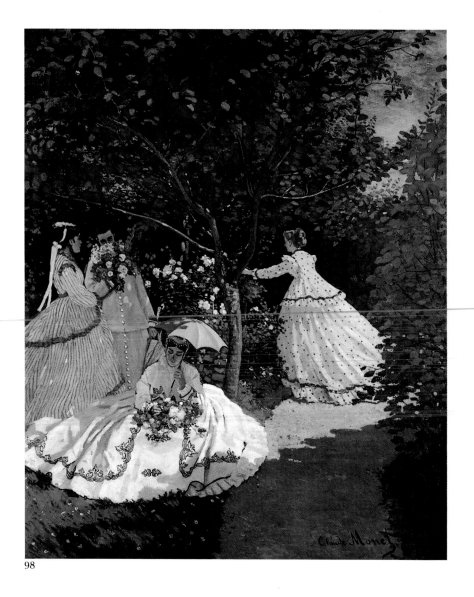

98

98 *C. Monet:* Femmes au jardin (Women in the Garden), *1866–67*
255 × 205 (100.4 × 80.7).
Rejected at Salon of 1867.
Acquired from the artist, 1921

99 *P. A. Renoir:* Frédéric Bazille peignant à son chevalet (Frédéric Bazille at his Easel), *1867*
105 × 73.5 (41.3 × 28.9). The still-life Bazille is seen painting is now in the Musée de Montpellier; hanging on the wall is a canvas by Claude Monet, who shared Bazille's studio at this time. Bequest of Marc Bazille, the artist's brother, 1924

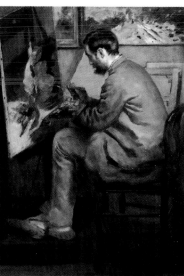

99

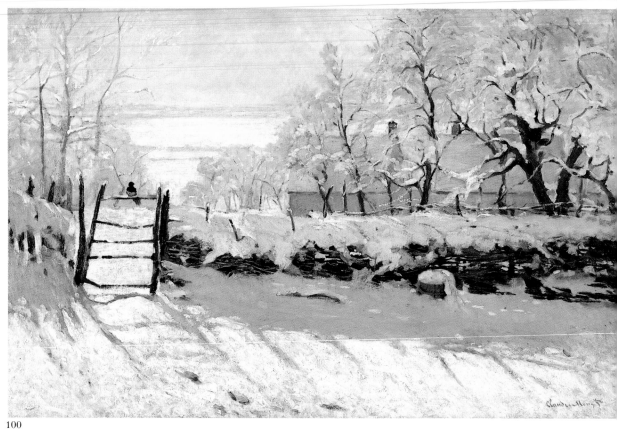

100

air painting (which, given the size of the canvas, was in itself a major achievement), the purpose being to retain the freshness of the original vision in the finished work; the canvas was in fact extensively reworked in the studio. The sharp silhouetting of the figures, the contrasts of light and shade, and the choice of a subject from modern life with no anecdotal detail whatsoever, could not but offend the conservative Salon jury, who maintained an implacable hostility towards this style of painting which had grown up in the wake of Courbet and Manet. It fell to Zola to defend Monet's picture, just as he had pleaded the cause of Manet and Pissarro before him. That Monet was undeterred by the virulence of the attacks is brilliantly attested by the other masterpieces of this period in the Musée d'Orsay, notably *La pie* (*The Magpie*) and *Hôtel des Roches-Noires à Trouville* (*Hôtel des Roches-Noires, Trouville*).

100 *C. Monet:* La pie (The Magpie), c. *1868–69* *89 × 130 (35 × 51.2). Acquired 1984*

101 *F. Bazille:* Réunion de famille (The Artist's family on a Terrace), *1867* *152 × 230 (59.8 × 90.6). Salon of 1868. Acquired in association with Marc Bazille, the artist's brother, 1905*

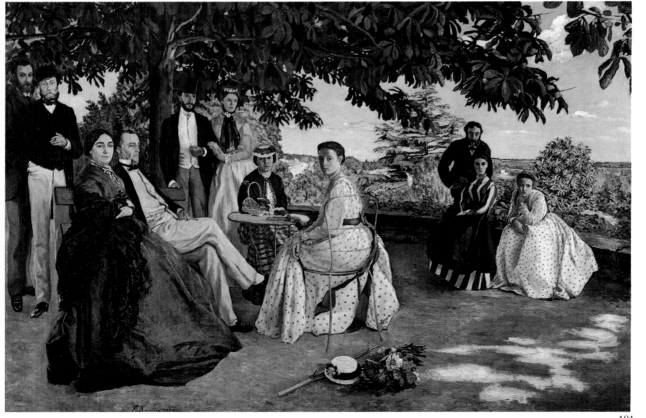

Drawing and watercolour

102 *J. B. Jongkind:*
Autoportrait sous le soleil
(Self-portrait, sunshine),
c. *1850–60*
*Watercolour. 20 × 17
(7.9 × 6.7). Gift of Etienne
Moreau-Nélaton, 1906*

103 *G. Doré:* Catastrophe du
Mont-Cervin; la chute
(Tragedy on the Matterhorn;
the Fall), *1865*
*Pen and brown ink, India ink
wash, brown wash, highlights
in white gouache. 79 × 58.5
(31 × 23). Gift of
Mademoiselle de Viefville,
1952*

Complementing the collections of painting, sculpture and decorative arts in the Musée d'Orsay, there will also be opportunities to see drawings by the various artists represented. These temporary exhibitions (it being possible to display the drawings only for restricted periods and in precise lighting conditions) are intended to serve very much as an introduction to the permanent collections of the Cabinet des Dessins in the Louvre. That vast repository includes examples of work, both individual items and major series, by most of the leading artists of the period covered by the Musée d'Orsay. A mention of just a few of the artists represented from the early years of that period will suggest something of the richness and diversity of the collections: the fantastical and meticulous storytelling of Gustave Doré is worlds away from the pungent Realism of Daumier or the poetic Realism of Millet (particularly well represented here) or from Jongkind, who anticipated the Impressionist style in a series of watercolours donated to the Louvre as part of the Moreau-Nélaton collection.

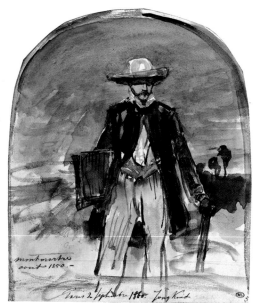

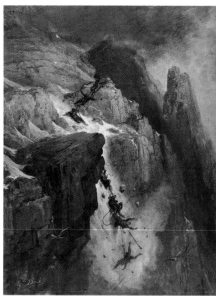

102

103

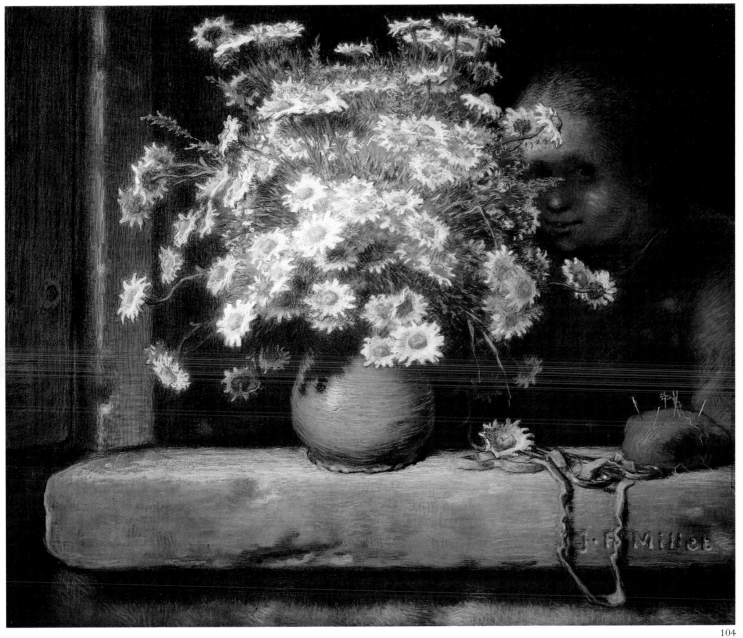

104

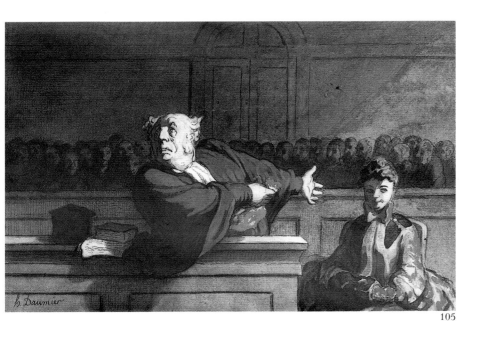

105

104 *J. F. Millet:* Le bouquet de marguerites (The Bunch of Daisies), *1871–74*
Pastel. 68 × 83 (26.8 × 32.7). Acquired out of income from bequest of Madame Dol-Lair, 1949

105 *H. Daumier:* Le défenseur (Counsel for the Defence)
Pen and black ink, watercolour and gouache over a pencil outline. 19 × 29 (7.5 × 11.4). Acquired in lieu of estate duties, 1977

Photography

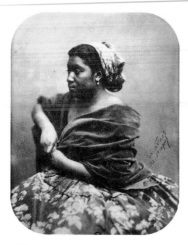

106

106 *F. Nadar:* Portrait d'une antillaise (Portrait of a West Indian Woman), c. *1855*
Salt print from wet-collodion glass-plate negative. 25 × 19 (9.8 × 7.5). Acquired 1981

107 *G. Le Gray:* Le vapeur (The Steamer), *1857*
Albumen print from two wet-collodion glass plate negatives. 32 × 41.3 (12.6 × 16.3). Acquired 1985

Long overlooked and even now largely neglected, the photography of the nineteenth century is given proper coverage for the first time with the opening of the Musée d'Orsay. The displays have been organized to illustrate the significant developments in the history of photography, both in France and abroad, starting with the daguerreotype and ending with the snapshot and the rise of the 'pictorialist' movement. At this point the Musée National d'Art Moderne in the Centre Pompidou takes over, with the abstract and experimental photography that first appeared in Europe and America towards the end of the First World War.

When work was started on assembling the Musée d'Orsay collection, in 1979, it was decided to concentrate specifically on photography as a creative art, thus supplying a different emphasis from the archive of the Bibliothèque Nationale, which, according to a law passed in 1851, receives copies of all commercially used photographs. The principal criterion of 'artistic' quality is originality in the interpretation of subject matter, and yet some of the most imaginative uses of the medium in the nineteenth century were in the form of documentary records – one thinks in particular of the views of Egypt by J. B. Greene (1832–57) or the Parisian scenes of Eugène Atget (1857–1923). The museum is not interested exclusively in the work of professional photographers; it is also concerned with artists working in other fields who at certain times experimented with photography for particular purposes of their own, whether visual artists (Degas, Bonnard, Gallé) or writers (such as Victor Hugo or Lewis Carroll).

The Musée d'Orsay collections are particularly well endowed with the works of the so-called 'primitives', active first in England and later in France when photographs first began to be printed on paper (c. 1850–60). Within that short period the expressive potential of the new medium was explored with startling inventiveness and variety, already suggesting many of the techniques that were to be developed in the future.

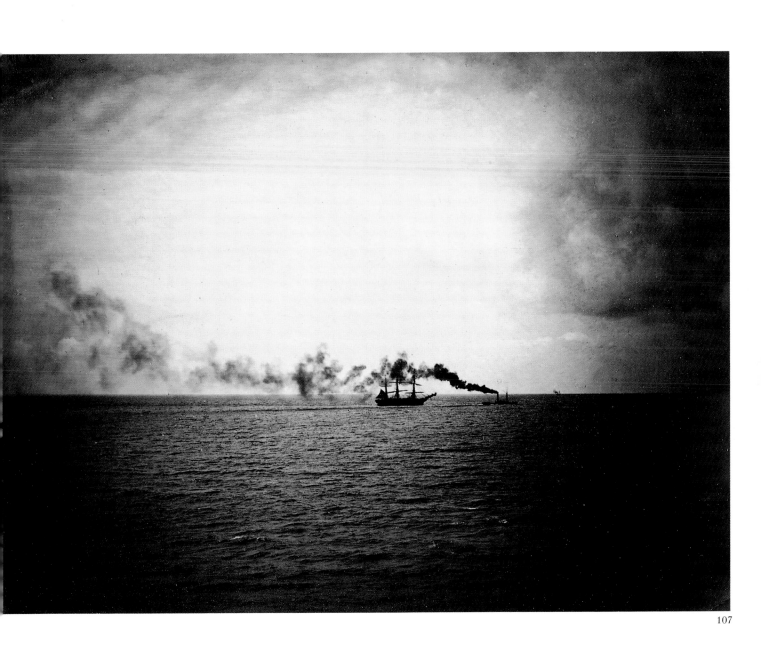

107

108　*T. Annan:* Plate from the album 'Photographs of the Old Closes and Streets of Glasgow', *1868–77*
Albumen print from wet collodion glass-plate negative. 27.7 × 22.7 (10.9 × 8.9).
Acquired 1983

109　*C. Hugo:* Victor Hugo sur un rocher, Jersey (Victor Hugo on a Rock, Jersey), *1853*
Salt print from albumen on glass negative. 15.4 × 21.6 (6.1 × 8.5). Gift of André and Marie-Thérèse Jammes, 1984

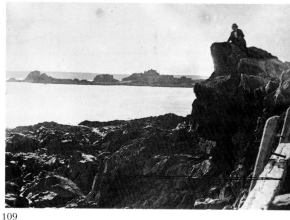

109

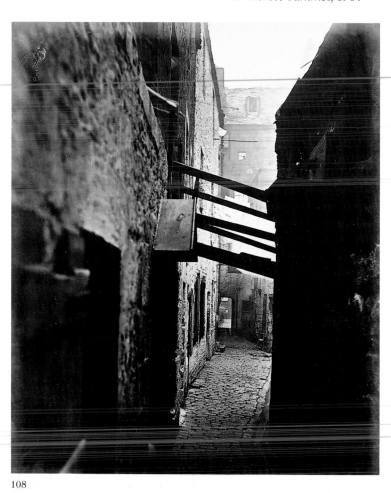

108

110　*J. C. Langlois:* Trois planches du Panorama de Sébastopol pris de la Tour Malakoff (guerre de Crimée) (Three Plates from the panorama of Sebastopol taken from the Malakoff Tower, Crimean War), *November 1855*
Salt print with albumen from a waxed paper negative. 35 × 31 (13.8 × 12.2). Acquired 1982 with the aid of a grant from Mission pour le patrimoine photographique (Direction du Patrimoine)

111　*Baron Gros:* Bas-relief du Parthénon, Athènes (Bas-relief, the Parthenon, Athens), *c. 1850*
Daguerreotype. 11 × 14.5 (4.3 × 5.7). Gift of Roger Thérond, 1985

112　*A. Braun:* Couronne de fleurs (Garland), *1856*

Albumen print from wet-collodion glass-plate negative. 44.2 × 48.1 (17.4 × 18.9). Acquired 1981

113　*L. Carroll (C. L. Dodgson):* Xie Kitchin Asleep, *12 June 1873*
Albumen print from glass-plate negative. 12 × 14.5 (4.7 × 5.7). Acquired 1982

114　*C. Nègre:* Nu allongé dans l'atelier de l'artiste (Reclining Nude in the Artist's Studio), *c. 1850*
From waxed paper negative. 11.3 × 18.7 (4.4 × 7.4). Gift of Kodak-Pathé Foundation, 1983

115　*E. Baldus:* Groupe dans un parc (Group in Park), *185*
Salt print, from wet collodion glass-plate negative. 29 × 40.8 (11.4 × 16.1). Gift of Kodak-Pathé Foundation, 1983

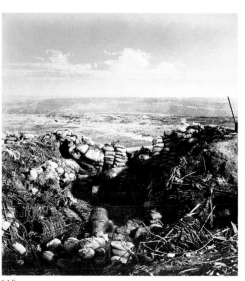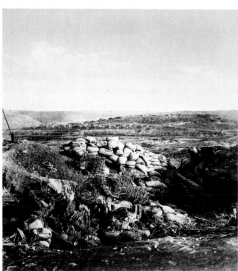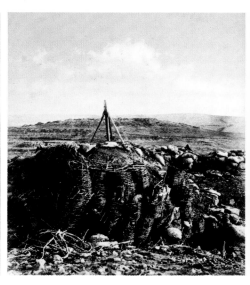

110

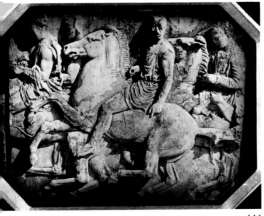

111

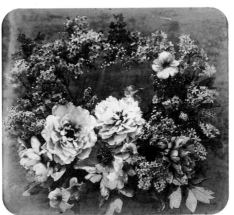

112

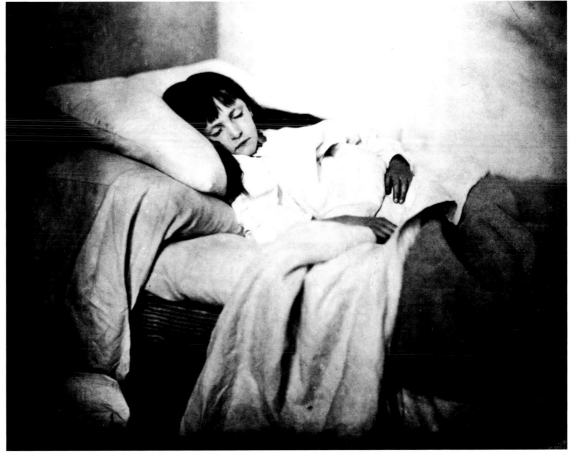

113

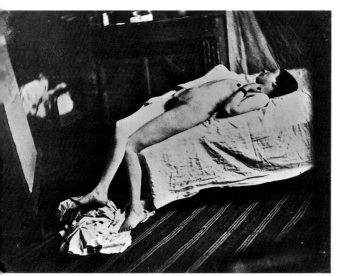

114

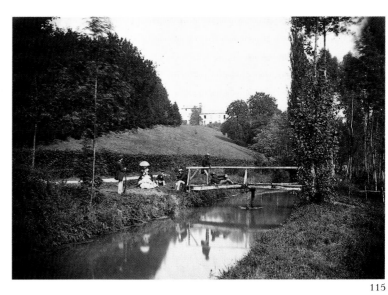

115

Architecture
and town-planning

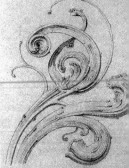

116

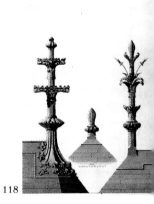

117

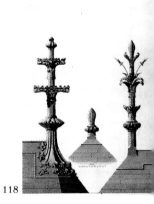

118

In architecture, the second half of the nineteenth century was a time of expansion. There was extensive urban redevelopment, not only in Haussmann's Paris but in comparable programmes in provincial France and abroad. A vast construction programme was undertaken – railway stations, factories, town halls, museums, schools and colleges, grand hotels. Technology was making rapid strides; iron was in widespread use, and concrete began to make an appearance. The architecture of this period can all too easily seem to be bogged down in a more or less slavish imitation of bygone styles. Yet the historicism of Eugène Viollet-le-Duc (1814–79) or Victor Ruprich-Robert (1859–1953) cannot simply be dismissed as a sterile reproduction of the forms of a previous age; these architects were, in their own way, as interested as was the Arts and Crafts Movement in England in extending their designs to include even the smallest detail of interior decoration. Using medieval architecture as a source of new design ideas, they paved the way for the movement we now call Art Nouveau. Among the more prominent landmarks of the architecture of this period are buildings erected for the World Fairs held in Paris between 1855 and 1900, notably the Palais de l'Industrie (1855) and the Eiffel Tower (1889).

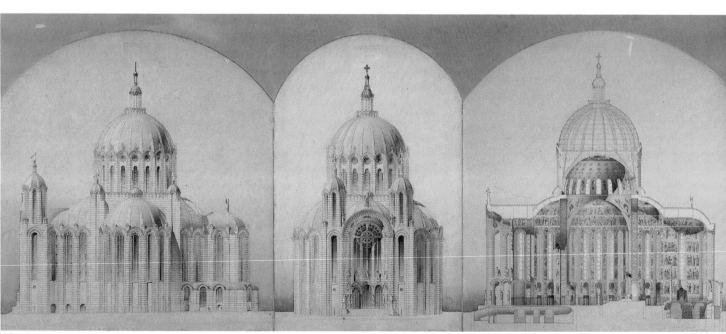

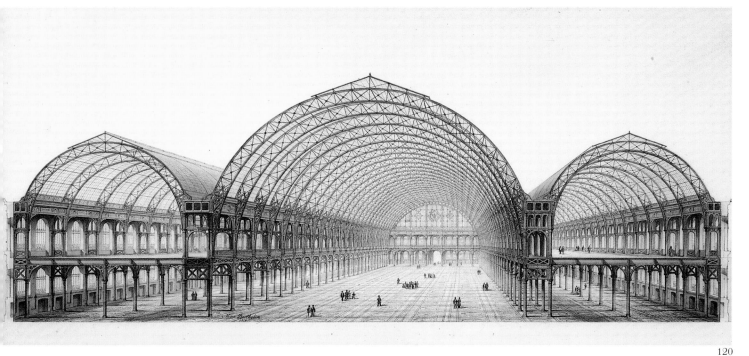

120

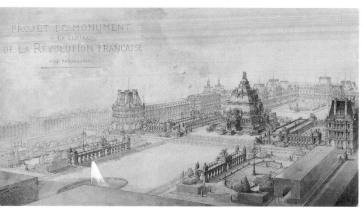

121

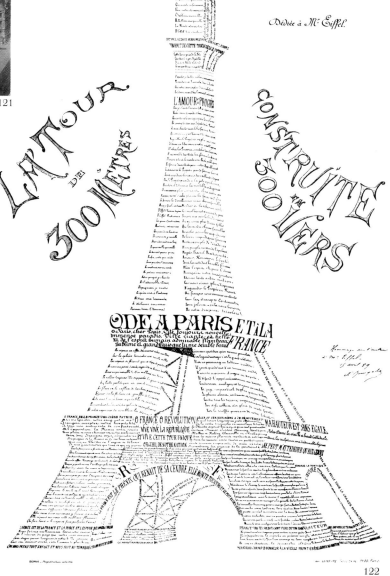

120 *M. Berthelin:* Palais de l'Industrie: cross section, *1854 Pen and black ink, watercolour. 31 × 67.3 (12.2 × 26.5). Acquired 1979*

121 *L. E. Lheureux:* Design for a monument celebrating the French Revolution *Perspective drawing. Crayon, pen and ink, wash, watercolour, gold highlights. 48 × 86.5 (18.9 × 34.1). Salon des Artistes français, 1889. Acquired 1981*

122 *A. Bourgade:* Calligram or word-picture of the Eiffel Tower, *1889 Drawing. 80 × 57 (31.5 × 22.4). Eiffel archives. Gift of Mademoiselle Solange Granet, Madame Bernard Granet and children, descendants of Gustave Eiffel, 1981*

122

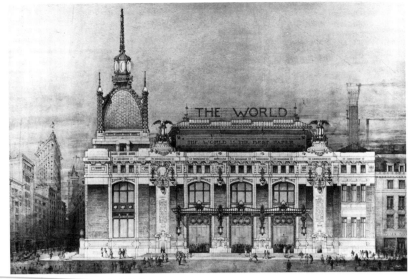

123

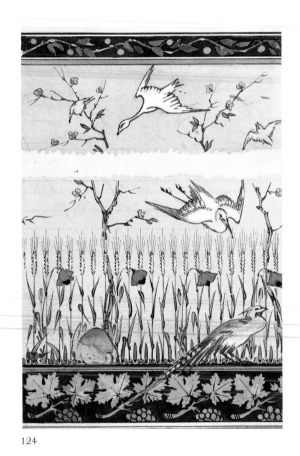

124

123 *M. Boille:* Student
project: newspaper offices
*Crayon and watercolour.
54.2 × 81.8 (21.3 × 32.2). Gift
of Pierre and Jacques Boille,
sons of the architect, 1982*

124 *E. Viollet-le-Duc:*
Furnishing fabric, design for
'Histoire d'une maison',
c. 1870–73
*Watercolour. 19.6 × 11.2
(7.7 × 4.4). Acquired 1980*

125 *G. M. Niedecken:* Design
for the living-room of the
M.E.P. Irving house, Decatur,
Ill.
*The house was built by Frank
Lloyd Wright in 1909–10. Pen
and black ink and watercolour
on canvas. 71 × 66 (28 × 26).
Acquired 1985*

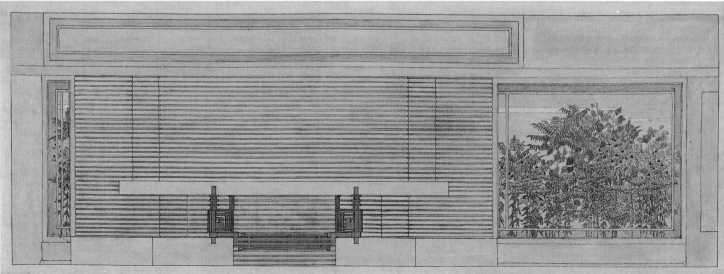

125

Impressionism

Tired of constant rebuffs from the Salon jury, a few artists decided in the spring of 1874 to stage an independent exhibition of their works in rooms on the Boulevard des Capucines in Paris. Among them were Edgar Degas, Auguste Renoir, Camille Pissarro, Paul Cézanne, Alfred Sisley, Armand Guillaumin, Berthe Morisot, and Claude Monet, who showed a canvas called *Impression, soleil levant* (*Impression: Sunrise*). An incensed critic coined the mocking epithet 'impressionist', and the name stuck. There was one notable absentee from their ranks, a painter who had crossed swords more than once with the Salon jury and chose not to risk further offence. This was Edouard Manet, who, by public

126 *C. Monet:* Régates à Argenteuil (Sailing Boats at Argenteuil), c. *1872*
48 × 75 (18.9 × 29.5). Bequest of Gustave Caillebotte, 1894

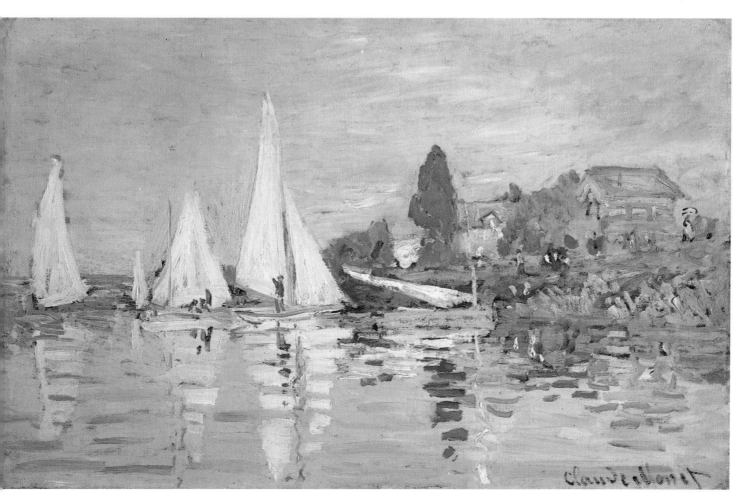

126

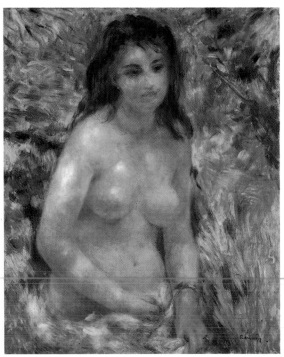

127　·

127　*P. A. Renoir:* Etude:
torse, effet de soleil (Study:
Nude in the Sunlight), *1875
81 × 65 (31.9 × 25.6). Shown at
second Impressionist
exhibition, 1876. Bequest of
Gustave Caillebotte, 1894*

128　*P. A. Renoir:* Bal du
Moulin de la Galette
(Dancing at the Moulin de la
Galette), *1876
131 × 175 (51.6 × 68.9).
Exhibited at the third
Impressionist exhibition, 1877.
Bequest of Gustave Caillebotte,
1894*

and critics alike, was regarded as the leader of the group,
which assembled regularly at the Café Guerbois and later the
Café de la Nouvelle Athènes. The experiment of a group
exhibition was repeated in 1876, 1877, 1879, 1880, 1881, 1882
and 1886. Although there was some internal dissension and a
number of defections, there were always newcomers keen to
participate, among them Gustave Caillebotte (1848–94), in
1876, who helped his friends by buying their paintings. He
left his magnificent collection to the nation in 1894, and so
ensured, in the face of fierce opposition at the time, the
presence in the state collections of a superb body of
Impressionist painting, today one of the glories of the Musée
d'Orsay. In 1879, at the time of the fourth independent
exhibition, the group was joined by Mary Cassatt, a friend of
Degas, and also by Albert Lebourg and Paul Gauguin, closely
associated with Pissarro. The participation of Georges Seurat
and Paul Signac in the last exhibition, of 1886, effectively
marked the end of one era and the beginning of the next.

It was only because of the loyalty of a small number of
collectors and critics, among them Paul Durand-Ruel, that
these painters managed to survive the hardships of those
difficult years. Most of them had started their careers in the
1860s and had reached artistic maturity without receiving
official recognition. By then, though they were still united in
their opposition to academic art and in their desire to be
painters of the modern age, their divergent personalities had
begun to lead them in very different directions.

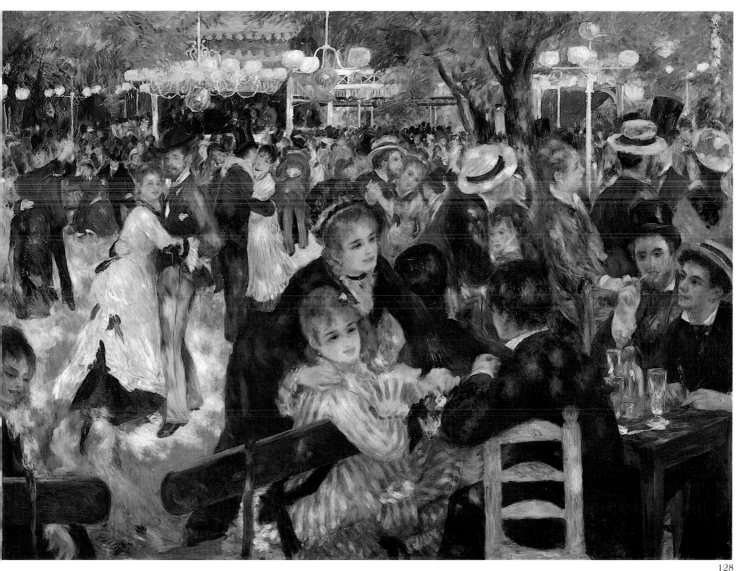

128

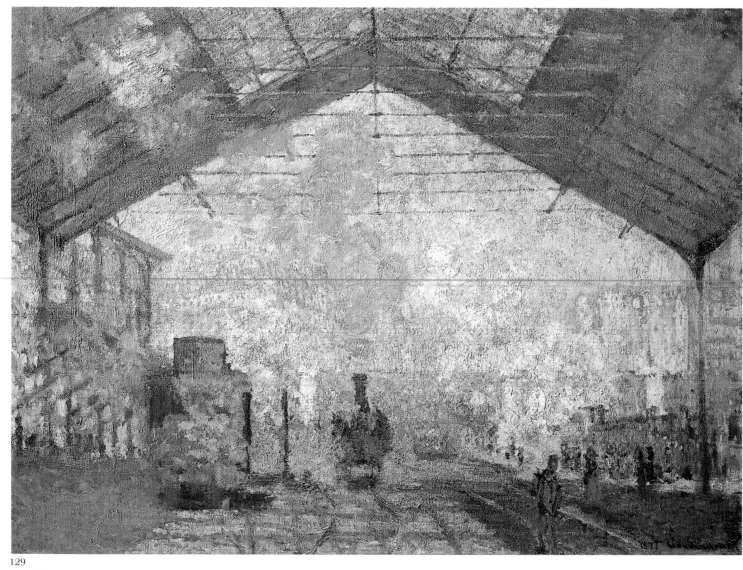

129

129 *C. Monet:* La gare Saint-Lazare (Saint-Lazare Station) *75.5 × 104 (29.7 × 40.9). Shown at third Impressionist exhibition, 1877. Bequest of Gustave Caillebotte, 1894*

130 *C. Monet:* La rue Montorgueil, fête du 30 juin 1878 (Rue Montorgueil Decked Out with Flags, 30 June 1878) *81 × 50 (31.9 × 19.7). Shown at fourth Impressionist exhibition, 1879. Acquired in lieu of estate duties, 1982*

131 *C. Pissarro:* Les toits rouges (Red Roofs), 1877 *54.5 × 65.5 (21.5 × 25.8). Bequest of Gustave Caillebotte, 1894*

132 *P. Cézanne:* La maison du pendu (House of the Hanged Man), 1873 *55 × 66 (21.7 × 26). Bequest of Isaac de Camondo, 1911*

133 *B. Morisot:* Le berceau (The Cradle), 1872 *56 × 46 (22 × 18.1). Shown at first Impressionist exhibition, 1874. Acquired 1930*

134 *C. Monet:* Les coquelicots (Wild Poppies), 1873 *50 × 65 (19.7 × 25.6). Shown at first Impressionist exhibition, 1874. Gift of Etienne Moreau-Nélaton, 1906*

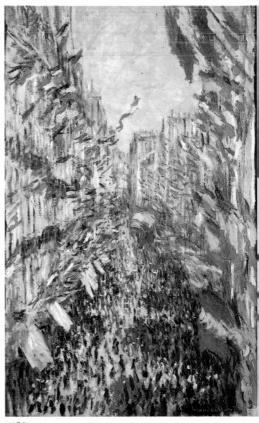

130

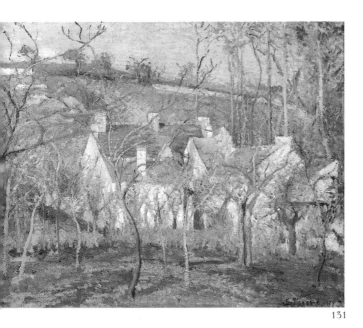

131

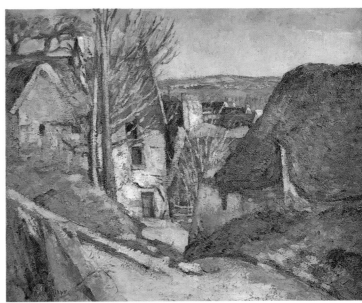

132

Monet moved away from huge canvases and figure painting in order to devote himself to studying the vibrant effects of light, concentrating on landscapes of the Seine valley around Argenteuil – a magnet for all the Impressionists, and even for Manet, in the early 1870s. Monet's *Régates à Argenteuil* (*Sailing Boats at Argenteuil*), which has all the spontaneity and charm of a sketch, and his *Coquelicots* (*Wild Poppies*), a subtly rhythmic composition echoing the forms of two figures in a landscape – these are paintings that typify Impressionism at its peak.

Monet also painted scenes of Paris, and the wonderfully luminous series based on the Gare Saint-Lazare – a modern subject if ever there was one – anticipated later developments in his work.

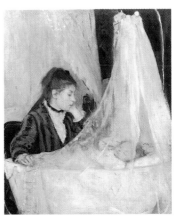

133

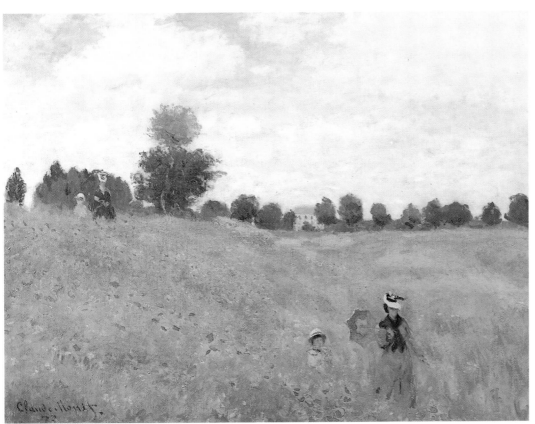

134

103

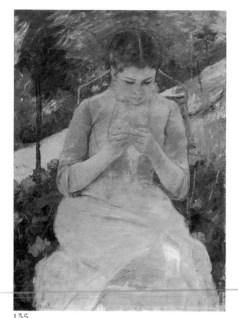

135

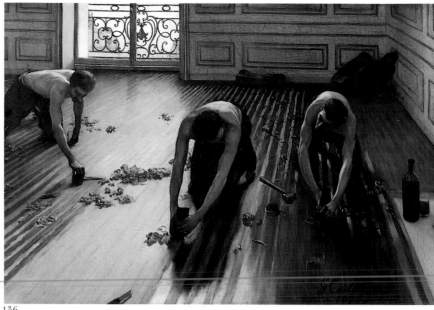

136

Renoir continued his love affair with the human figure. His *Etude: torse, effet de soleil* (*Study: Nude in the Sunlight*), accused by hostile critics of suggesting 'a pile of decomposing flesh', shows how he pursued the study of colour to the point where the forms seem almost to dissolve in a shimmering haze of varying intensity. Nevertheless his acknowledged masterpiece of this period is *Bal du Moulin de la Galette* (*Dancing at the Moulin de la Galette*), an evocation of life in Montmartre.

Pissarro (1830–1903) lived at Pontoise, north-east of Paris, and concentrated for the most part on landscapes. Like his friend Cézanne, who regularly worked with him, he was much concerned with the structure of forms. Alfred Sisley (1839–99) developed a style close to Monet's, working mainly at Louveciennes and Marly.

Two women were closely associated with the Impressionist group: Berthe Morisot (1841–99), whose painting has many points in common with that of her brother-in-law, Manet, and Mary Cassatt (1844–1926), on whom Degas was the crucial influence.

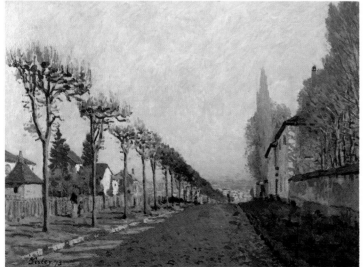

137

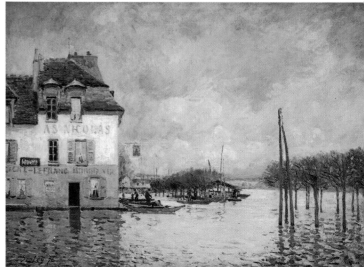

138

Degas

Edgar Degas (1834–1917) figured prominently in the first exhibition of the embryonic Impressionist group in 1874. Although his career in the 1860s had appeared to be proceeding along traditional lines, it was above all his choice of subjects from contemporary reality – the ballet, Parisian cafés, working girls, milliners and washerwomen, the races – and the Naturalism of his portraits that transformed him within the space of a few years into one of the most masterly exponents of the 'new painting'. Degas' love of unusual angles and viewpoints was accompanied by precise draughtsmanship and bold, flowing forms; his palette, which was initially dark and austere, later expanded to include a range of acid tones.

139 *E. Degas:* Au café, *dit* L'absinthe (At the Café, *known as* Absinthe), *1876 92 × 68 (36.2 × 26.8). Bequest of Isaac de Camondo, 1911*

140 *E. Degas:* Chevaux de courses devant les tribunes (Race-horses in Front of the Stands), c. *1869 46 × 61 (18.1 × 24). Bequest of Isaac de Camondo, 1911*

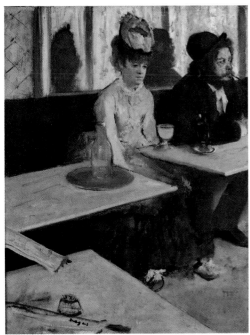

139

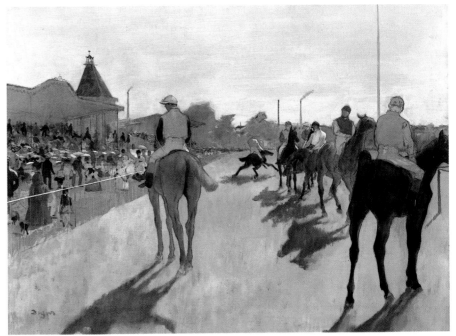

140

141 *E. Degas:* L'étoile (The Star), c. 1878
Pastel. 60 × 44 (23.6 × 17.3).
Bequest of Gustave Caillebotte,
1894

142 *E. Degas:* Les repasseuses (Women Ironing), c. 1884
76 × 81.5 (29.9 × 32.1). Bequest of Isaac de Camondo, 1911

143 *E. Degas:* Grande danseuse habillée (Little Dancer of Fourteen Years or Large Dancer, Clothed)
Bronze cast of the original wax model shown at sixth Impressionist exhibition, 1881. 98 (38.6). Acquired 1930 through the generosity of the artist's heirs and the metal founder, Hébrard.

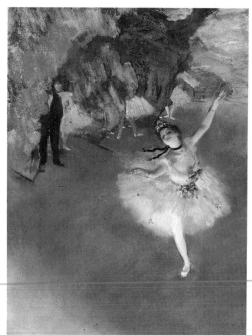

141

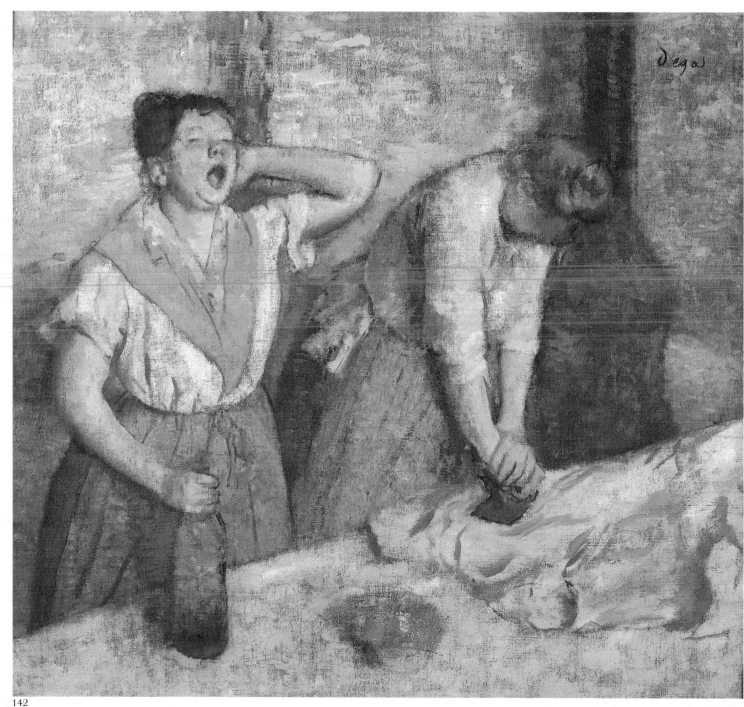

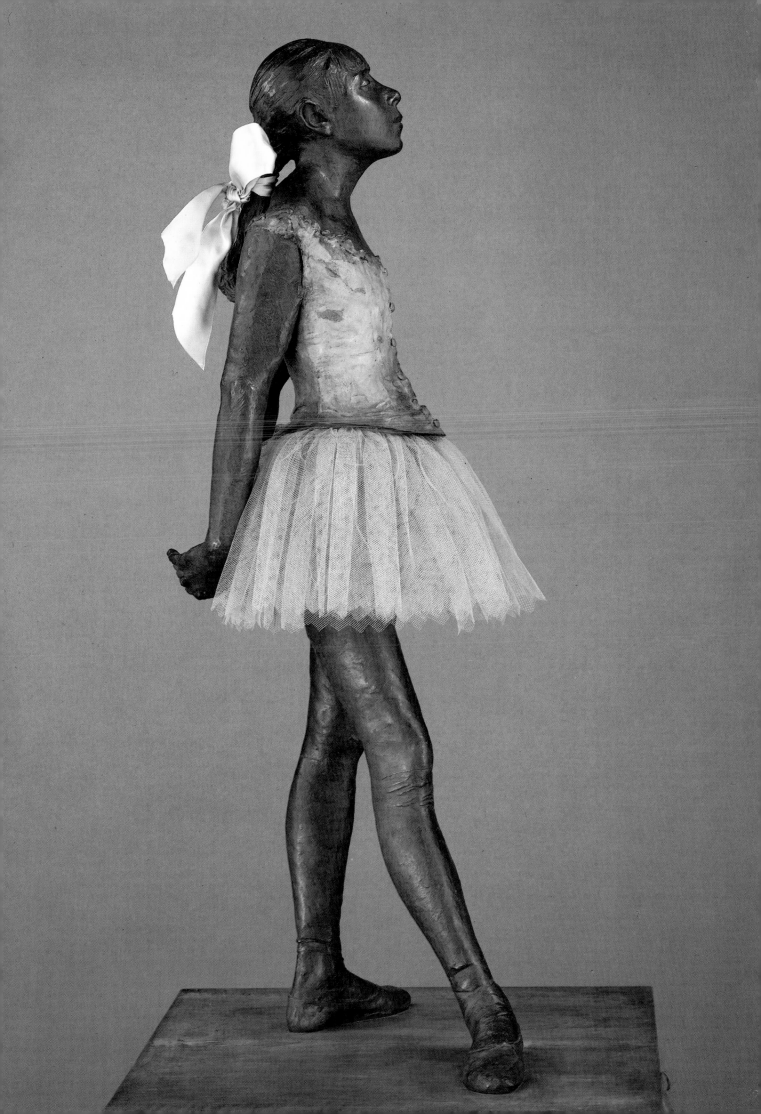

Manet

144 *E. Manet:* Sur la plage
(On the Beach), *1873*
59.5 × 73 (23.4 × 28.7). Gift of
Jean Edouard Dubrujeaud,
subject to a life interest, 1953;
entered national collection
1970

145 *E. Manet:* Georges
Clemenceau *(1841–1929),*
1879
94.5 × 74 (37.2 × 29.1). Gift of
Mrs Louisine W. Havemeyer,
1927

Sur la plage (*On the Beach*) was painted in 1873 at Berck-sur-Mer, presumably as a *plein-air* picture. It represents Manet's wife Suzanne, who frequently modelled for her husband, and his brother Eugène, shortly to marry Berthe Morisot. A work like this illustrates just how different Manet's style of painting was from that of his young Impressionist friends, even where the subject matter was analogous. Manet's vision was essentially a blend of classical and Japanese influences: the gradation of shades of grey in the foreground is worthy of Frans Hals or Velázquez. Around 1874 he painted extensively in Argenteuil, with Monet, but refused to take part in the group exhibitions of the so-called independents, continuing to submit his work to the official Salon in spite of the unrelenting hostility of the critics. Afflicted with partial paralysis in 1880, he died in 1883.

The Musée d'Orsay is the possessor of a fine portrait by Manet of Georges Clemenceau (1841–1929), a fitting tribute to the politician who did so much to help the Impressionists. It was he who gave official blessing to Monet's campaign to purchase Manet's *Olympia* for the Louvre, in 1907, and he was also responsible for the commission issued to Monet in the latter years of his life for the great sequence of paintings of waterlilies (*Nymphéas*) in the Orangerie.

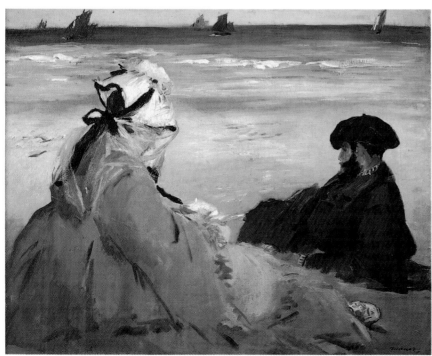

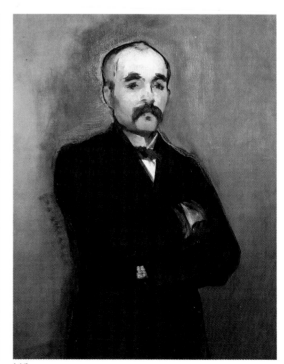

144

145

Renoir, Monet, Pissarro

For all the artists in the Impressionist group, the early 1880s were a time for taking stock, if not actually one of artistic crisis. Renoir had been exhibiting again at the Salon since 1878, enjoying a fair degree of success. His improved financial situation enabled him to travel, and he visited Algeria in 1881; the Musée d'Orsay possesses several major canvases from this trip, notable for their treatment of the strong southern light and for the many echoes of Delacroix. A trip to Italy later that year led him to rediscover the Renaissance masters he had admired in the Louvre as a young man, and his first-hand experience of classical antiquity, for example the paintings of Pompeii, had an undoubted influence on his own work. A new concern for drawing is apparent in two major compositions of 1883, *Danse à la ville* (*Dance in the City*) — the female model is Suzanne Valadon, later a painter herself and the mother of Maurice Utrillo — and *Danse à la campagne* (*Dance in the Country*), where the model is Aline Charigot, later to become Renoir's wife. Renoir's palette became simpler and took on the acid tones that typify his work at this period. Yet with *Jeunes filles au piano* (*Young Girls at the Piano*), the first painting by Renoir ever purchased for the nation (at Mallarmé's suggestion, in 1892), there is clear evidence of a move towards an altogether softer style and warmer colours. Renoir continued to paint the relaxed and charming scenes he preferred, returning again and again to the theme of female *Bathers* (*Baigneuses*), which found its culmination in the great composition of 1918–19, executed in the last few months of his life. Crippled with rheumatism, the old painter had retired to Cagnes-sur-Mer in the South of France, and there he produced this dazzling pictorial testament, in which the human forms, sensual and exuberantly coloured in the manner of Rubens, blend and coalesce in an incandescent landscape.

Like Renoir, Monet was active well into the twentieth century, the different stages of his artistic development being directly linked to particular motifs, which in turn were conditioned largely by his place of residence. Late in 1878 he

146 *C. Pissarro:* Jeune fille à la baguette (Peasant Girl with Stick), *1881*
81 × 65 (31.9 × 25.6). Bequest of Isaac de Camondo, 1911

147 *P. A. Renoir:* Jeunes filles au piano (Young Girls at the Piano), *1892*
116 × 90 (45.7 × 35.4). Acquired 1892

moved to Vétheuil, a small village in the Seine valley between Paris and Rouen, and until 1891 he found his subject matter in the surrounding area, landscapes that reflected the changing seasons. When the Seine was frozen over during the harsh winter of 1879–80, he produced a sequence of paintings on this theme, several of which are in the museum's possession. The move down river to Giverny corresponded to a further development in his work. Monet had always liked to produce many different interpretations of a single motif, studying ephemeral effects of light as it altered through the day or over the different seasons of the year. Yet it was only with the *Meules* (*Haystacks*) that the 'series' became a feature of his working method. He wrote to his friend, the critic Gustave Geffroy: 'I am persisting with a series of different effects, but at this time of the year the sun sets so fast I cannot keep up with it ... the further I get, the more I see that it will take a great deal of work to succeed in conveying what I want: "instantaneity", and above all the external "envelope", the same light spread overall.'

Other series were to follow, notably that based on Rouen Cathedral, which although dated 1894 was in fact painted in two bursts in 1892 and 1893; the sequence is well represented in the Musée d'Orsay by the bequest of Comte Isaac de

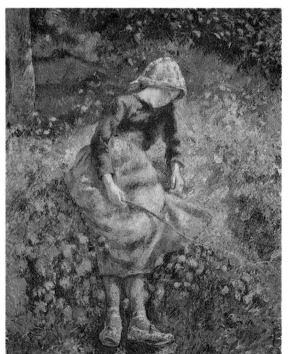

146

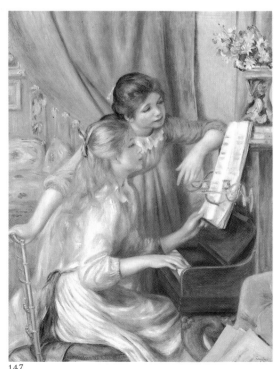

147

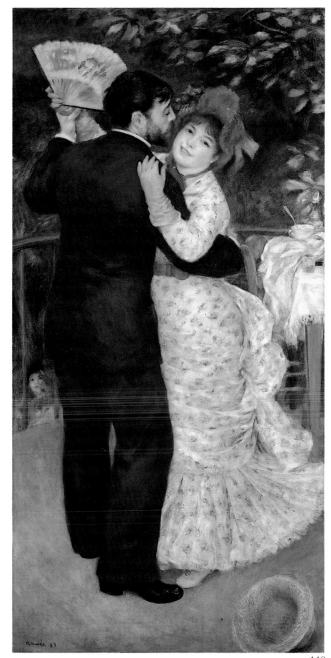

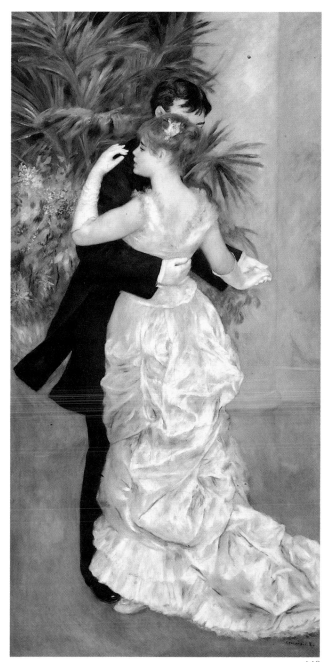

148

149

Camondo, a collector with a passion for Monet's work, and by one canvas purchased by the state (coming to terms with Monet's reputation rather late in the day) in 1907.

Around the turn of the century Monet painted other series based on Giverny and London. At that time he often used canvases that were almost square, and this is also the format of his earliest paintings of waterlilies in his garden at Giverny, exhibited under the collective title *Bassin aux nymphéas* (*Waterlily Pool*). This motif was Monet's central preoccupation throughout the latter period of his career, culminating in the vast decorative scheme for the two rooms of the Musée de l'Orangerie, opened to the public in 1927 after the painter's death, but planned by him with the assistance of his devoted friend Clemenceau.

148 *P. A. Renoir:* Danse à la campagne (Dance in the Country), *1883*
180 × 90 (70.9 × 35.4).
Acquired 1979

149 *P. A. Renoir:* Danse à la ville (Dance in the City), *1883*
180 × 90 (70.9 × 35.4).
Acquired in lieu of estate duties, 1978

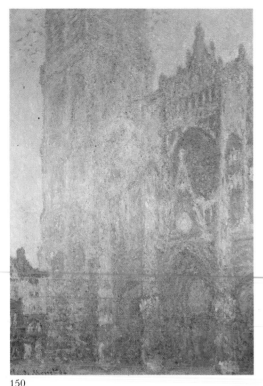
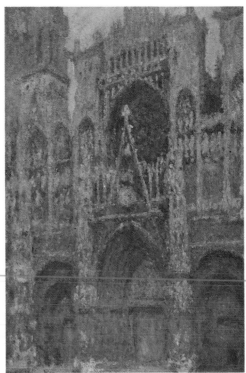
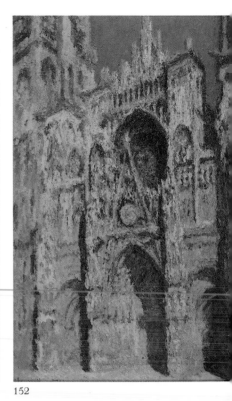

150   151   152

150–154 *C. Monet:* La
cathédrale de Rouen (Rouen
Cathedral)
106 × 73 (41.7 × 28.7);
100 × 65 (39.4 × 25.6);
107 × 73 (42.1 × 28.7);
107 × 73 (42.1 × 28.7); 91 × 63
(35.8 × 24.8). Although dated
1894, these five works from a
series were painted in 1892
and 1893. Harmonie brune
(Harmony in Brown, *153*) *was*
acquired in 1907. Effet du
matin, harmonie blanche
(Morning Effect, Harmony in
White, *150*), Temps gris
(Overcast Weather, *151*),
Plein soleil, harmonie bleue
et or (Full Sunlight,
Harmony in Blue and Gold,
152), Soleil matinal,
harmonie bleue (Morning
Sun, Harmony in Blue, *154*)
were part of the bequest of
Isaac de Camondo, 1911.

Sisley's development, like Monet's, can be traced through the different motifs he adopted at various periods. After moving to Moret-sur-Loing in 1882, he worked almost exclusively on landscapes of that area. He died in 1899, too soon to experience his fame.

Pissarro was the only one of the Impressionists to take part in all the group exhibitions. His work, too, changed radically in the early 1880s. Previously a landscapist, he began to develop an interest in the human figure, embarking on a series of paintings of the peasants of Pontoise. *Jeune Fille à la baguette (Peasant Girl with Stick)* is a good example of his work in this period, combining sensitivity with solid construction; the alternation of fine brushwork and heavy impasto is evidence of his almost obsessive concern for technical experiment. Indeed it was this enthusiasm for new effects that led him to adopt the Neo-Impressionist or Divisionist theories of Seurat and Signac in 1886–87. It fairly rapidly became apparent that the application of strict rules did not suit his temperament, and he abandoned the method in favour of the more fluid handling that is typical of his late works – landscapes of Eragny-sur-Epte (where he moved in 1884) and views of Paris and Rouen.

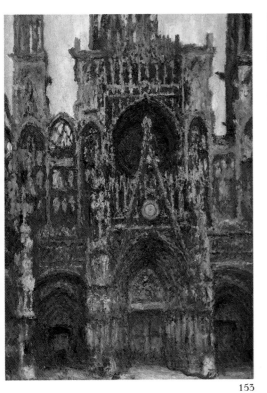

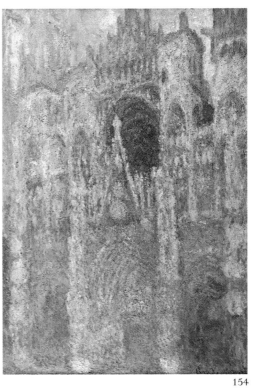

153

154

155 *P. A. Renoir:* Baigneuses (Bathers), *1918–19*
110 × 160 (43.3 × 63). Gift of the artist's sons, 1923

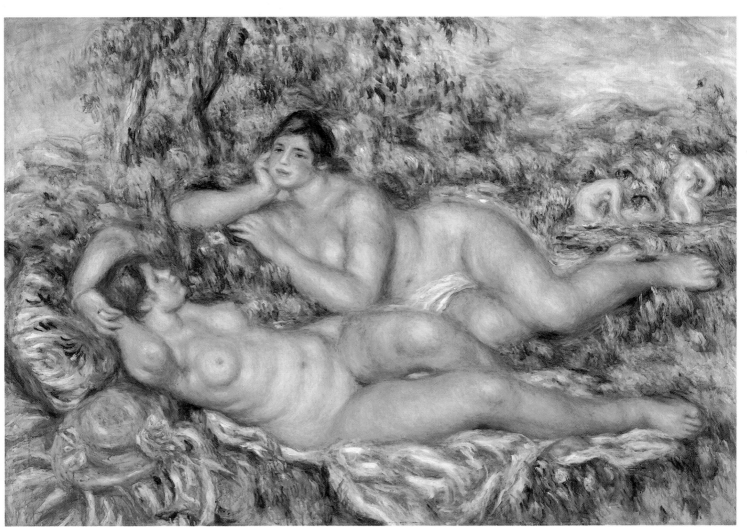

155

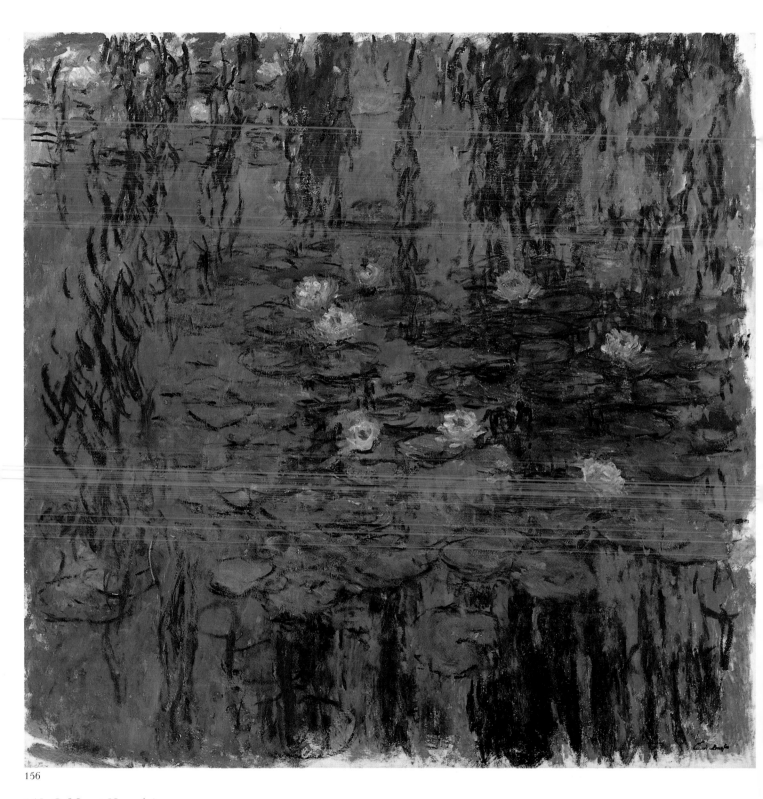

156

156 *C. Monet:* Nymphéas
bleus (Blue Waterlilies), *after*
1916
200 × 200 (78.7 × 78.7).
Acquired 1981

Cézanne

The collections of the Musée d'Orsay contain many fine works by Paul Cézanne (1839–1906), well representing the diversity of themes treated by the painter and showing his evolution through the different stages of his career.

In his early years, Cézanne (born, like his friend Emile Zola, in Aix-en-Provence) was strongly influenced by Delacroix and the old masters, in particular the Venetian school; that debt is clearly indicated in works like *La Madeleine* (*Mary Magdalen*), of *c.* 1868–69, and *Pastorale* (*Pastoral*) of 1870. Inevitably he was torn between his Romantic inclinations, evident in *La femme étranglée* (*Strangled Woman*), and the Realist spirit abroad among the other painters of the day, following in Manet's wake. At the first Impressionist exhibition of 1874, two Cézanne canvases attracted a hail of abuse from public and critics alike: one was the famous *La Maison du pendu* (*House of the Hanged Man*), a landscape executed while the artist was staying with Dr Gachet at Auvers-sur-Oise (near Pontoise), working with Pissarro; the other was *Une Moderne Olympia* (*A Modern Olympia*), an interpretation of the theme treated previously by Manet in 1863. Another echo of Manet is the view of the bay of Marseille looking down from L'Estaque: 'It's like a playing card', Cézanne explained to Pissarro, recalling the effect in Manet's *Fifer*.

157 *P. Cézanne:* L'Estaque: vue du golfe de Marseille (L'Estaque: View of the Bay of Marseille), c. *1878–79* *59.5 × 73 (23.4 × 28.7). Bequest of Gustave Caillebotte, 1894*

158 *P. Cézanne:* Les joueurs de cartes (The Card Players), c. *1890–95* *47.5 × 57 (18.7 × 22.4). Bequest of Isaac de Camondo, 1911*

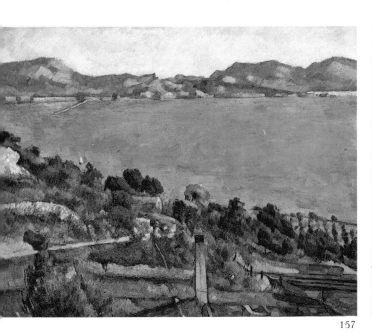

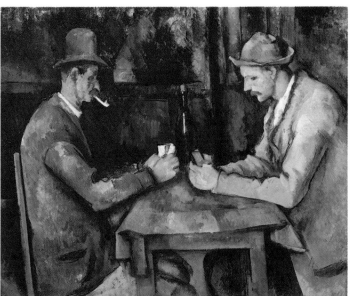

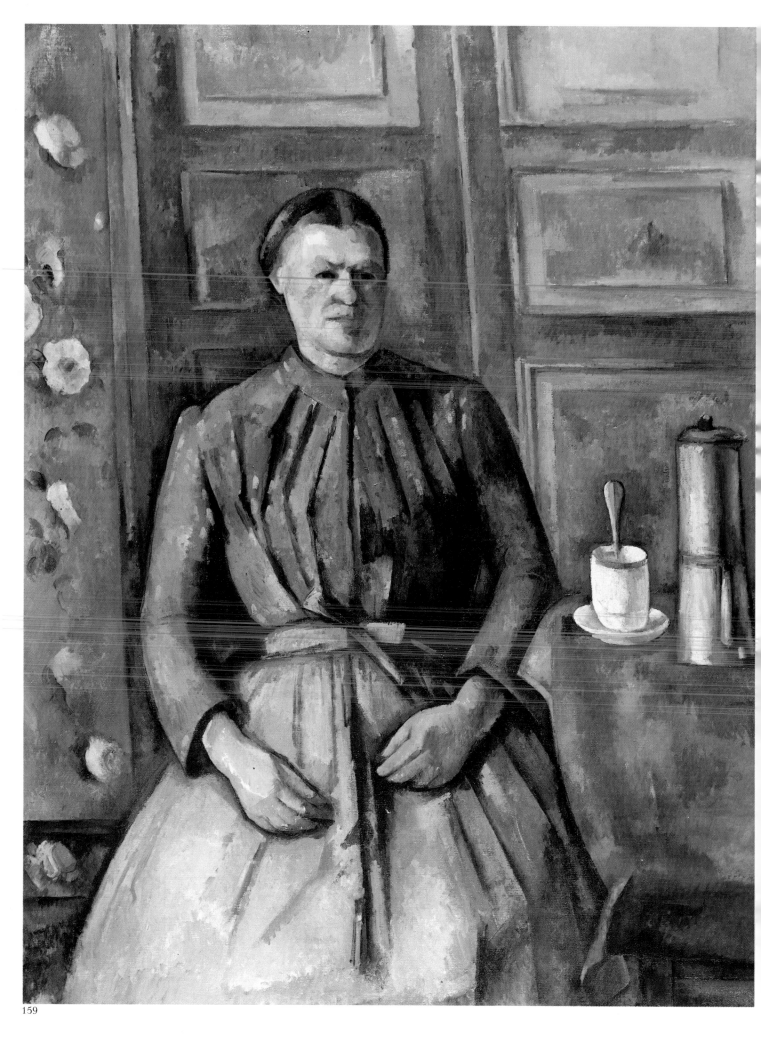

159

As well as his landscapes, and some early nudes in outdoor settings that look forward to the *Grandes Baigneuses* (*Great Bathers*) – a number of studies for which are in the Musée d'Orsay – the two genres that preoccupied Cézanne throughout his life were portraiture (or 'the figure' as he called it) and still-life. Possibly because he worked very slowly, possibly because of a certain shyness, he normally either painted self-portraits (two of which are in the Musée d'Orsay) or called on his family and friends to act as models, as in *Les joueurs de cartes* (*The Card Players*). His wife was his favourite sitter, and his paintings of her reveal a desire to look beyond transient facial expressions and express more abiding qualities: the study of forms predominates over psychological analysis, as in *La femme à la cafetière* (*Woman with a Coffee Pot*). The move in the direction of simplified volumes and geometricization of forms was to have a profound influence on the course of twentieth-century painting – as did Cézanne's abandonment of linear perspective in the late still-lifes. His innovations, in pictures such as *Pommes et oranges* (*Apples and Oranges*), helped to pave the way for the experiments of Cubism.

159 *P. Cézanne:* La Femme à la cafetière (Woman with a Coffee Pot), c. *1890–95* *130 × 96.5 (51.2 × 38). Gift of Monsieur and Madame Jean-Victor Pellerin, 1956*

160 *P. Cézanne:* Pommes et oranges (Apples and Oranges), c. *1895–1900* *74 × 93 (29.1 × 36.6). Bequest of Isaac de Camondo, 1911*

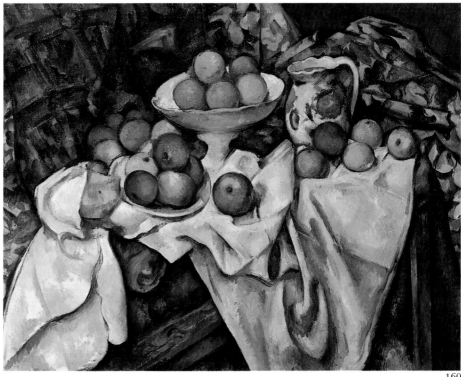

Van Gogh

It was not until 1880 that Vincent van Gogh (1853–90), the son of a Dutch pastor, discovered his vocation as a painter. Before that he had worked for the art dealer Goupil in The Hague, London and Paris, and studied theology. His early paintings include dark and heavily impastoed oils of Dutch peasants which even at this early stage reveal something of the artist's troubled nature. In 1886 Van Gogh went to live in Paris, where his brother Théo cared for him with great devotion and gave him much-needed financial assistance. Théo, who also worked for Goupil, was receptive to new ideas in painting, and the extensive correspondence between the two brothers forms one of the most moving documents in the history of art. In Paris, Van Gogh came into contact with a creative world in ferment. The encounter with the Impressionists had an immediate effect on his painting; his palette lightened, and his subjects became more varied. *L'Italienne* (*The Italian Woman*) is one of his most vivid portraits, probably representing Agostina Segatori who ran the Paris cabaret Le Tambourin, which was a regular haunt of painters and artists of all kinds: the heightened complementary colours (red-green, blue-orange) and the abstract simplification of the compositional elements reinforce the vigorous and expressive brushwork that marks Van Gogh so clearly as the precursor of the Fauves.

In February 1888 the artist went to live in Arles in the South of France, intending to found an artistic community in which he would be joined by, among others, Paul Gauguin, for whom he had the greatest admiration. Gauguin arrived in October, but the dream rapidly turned to nightmare when a violent argument broke out between the two men and Van Gogh cut off his own ear in a fit of madness. This was the prelude to a complete mental breakdown, with only brief periods of remission, which led to Van Gogh's hospitalization and eventual suicide in 1890.

La chambre de Van Gogh à Arles (*Van Gogh's Bedroom at Arles*) of which there are three versions, was painted while Van Gogh was an inmate of the asylum at Saint-Rémy. It

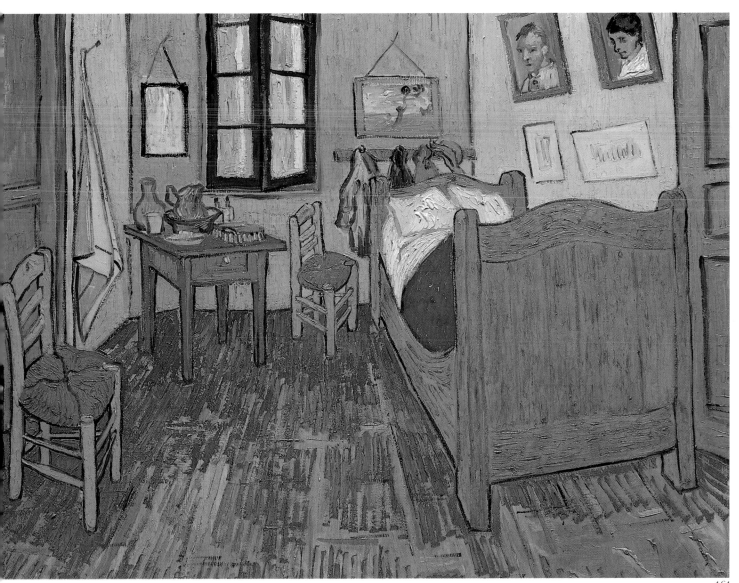

161

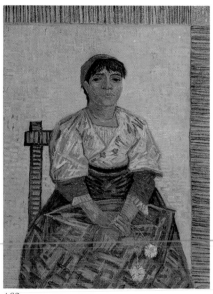

162

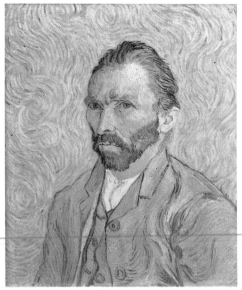

163

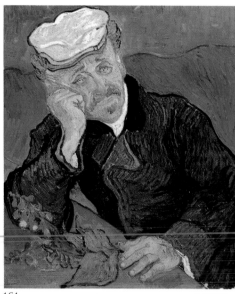

164

162 *V. van Gogh:* L'Italienne
(The Italian Woman),
painted in Paris, 1887
81 × 60 (31.9 × 23.6). Gift of
Baronne Eva Gebhard-
Gourgaud, 1965

163 *V. van Gogh:* Portrait de
l'artiste (Self-portrait), *1889*
65 × 54.5 (25.6 × 21.5). Gift of
Paul and Marguerite Gachet,
1949

164 *V. van Gogh:* Le docteur
Paul Gachet (Portrait of Dr
Gachet), *painted at Auvers-*
sur-Oise, June 1890
68 × 57 (26.8 × 22.4). Gift of
Paul and Marguerite Gachet,
1949

165 *V. van Gogh:* L'église
d'Auvers-sur-Oise (The
Church at Auvers-sur-Oise),
June 1890
94 × 74.5 (37 × 29.3). Acquired
with the help of Paul Gachet
and an anonymous donation,
1951

shows the room he had occupied at the time he painted his
famous *Tournesols* (*Sunflowers*). A glorious evocation of a
past life, with a brilliancy of colouring and dizzying
perspective that are in marked contrast to the orderliness of
the modest room, this canvas clearly represents some sort of
attempt at exorcism, for there can be little doubt that
painting served Van Gogh as a form of personal therapy.

That cathartic mechanism is seen most clearly at work in
the self-portraits, some forty in all, in which Van Gogh
explored his own image, often distorted by hallucinations –
as in the example, painted in 1889, in the Musée d'Orsay. The
classic representative of the 'doomed artist' beloved of the
nineteenth century, Van Gogh prefigured such painters of
pure expression as Edvard Munch, Alexei Jawlensky and
Oskar Kokoschka, who regarded art essentially as the process
of projecting an inner world. This particular self-portrait was
presented by Van Gogh to Dr Gachet, who was both a gifted
medical practitioner – with a particular interest in mental
illness – and also the friend and patron of numerous painters
including Renoir, Pissarro, Cézanne and Guillaumin, all of
whom stayed with him at Auvers-sur-Oise. It was to his house
that Van Gogh went in May 1890 to convalesce after his latest
attack, and it was there that he painted, in the little time left
to him, the famous *Eglise d'Auvers* (*The Church at Auvers*),
an extraordinary marriage of brushwork and colour that
reveals Van Gogh as the precursor of European
Expressionism.

One of the conditions imposed by the son and daughter of
Dr Gachet was that the paintings from his distinguished
collection should be grouped together; their wishes in this
matter have been respected in the hanging scheme adopted
in the Musée d'Orsay.

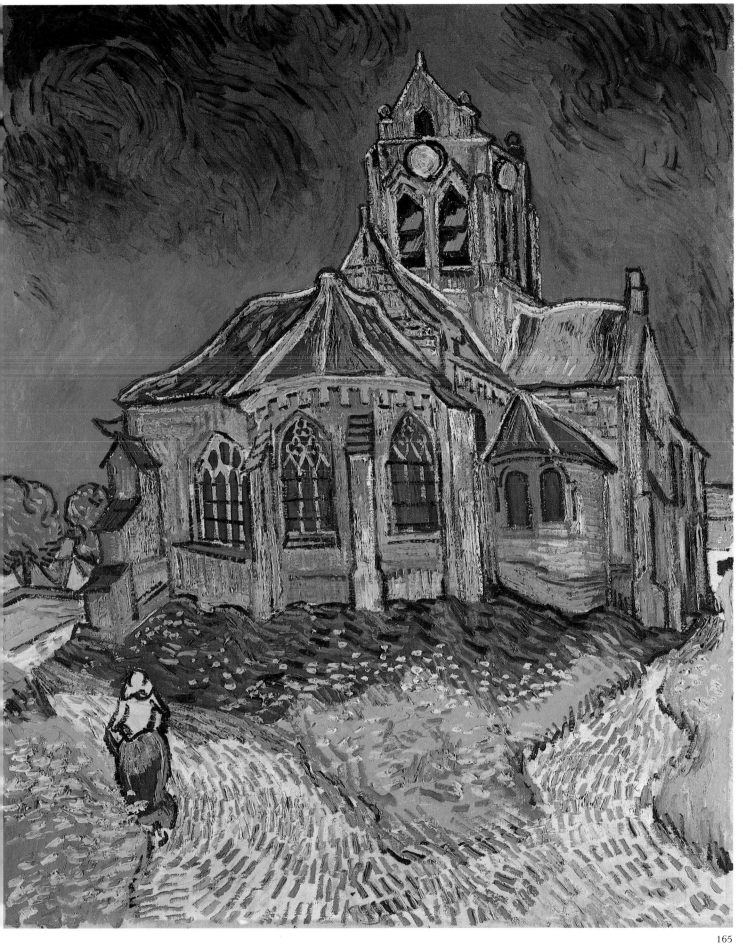

Seurat and
Neo-Impressionism

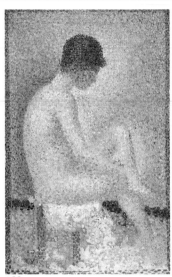

166

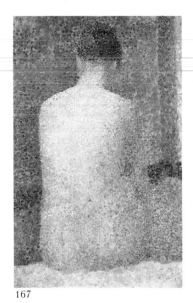

167

In the course of a brief but intensely active career Georges Seurat (1859–91) produced a small number of masterpieces, now largely dispersed in foreign museums. The result is that Seurat is relatively little known in his own country. *Une baignade, Asnières (Bathers at Asnières)*, of 1883–84, rejected by the Salon jury and exhibited at the first Salon of the Société des Artistes Indépendants in 1884, is now in London. *Une dimanche après-midi à l'Ile de la Grande Jatte (Sunday on the Island of La Grande Jatte)*, shown at the eighth and last Impressionist exhibition of 1886, is in Chicago. *Les poseuses (The Models)*, of 1886–88, is in the Barnes Foundation, Merion, Pa. The first two of these masterpieces are represented in the Musée d'Orsay by a few working sketches, the third by a number of more finished and meticulously executed studies. Otherwise, the only examples in the museum of his perfected technique, generally known as Neo-Impressionism, are one landscape, *Port-en-Bessin* (1888), and his last painting, *Le cirque (The Circus)*, of 1891. His method consisted in the application on the canvas of tiny dabs of pure, divided colour, according to a system of formal composition founded in the equilibrium of opposites, probably based on the Golden Section. In the course of a traditional classical training, Seurat had become interested in theories of line and colour, which he studied in the writings of Blanc, Rood and Chevreul, and later with his contemporary Charles Henry. Seurat hoped to found a new 'great tradition' that would build on the achievements of Impressionism, one based on his own interpretation of modernity as extending beyond subject matter to encompass rigorous 'scientific' method. In *The Circus* – not without wit – he uses the symbolism of colour and ascendant lines to convey a sense of animated movement and celebration.

Seurat's theories were taken up and developed by his friend Paul Signac (1863–1935) in a manifesto published at the end of the century, *D'Eugène Delacroix au néo-impressionnisme*. After Seurat's early death it fell to Signac to take over his mantle as leader of the movement, and he

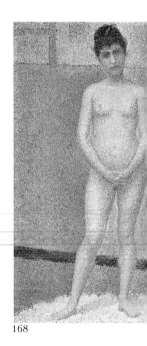

168

166–168 *G. Seurat:* Trois esquisses pour Les poseuses (Three Sketches for The Models), *1886–87*
25 × 16 (9.8 × 6.3); 24.5 × 15.5 (9.6 × 6.1); 25 × 16 (9.8 × 6.3).
Acquired 1947

169 *G. Seurat:* Le cirque (The Circus), *1891*
185.5 × 152.5 (73 × 60).
Bequest of John Quinn, 1924

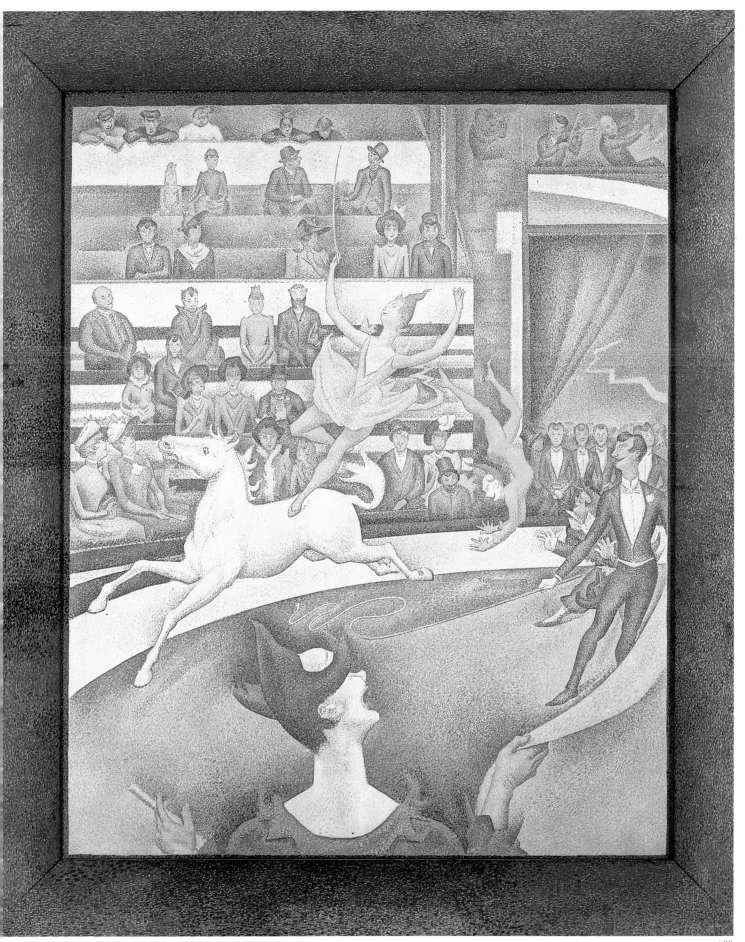

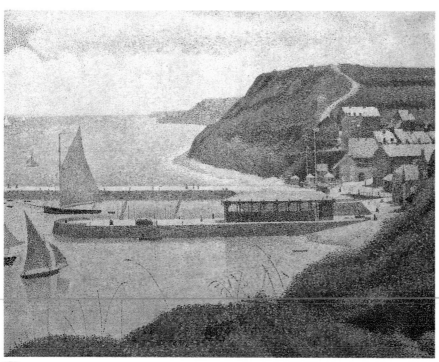

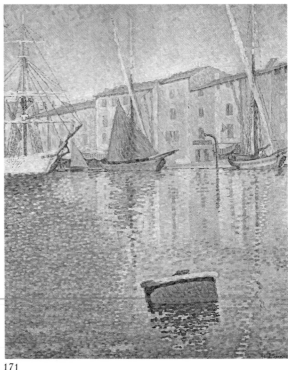

170

171

170 *G. Seurat:* Port-en-
Bessin, avant-port, marée
haute (Port-en-Bessin, Outer
Harbour, High Tide), *1888
67 × 82 (26.4 × 32.3). Proceeds
of anon. Canadian gift, 1952*

171 *P. Signac:* La bouée
rouge (The Red Buoy), *1895
81 × 65 (31.9 × 25.6). Gift of
Dr Pierre Hébert, subject to a
life interest, 1957; entered
national collection 1973*

172 *H. E. Cross:* L'air du soir
(Evening Breeze), *1894
115.5 × 163 (45.5 × 64.2). Gift
of Mme Ginette Signac, 1976*

developed a method that relied more on colour and broader
brushstrokes. From the late 1890s onwards he concentrated
increasingly on seascapes which, in their alliance of a true
Impressionist sensibility with disciplined technique, have
surprising affinities with French landscapes of the seventeenth and eighteenth centuries. Of the other members of the
group, which held together until the mid 1890s (Charles
Angrand, Maximilien Luce, Albert Dubois-Pillet, and for a
time Camille Pissarro and Théo van Rysselberghe, among
others), it was Henri-Edmond Cross (1856–1910) who,
alongside Signac, remained loyal to Seurat's technique for the
rest of his life. His *L'air du soir* (*Evening Breeze*), though
Neo-Impressionist or 'Divisionist' in manner, demonstrates a
fine aesthetic sense that is typical of the *fin de siècle* and
somewhat reminiscent of the Nabis, Maurice Denis in
particular.

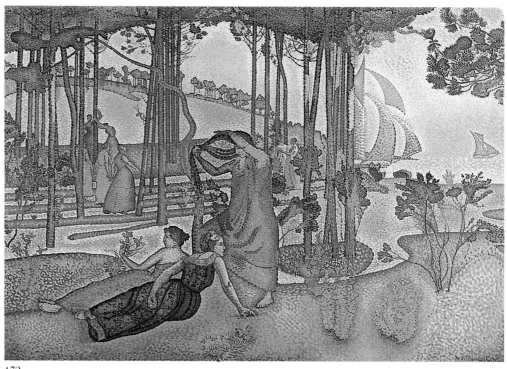

172

Toulouse-Lautrec

Born of an aristocratic family from south-west France, Henri de Toulouse-Lautrec (1864–1901) suffered in his youth a series of accidents that left him permanently disabled. It was the combination of piercing intelligence with physical deformity that created one of the most eccentric personalities of the *fin de siècle*, a man who could be intensely touching or woundingly sarcastic. Compensating for his infirmities by emancipating himself from bourgeois convention, Lautrec plunged into the nocturnal world of Paris theatres, clubs and brothels, finding there the models for his paintings, which are markedly influenced by Degas and Japanese prints. In true Baudelairian spirit, he sought beauty in degradation, and his oils, pastels and lithographs provide an exceptionally vivid picture of the world of entertainment in the late nineteenth century.

In 1895 the dancer La Goulue, formerly a celebrity of the Moulin Rouge, asked the artist to decorate a fairground booth at the Foire du Trône where she planned to present her new act. Lautrec was inspired to produce two large canvases in which he invested all his skill as a poster artist, one showing La Goulue dancing at the Moulin Rouge with her partner Valentin le Désossé, the other representing her as a Moorish dancer.

Women – whether actresses, society ladies or prostitutes – were in themselves a principal source of Lautrec's inspiration as in *La Toilette* of 1896 and the album of lithographs, *Elles*, published in the same year.

173 *H. de Toulouse-Lautrec:* La toilette, *1896*
67 × 54 (26.4 × 21.3). Bequest of Pierre Goujon, 1914

174 *H. de Toulouse-Lautrec:* Henry Samary, de la Comédie Française, dans le rôle de Raoul de Vaubert dans la comédie de J. Sandeau, 'Mademoiselle de la Seiglière' (Henry Samary Performing at the Comédie Française), *1889*
75 × 52 (29.5 × 20.5). Gift of Jacques Laroche, subject to a life interest, 1947; entered national collection 1976

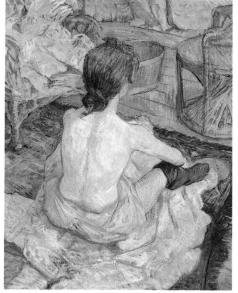

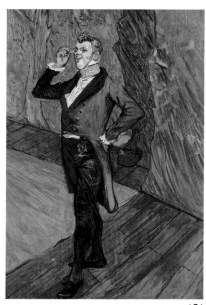

173

174

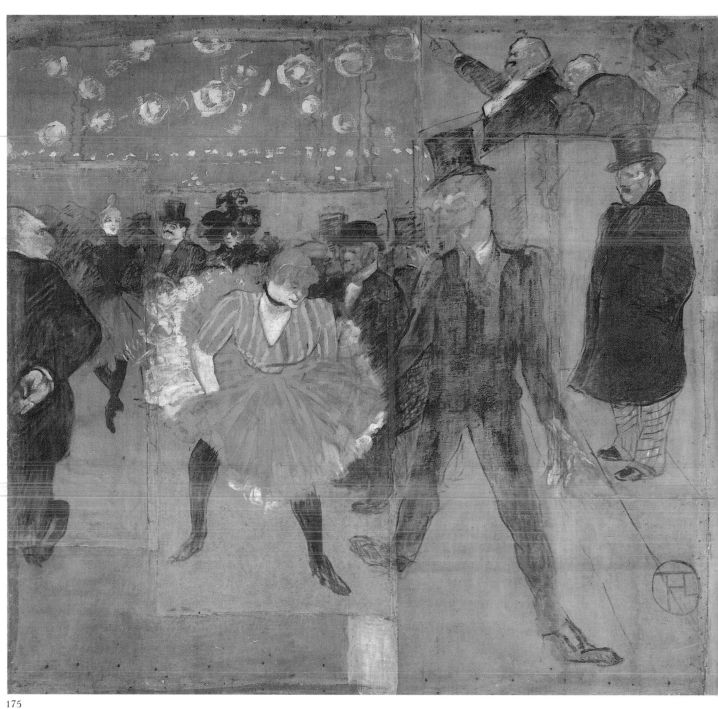

175

175–176 *H. de Toulouse-*
Lautrec: La danse au Moulin-
Rouge, La Goulue et Valentin
le Désossé (Dancing at the
Moulin-Rouge, La Goulue
and Valentin le Désossé)
La danse mauresque ou La
Goulue en almée (The
Moorish Dance or La Goulue
as a Moorish Dancer)

298 × 316 (117.3 × 124.4);
285 × 307.5 (112.2 × 121).
Panels decorating La Goulue's
booth at the Foire du Trône,
1895. Acquired, in fragments,
in 1929, with the exception of
the section showing Valentin
le Désossé, given by
Monsieur Auffray, 1929;
restored 1930

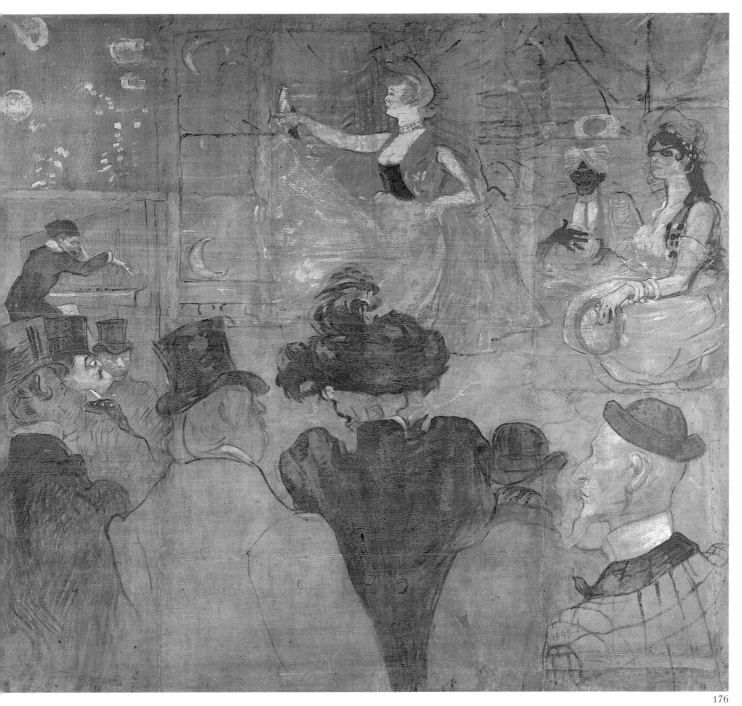

176

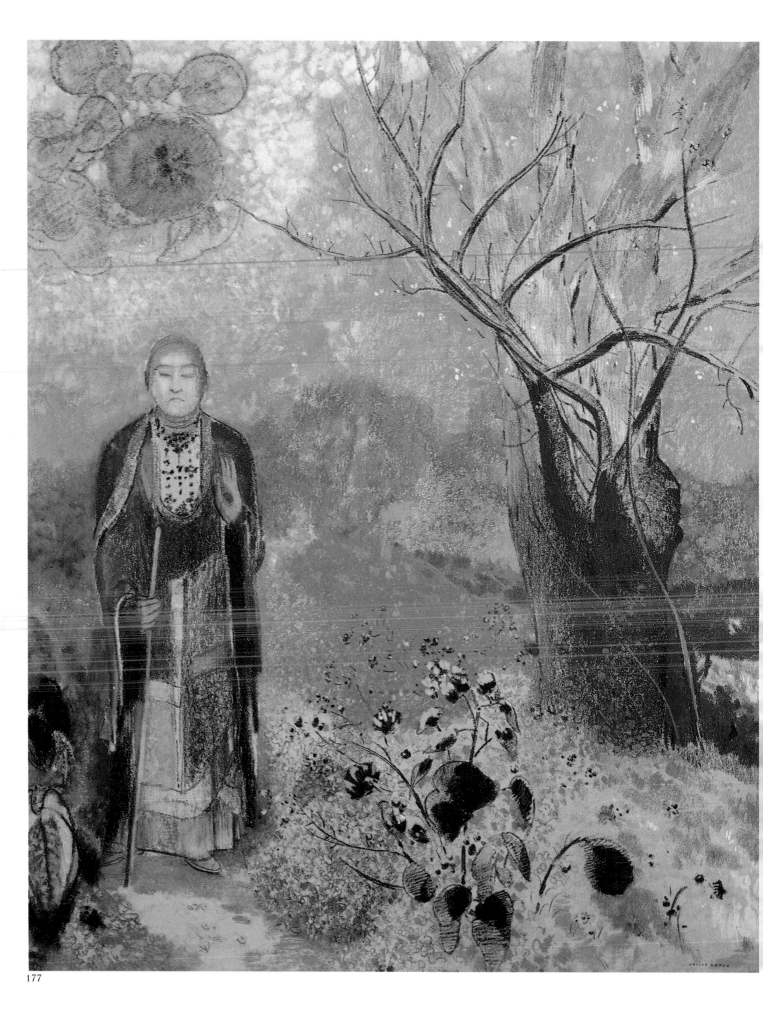

177

Redon

Working largely in isolation, Odilon Redon (1840–1916) produced a body of work of striking originality. Derived almost entirely from the unconscious and dreams, his pictures are peopled with mysterious creatures, gnomes and fantastic animals and flowers. Together with Puvis de Chavannes and Gustave Moreau, he is one of the principal representatives of French Symbolism.

Redon's early work is largely in black-and-white (charcoal drawings and lithographs) and, like the rest of his oeuvre, is often inspired by literature (Poe, Flaubert, etc.). His externalization of private fantasies is entirely characteristic of the climate that prevailed in the *fin-de-siècle* years, and of the vein of lyrical introspection that ran through French poetry from Baudelaire to Mallarmé. In 1890 Redon began to experiment with colour, still using the same subject matter. *Les yeux clos* (*Closed Eyes*) was the first of his works to be acquired for the nation. Ultimately it was pastel that provided Redon with the sumptuous effects best suited to convey his fantastic imagery. His virtuoso use of the medium is unsurpassed, as witness *Le Bouddha* (*Buddha*), one of the most famous of the many pastels by him in the Musée d'Orsay (a collection assembled for the most part from the gifts and bequests of the artist's widow Suzanne and son Arï, and from donations by Claude Roger-Marx).

177 *O. Redon:* Le bouddha (Buddha), c. *1905*
Pastel. 90 × 73 (35.4 × 28.7).
Salon d'Automne, Paris, 1906.
Acquired 1971

178 *O. Redon:* Les yeux clos (Eyes Closed), *1890*
44 × 36 (17.3 × 14.2). Acquired 1904

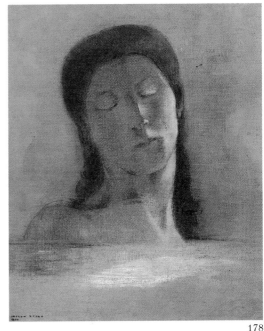

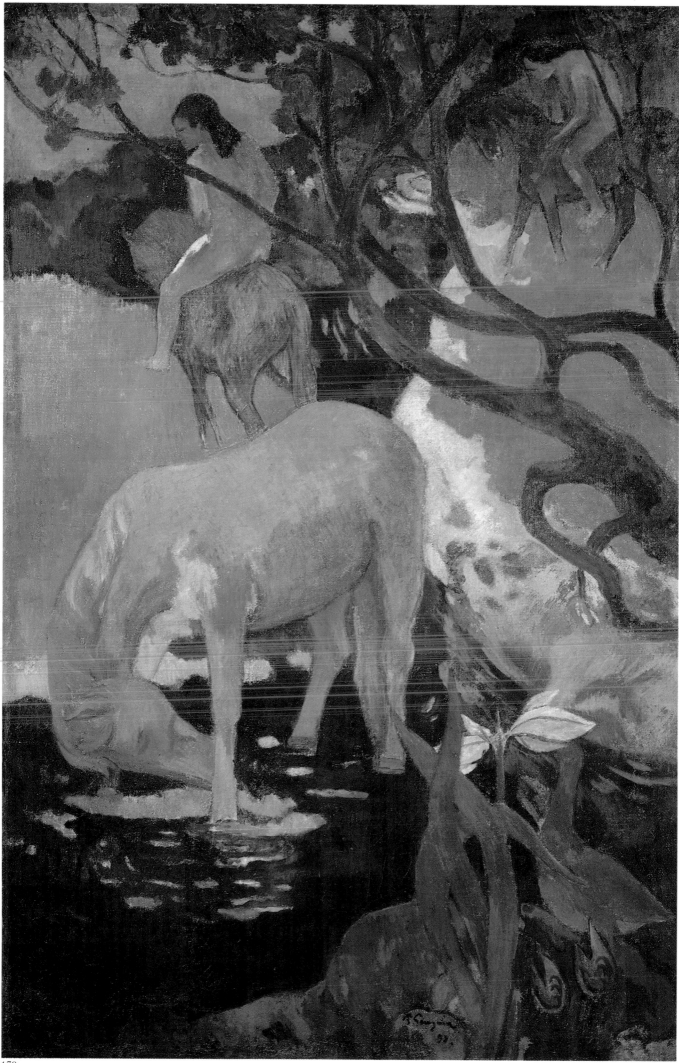

Gauguin

Paul Gauguin (1848–1903) began painting as an amateur, and it was because of his successes at the group exhibitions of the Impressionists, in which he participated from 1880 onwards, that he determined to make it his full-time career.

Pont-Aven in Brittany was the first port of call in a journey of discovery that was to last a lifetime. Gauguin stayed there in 1887, 1888, 1889–90, and again in 1894, associating with the painters who have come to be known collectively as the Pont-Aven School, some of whom were manifestly influenced by him.

In between trips to Brittany, Gauguin also travelled to Martinique, paid a brief visit to Van Gogh in Arles, and spent time in Paris. *La belle Angèle*, of 1889, is a good illustration of Gaugin's distinctive synthesis of *Cloisonnisme* (the use of black outlines) and Symbolism, incorporating Japanese influences and a feeling for decorative symplicity inherited from Puvis de Chavannes. It expresses, too, the love of the primitive world that took him to Tahiti for the first time in 1891–93. There Gauguin found the themes and the spiritual significance his work demanded, and he developed an interest in the native religions and crafts that powerfully influenced the nature of his later sculptures.

His return to France in 1893 proved to be no more than an interlude, and in 1895 he left again for Polynesia, this time for good.

179 *P. Gauguin:* Le cheval blanc (The White Horse), *1898*
140 × 91.5 (55.1 × 36). Acquired 1927

180 *P. Gauguin:* La belle Angèle, *1889*
92 × 73 (36.2 × 28.7). Gift of Ambroise Vollard, 1927

181 *P. Gauguin:* Le repas (The Meal), *1891*
73 × 92 (28.7 × 36.2). Gift of Monsieur and Madame André Meyer, subject to a life interest, 1954; entered national collection 1975

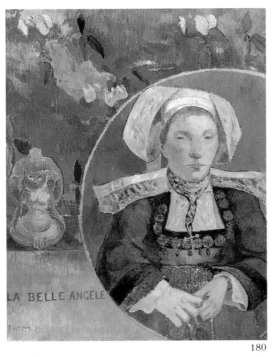

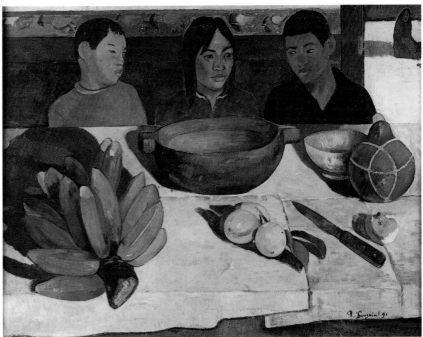

180

181

The Pont-Aven School

182 *E. Bernard:* Madeleine
au Bois d'Amour (Madeleine
in the Bois d'Amour), *1888*
137 × 164 (53.9 × 64.6).
Acquired 1977

183 *P. Sérusier:* Le talisman
(The Talisman), *1888*
27 × 22 (10.6 × 8.7). Acquired
1985, with the generous
assistance of M.P.M., through
the Lutèce Foundation

Pont-Aven is a Breton village near Concarneau where a number of artists congregated, united in their desire to emphasize their differences from Impressionism. Gauguin went there in 1888. Emile Bernard (1868–1941), who arrived in August 1888, became the group's theoretician: 'Synthetism' and 'simplification' are the key-words he noted down on the back of his *Nature morte au pot de grès* (*Still-life with Stoneware Pot*), in the Musée d'Orsay. For the portrait of his sister Madeleine reclining in the Bois d'Amour at Pont-Aven, he adopted a downward perspective and outlined the flat areas of colour in black. It was a lesson effortlessly absorbed by Paul Sérusier (1863–1927), who also worked at Pont-Aven. On the back of one of his pictures he noted that it was painted 'in October 1888 under Gauguin's guidance': this landscape, without perspective, dominated by intense, pure tones of colour, was to become the famous *Talisman* of the Nabis (see p. 137). Other painters such as Charles Laval (1862–94) and Charles Filiger (1863–1928) seized on these simple motifs, and Brittany came to represent, for them and many others, the mystic innocence of a primitive society.

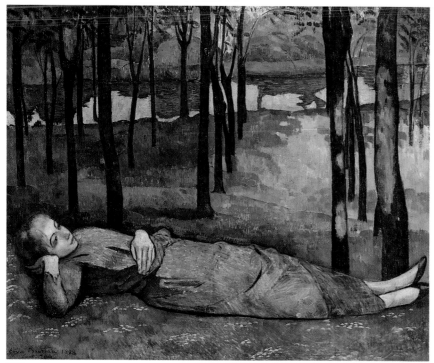

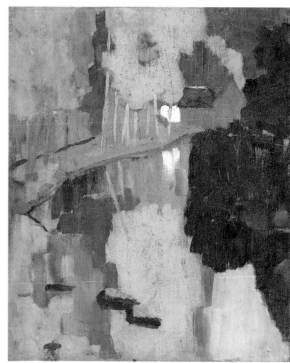

Sculpture: Gauguin and the Nabis

Following on from a brief experiment with ceramics in 1886–87, Gauguin produced a number of painted wooden sculptures, among them a relief called *Soyez mystérieuses* (*Be Mysterious*), on which he worked at Le Pouldu, in Brittany, in 1890. The style he adopted – polychrome effects, simplified forms with flattened planes and areas of contrasting shadow – was influenced by his acquaintance with Breton folk art and the so-called primitive arts in general. His distinctive combination of modelling, colour and abbreviated formal construction transforms these works from representational objects into archaic emblems.

An artist who shared Gauguin's appreciation of pagan idols was Georges Lacombe (1868–1916), introduced to the Nabi group by Sérusier. His *Danses bretonnes* (*Breton Dances*) of 1894 is a subtle conjunction of flattened surfaces with fluid line; and he showed this same ability to blend sophisticated technique with primitivism in transforming a carved bed into a symbol of the mystery of human life. Another emblem of the recurring cycle of life and death is his *Isis*, which shows the goddess clasping her breasts and expressing two streams of blood, representing the life force. The freedom and spontaneity of this type of direct sculpture is reflected in its bold polychrome effects, expressive deformations and accentuated physical characteristics.

184–185 *P. Gauguin:* Idole à la coquille (Idol with Shell), *1893*
Idole à la perle (Idol with Pearl), c. *1892–93*
*Wood. 34.4 (13.5); 23.7 (9.3).
Acquired 1951, with assistance from Madame Huc de Monfreid; entered national collection 1968*

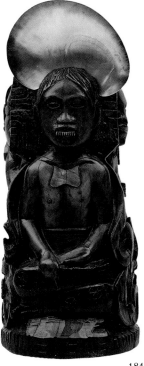

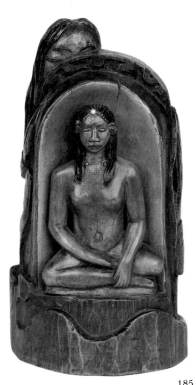

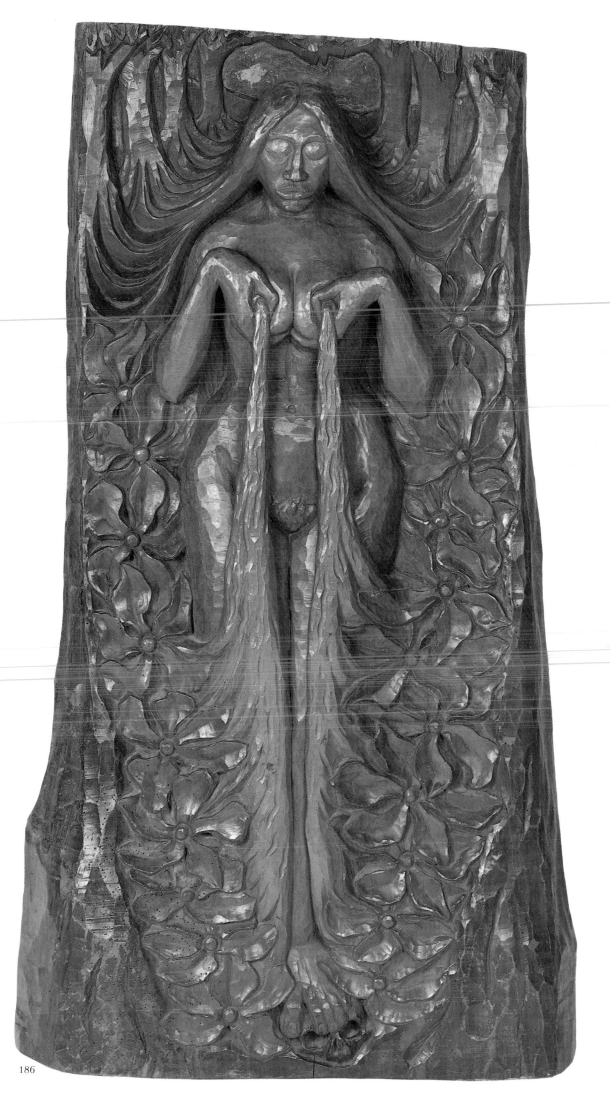

186

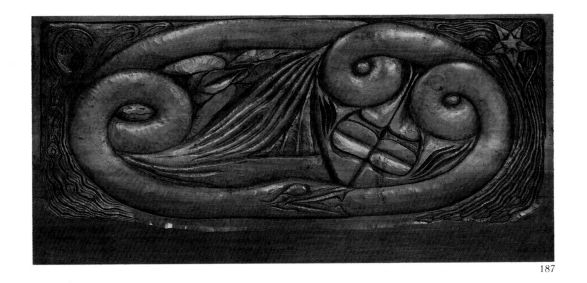

187

186 *G. Lacombe:* Isis,
c. *1893–94*
Polychrome wood. 111 × 62
(43.7 × 24.4). Salon des Indé-
pendants, 1895. Acquired 1982

187 *G. Lacombe:* L'existence
(Existence), *1892*
Wood. 68.5 × 41.5 (27 × 16.3).
Headboard of bed from the
Nabis' studio. Acquired 1956

188 *P. Gauguin:* Soyez
mystérieuses (Be Mysterious),
1890
Polychrome wood. 73 × 95
(28.7 × 37.4). Acquired 1978

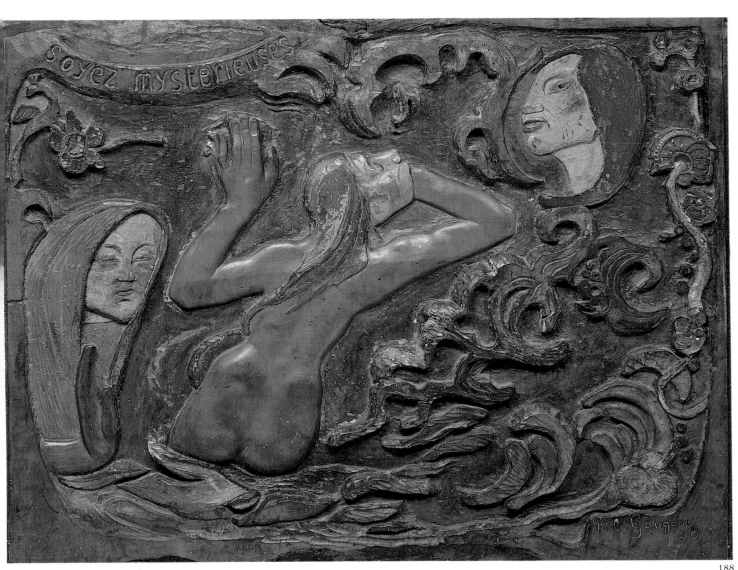

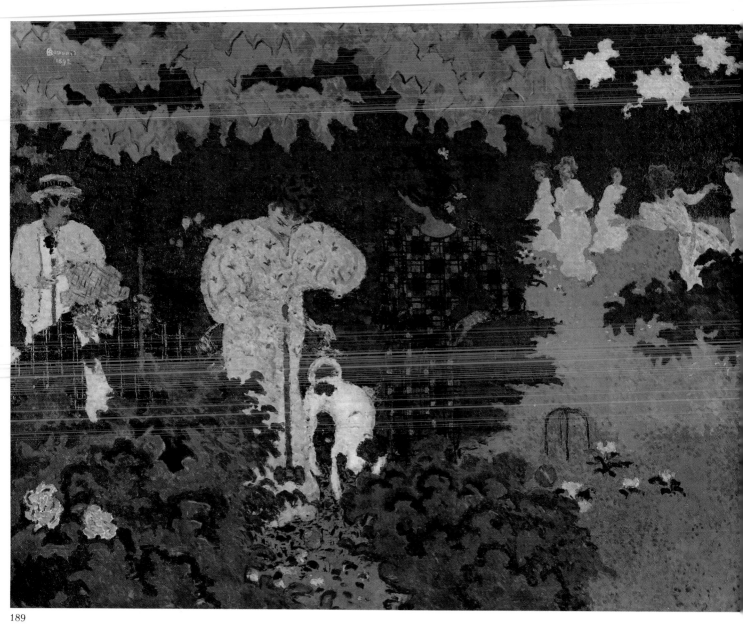

189

The Nabis

The Nabis did not in the strict sense constitute a school; rather they were a group of painters who were friends and who between 1888 and 1900 shared a common desire to breathe new life into painting. The members of the original group were Pierre Bonnard (1867–1947), Edouard Vuillard (1868–1940), Maurice Denis (1870–1943), Ker-Xavier Roussel (1867–1944) and Paul Ranson (1864–1909), who were students together at the Académie Julian and the Ecole des Beaux-Arts, joined soon afterwards by Félix Vallotton (1865–1925), of Swiss origin, and the sculptor Aristide Maillol (1861–1944). Their hero was Gauguin, whose famous watchword 'the freedom to dare all' was passed on to them by Sérusier on the fateful day in October 1888 when he showed them his *Talisman*, painted under Gauguin's guidance. They also admired Puvis de Chavannes, Redon and Cézanne. Denis painted a *Hommage à Cézanne* (*Homage to Cézanne*), now in the Musée d'Orsay, which shows the members of the Nabi group.

The young men regarded themselves as prophets of a new painting; the Hebrew word *nabi* means 'prophet'. Admiring Japanese prints, they copied their simplified forms, flat colour and lack of depth. Thus Bonnard, dubbed by his fellows '*le nabi japonard*', treats the members of his family in his *Partie de croquet* (*The Game of Croquet*), as silhouettes standing out sharply against a background composed of a series of large decorative masses.

As a group, they wanted to get away from easel painting and therefore tended to look to the arts of décor, from theatre design to paintings for domestic interiors, a field in which their talents flourished. The Musée d'Orsay possesses five of the nine panels painted by Vuillard in 1894 for Alexandre Natanson, editor of the famous *Revue blanche*, who commissioned the sequence for his Paris flat on the avenue du Bois, now avenue Foch. In this decorative scheme, spatial depth is conveyed by a rhythmic interpenetration of planes – suggested, perhaps, by no more than the vertical of a tree-trunk or the curved outline of a clump of trees. The same rhythmic composition is apparent in Maurice Denis's modern

189 *P. Bonnard:* La partie de croquet *ou* Le crépuscule (The Game of Croquet, *or* Twilight), *1892* *130 × 162 (51.2 × 63.8). Salon des Indépendants, Paris, 1892. Gift of Daniel Wildenstein, by the agency of the Société des Amis d'Orsay, 1985*

190–191 *E. Vuillard:* Jardins publics (The Park), *five of nine decorative panels executed for Alexandre Natanson, 1894 215 × 88 (84.6 × 34.6); 215 × 92 (84.6 × 36.2); 212 × 152 (83.5 × 59.8); 212 × 80 (83.5 × 31.5); 212 × 80 (83.5 × 31.5). Left to right:* Les fillettes jouant (Girls Playing), L'interrogatoire (The Interrogation), *Radot bequest, 1978;* La conversation (The Conversation), Les nourrices (Nannies), L'ombrelle rouge (The Red Parasol), *acquired 1929*

192 *F. Vallotton:* Le ballon (The Ball), *1899 Bequest of Carle Dreyfus, 1953*

193 *M. Denis:* Les muses (The Muses), *1893 49.5 × 62 (19.5 × 24.4). Acquired 1932*

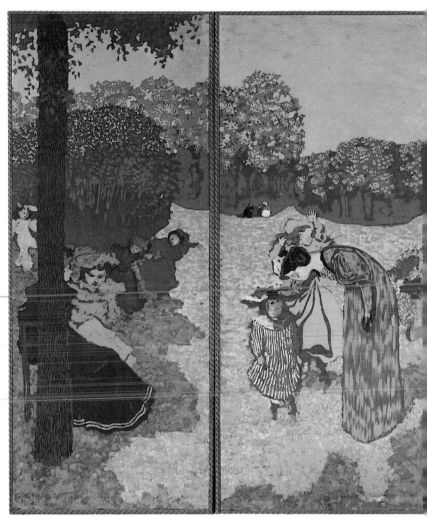

190

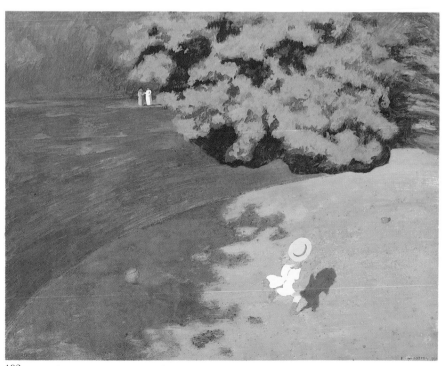

192

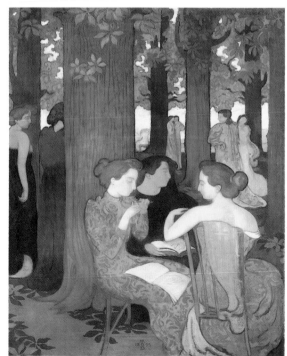

193

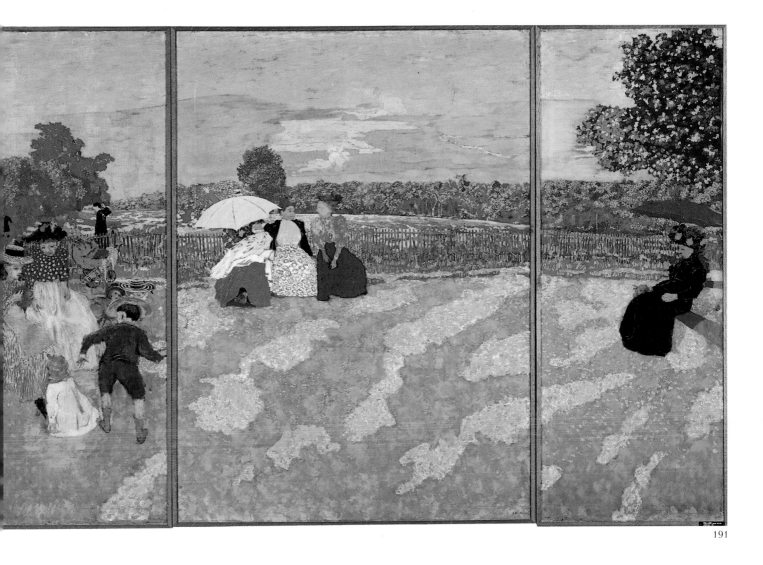

interpretation of the mythological *Muses*, very much in the spirit of Art Nouveau with its emphasis on such decorative elements as the leaves of the chestnut trees and the generous deployment of serpentine curves.

Vallotton made eloquent use of foreshortening, influenced by his experience of wood-engraving, and conveyed a sense of space by the juxtaposition of dark and light areas, set in a rising, horizonless perspective.

It is this free handling of motifs, often accompanied by marvellously subtle distortions, this fundamentally decorative approach, that makes the Nabi movement so significant in the development of painting towards autonomy, one of the mainsprings of modern art.

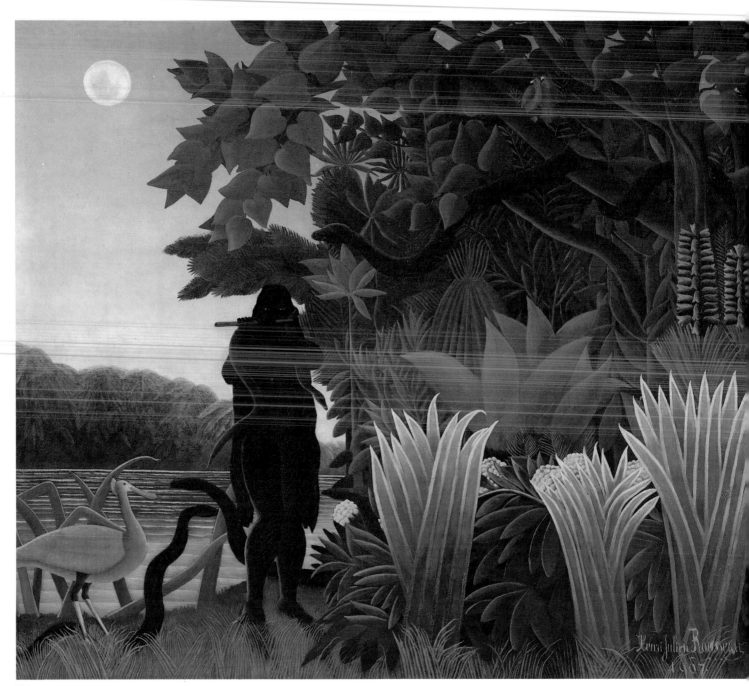

194

Douanier Rousseau

Although of the same generation as the major Impressionists, Henri Rousseau (1844–1910), born at Laval, stands quite apart from the mainstream of art at the turn of the century. He worked as a toll-collector in Paris – hence the nickname *Douanier* or 'customs-officer' – and was initially an amateur painter. Self-taught, he used to copy the Old Masters in the Louvre, and proclaimed his admiration for the great academic painters of the period, such as Gérôme. The circumstances of his life were otherwise quite ordinary, and the man remains as much of an enigma as the works he produced, the modernity of which disconcerted not a few of his contemporaries.

With encouragement from Signac, he exhibited at the Salon des Indépendants in 1880, and continued to do so right up to his death; he was also represented at the Salon d'Automne of 1905, where the Fauves made their explosive entry onto the artistic scene.

Rousseau created a strange world often overlaid with symbolic references, as in *La guerre* (*War*) of 1894, in the Musée d'Orsay, which contains echoes of the Italian Primitives. He took liberties with form, as his imagination dictated; compositional audacities such as his have been quite consciously cultivated by modern artists. No doubt it was for reasons such as these that poets and painters of the avant-garde sought him out, among them Jarry, Apollinaire, Delaunay and Picasso – whose collection of Rousseau's pictures is now in the Musée Picasso in Paris.

As well as many portraits, landscapes and historical scenes, painted in a style of deceptive naivety, Rousseau also produced a jungle series: beasts of prey attacking antelopes or staring out at the onlooker, surrounded by luxuriant tropical vegetation (which Rousseau modelled on plants he had seen in the Botanical Gardens in Paris). His fabulous exoticism is essentially a framework for an exuberant decorative impulse of great power and charm. This is particularly true of works such as *Charmeuse de serpents* (*The Snake Charmer*), a mythical Eden painted in 1907 for the mother of the painter Robert Delaunay.

194 *H. ('Le Douanier') Rousseau:* La charmeuse de serpents (The Snake Charmer), *1907*
169 × 189 (66.5 × 74.6). Bequest of Jacques Doucet, 1936

195 *P. Bonnard:* La Revue
Blanche, *1894*
Poster; colour lithograph.
80.5 × 62.5 (31.7 × 24.6)

196 *Bertall:* Le Salon dépeint
et dessiné par Bertall (The
Salon Depicted and Drawn
by Bertall), *1853*
Le Journal pour rire, no. 91, 25
June 1853, coloured wood-
engravings. 42 × 29.7
(16.5 × 11.7) overall

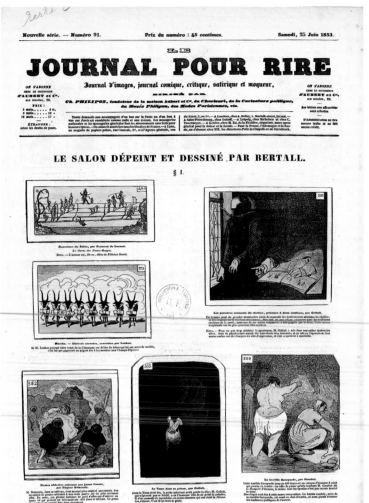

196

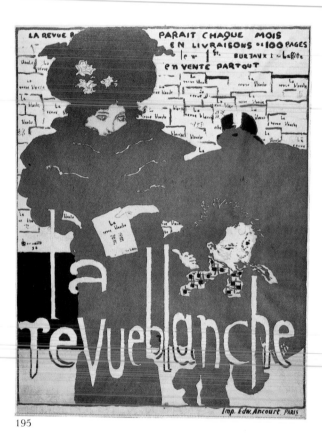

195

197 *J. J. Granville:* Derniers
dessins de J. J. Granville –
Premier rêve, Crime et
expiation (Latest Drawings
by J. J. Granville – First
Dream, Crime and
Expiation), *1847*
Wood-engraving by P. Soyer
for Magasin Pittoresque, 1847,
p. 212. 23.6 × 15.5 (9.3 × 6.1)
overall

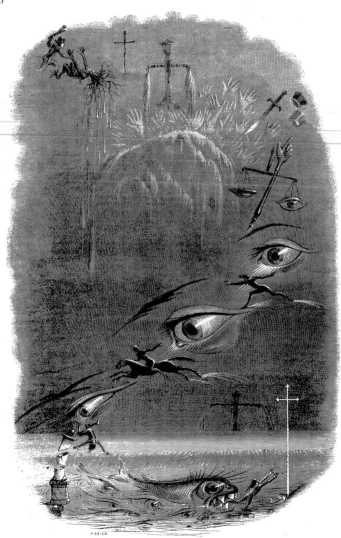

197

Posters, book illustrations, journalism

The nineteenth century was associated with the emergence of illustration as a form in its own right, taking the term in its widest possible sense, that of an image produced in association with a text. Reading was becoming more widespread with the growth of literacy in the population, and the notion of co-operation between the disciplines corresponded to the ideals of artistic synthesis propounded by Symbolist aesthetes and Romantic brotherhoods alike. As far back as the early 1830s, technical developments in lithography and wood-engraving had facilitated the expansion of newspaper publishing and poster production; to these techniques were added in the second half of the century photomechanical reproduction processes – which had the perverse effect, often, of reviving interest in original prints, craft presses and *éditions de luxe*. The Galerie de la Presse in the Musée d'Orsay retraces the main stages in the development of the illustrated press during the nineteenth century, showing its origins in political caricature (1830–35), which softened into more generalized social satire with the introduction of censorship (1835–48), and reverted again to a political role during the 1848 Republic, before proliferating in a number of small illustrated periodicals in the Second Empire – devoted to literature, the theatre, the arts or politics, or aimed at a particular readership, such as women or children. Small 'dossier' exhibitions will be used to give information about the press, posters and books, either as separate topics or by showing the relationships between them. Posters advertising newspapers or books form a distinct category, being among the earliest examples of illustrated posters: sometimes the colour lithograph used would simply be a copy of the frontispiece of the relevant book. Often the poster would show the sort of reader at whom the publication was aimed, such as the woman buying *La Revue blanche* (1889–1903), observed by Bonnard in the first of a famous series of posters for the Natansons' literary and artistic magazine. The illustrated book itself tended to be of three main types, appealing to quite distinct readerships: the juvenile market discovered by the firm of Hetzel among others, the general reader, and the specialist collector.

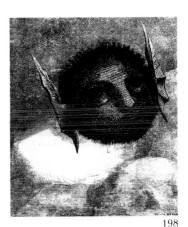

198

199

198 *O. Redon:* Gnome, *1879*
Lithograph for the album
Dans le rêve, *Paris, Lemercier,*
1879, pl. VI. 27.2 × 22
(10.7 × 8.7). Unlike his other
albums, which were literary in
inspiration, this one was,
according to Redon himself,
'created without any literary
reference at all. The title ... was
merely a rough indication of
the contents' (letter to
André Mellerio, 21 July
1898)

199 *C. Schwabe:* Cover for Le
Rêve *by Zola (Paris, Marpon*
et Flammarion), 1892
Chromolithograph. 28.2 × 19.2
(11.1 × 7.6). Based on an 1891
watercolour now in the Cabinet
des Dessins at the Louvre

Drawing and watercolour

From youthful iconoclasts to upholders of academicism, practically all the artists active between 1870 and the end of the century did a great deal of drawing, employing the whole range of established techniques. Thus the tradition of Ingres lived on, not only among the ranks of official painters but through Puvis de Chavannes, Degas, Seurat and Renoir, to mention but a few of those whose graphic work figures extensively in the collections.

Boudin, whose pastels and watercolours were praised by Baudelaire, is represented here by a superb series of small-scale studies. The Impressionists (notably Pissarro) all practised drawing, as did their precursor Manet and their immediate successors. If Degas was the master in the use of pastel, there were many others, including Mary Cassatt, who also made brilliant use of the medium. It was adopted to great effect by Redon, who in the early part of his career was known as the master of black-and-white. Nor should one forget Cézanne's watercolours, with their transparent ordered masses, a major element of his oeuvre, or the watercolours of a very different style executed by Signac and his Neo-Impressionist friends.

It is perhaps Gauguin who makes the most impressive contribution, with his manuscript *Noa-Noa*, written in collaboration with Charles Morice and illustrated with watercolours and colour engravings, together with various other figures and photographs; based on Gauguin's reminiscences of his first visit to Tahiti, the book is a living testament to all that the painter held most dear.

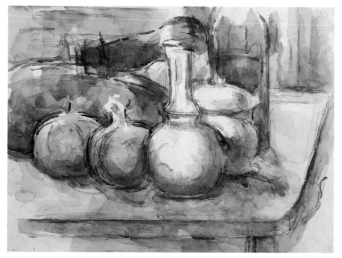

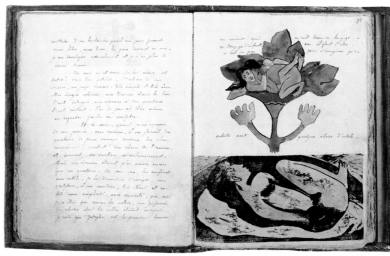

200   201

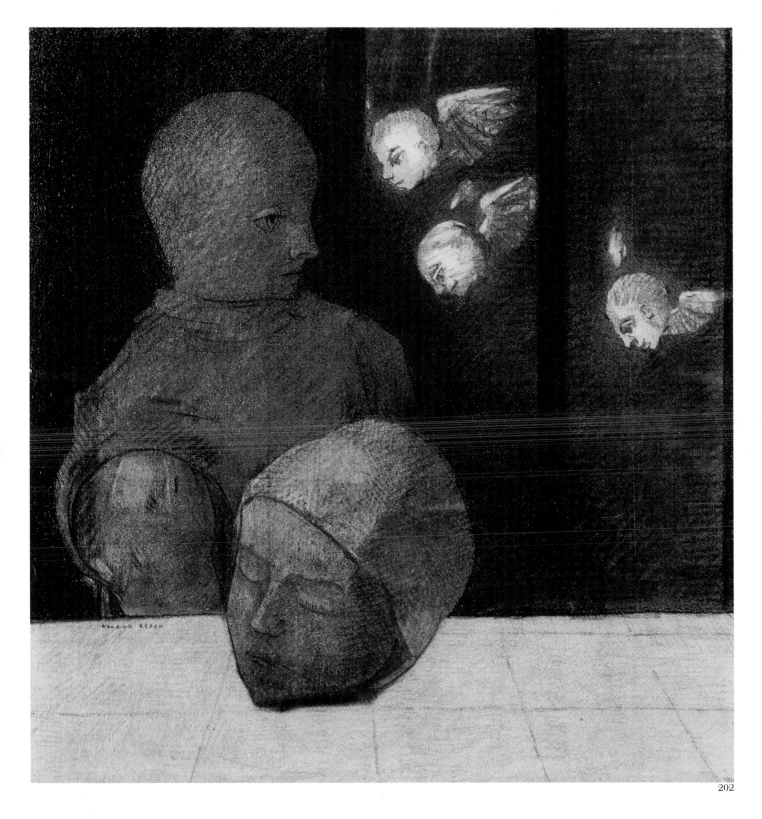

202

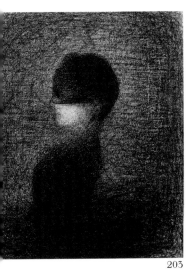

203

Photography

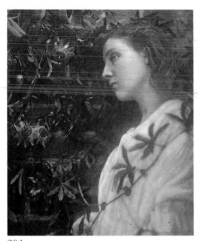

204

204 *J. M. Cameron:* Maud
(*illustration for* The Idylls of
the King and Other Poems *by
Tennyson, variant*), 1874–75
*Carbon print. 32.5 × 26.5
(12.8 × 10.4). Acquired 1985*

Spreading through advanced artistic organizations at the turn of the century – notably in the English-speaking countries – the movement towards 'art' or 'pictorialist' photography marked a decisive stage in the realization of the creative potential of the medium. It established the validity of the photographer's subjective vision and legitimized the role of imagination in photography. Pride of place is therefore given in the museum displays to this type of photography, which is closely related to the aesthetics of Art Nouveau and the paintings of the Impressionists, Symbolists and Nabis exhibited elsewhere in the collections.

It was in England, as photographers began to draw on literary and Romantic sources in the composition of their works, that the debate raged most fiercely. Could a photograph be a work of art? Could it be a picture comparable with a painting? Julia Margaret Cameron (1815–79) succeeded in revolutionizing the whole concept of portrait photography. Using purely photographic means (close-up and soft-focus) she anticipated certain effects of film in her timeless transpositions of scenes from Italian Renaissance painting. Cameron's innovations (though not her Italianate subjects) were assimilated in the work of Edward Steichen (1879–1973), one of the members of the American Photo-Secession group founded in 1902 by Alfred Stieglitz (1864–1946), himself one of the great portrait photographers. *The Kiss* by Clarence White (1871–1925), another member of the group, takes its inspiration directly from the illustrations of Aubrey Beardsley and the paintings of the Pre-Raphaelites. In contrast Stieglitz's series *City of Ambition* presents a wonderfully vivid symbolic portrait of New York. His shot of immigrants travelling steerage, of 1907 – an image admired by Picasso – marks the definitive emergence of a new photography.

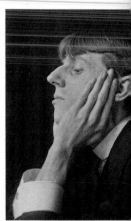

205

205 *F. Evans:* The Illustrator
Aubrey Beardsley *(1872–98),
1894*
*Platinotype. 15 × 10
(5.9 × 3.9). Acquired 1985*

206 *C. H. White:* The Kiss,
1899
*Platinotype, gelatin treated
with bichromate. 24.7 × 14.8
(9.7 × 5.8). Gift of Société C.D.F.
Chimie Terpolymères, 1985*

207 *A. Stieglitz:* New York,
City of Ambition, *1910*
*Printed by photogravure on
Japan paper 1910–15.
33.7 × 25.9 (13.3 × 10.2).
Acquired 1980*

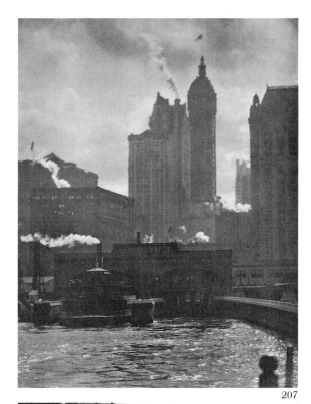

207

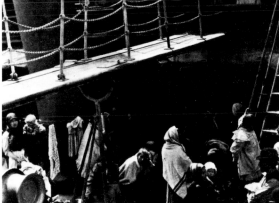

208

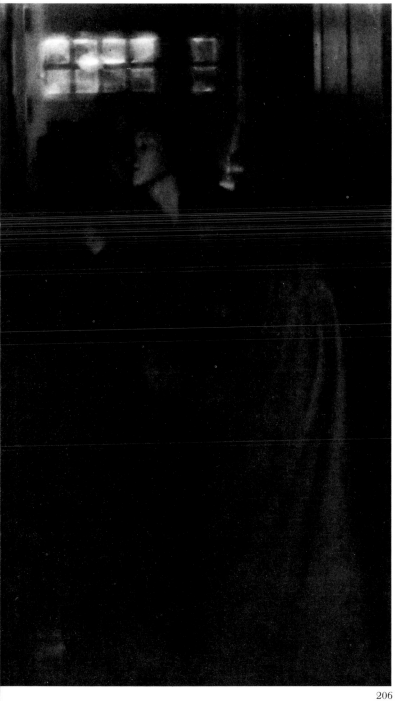

206

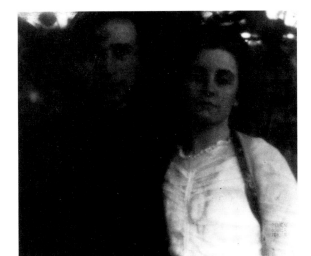

209

208 *A. Stieglitz:* The
Steerage, *1907*
Printed by photogravure on
Japan paper in 1915 for the
review 291. 34 × 26.5
(13.4 × 10.4). Acquired 1984

209 *E. Steichen:* The Artist
and his Wife on Honeymoon
at Lake George, *1903*
Platinotype, glycerine.
22.3 × 25.4 (8.8 × 10).
Acquired 1982

210 *E. Barrias:* La Nature se dévoilant à la Science (Nature Unveiling Herself to Science), *1899*
Marble, onyx, malachite, lapis lazuli, granite. 200 (78.7). Commissioned for Conservatoire des Arts et Métiers in 1899. Assigned to national collection 1903

211 *W. Guérin et Cie, porcelain manufacturers in Limoges; E. Cavaillé-Coll, architect; M. Rouillard, painter, decorator:* Monumental basin
Hard-paste porcelain, with painted decoration. 95, d. 80 (37.4, d. 31.5). Designed 1882. Entered national collection 1892

212 *J. P. Aubé, sculptor; Thiébault Frères, metal-founders; Berquin-Varangoz, lapidary:* La France convie la Russie à visiter la capitale (France Invites Russia to View the Capital). *1899*
Table centrepiece. Silver and rock-crystal. 64 × 95 × 42 (25.2 × 37.4 × 16.5). Commissioned by the state to commemorate the visit of Tsar Nicholas II on 6–8 October 1896

213 *J. P. Aubé, sculptor; L. C. Boileau, architect:* Monument à Gambetta (Memorial to Gambetta), *1884*
Plaster. 240 (94.5). Winning design in competition of 1884. Loaned by Musée des Arts Décoratifs, 1980

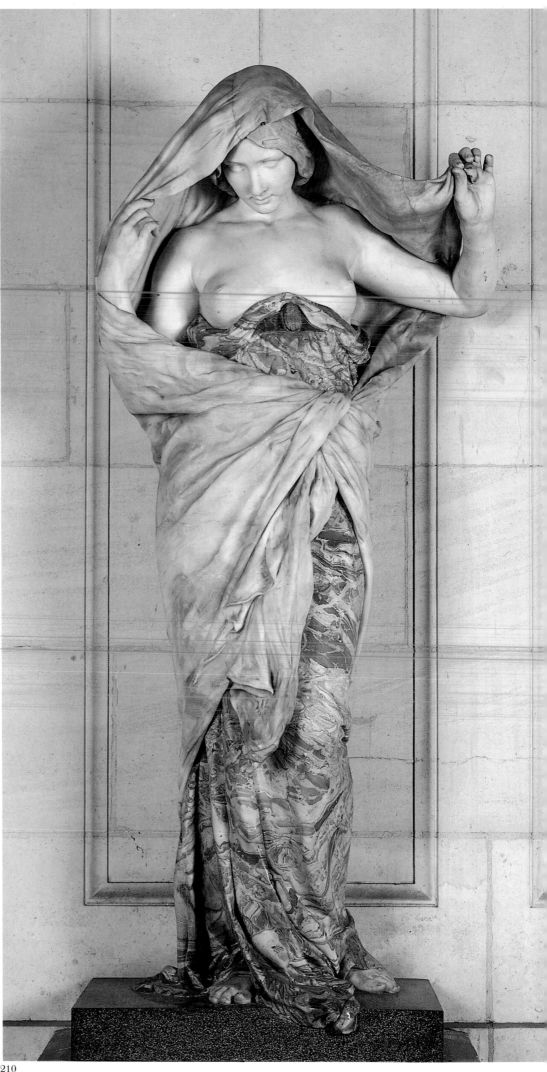

210

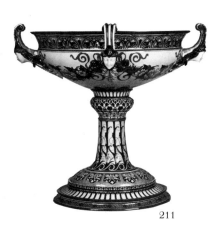

211

Art and decoration
in the Third Republic

The Third Republic (which lasted from 1870 to 1940) sought to demonstrate its permanence and stability by erecting monuments to its glory. In 1879 the Paris municipal authorities held a competition which resulted in the construction of Charles Morice's monument in the place de la République, and the *Triomphe de la République* (*The Triumph of the Republic*) by Jules Dalou (1838–1902) in the place de la Nation. When the statesman Léon Gambetta died, in 1882, the moment was seized upon to celebrate his achievements in defending France and founding the Republic. A competition was held – this was thought to be the most democratic method – for a design to be financed by public subscription. The winners were the architect Louis-Charles Boileau and the sculptor Jean-Paul Aubé, who chose a site on the cour Napoléon, facing the Second Empire portion of the Louvre. From the first, the 36-foot-high memorial attracted criticism. The bronzes were melted down during the German Occupation, and the stonework was removed in 1954. The remaining part of the central group was re-erected behind the *mairie* of the 20th arrondissement in Paris to commemorate the centenary of Gambetta's death, but it gives a very incomplete idea of the symbolic and didactic scheme of the original. The model which won the competition has been restored for the Musée d'Orsay; it is highly typical of a type of monument that remained in vogue up to the early years of the twentieth century.

Aubé was also responsible for a table centrepiece in rock crystal, an object appropriate to the sumptuous and leisurely banquets of a bygone age.

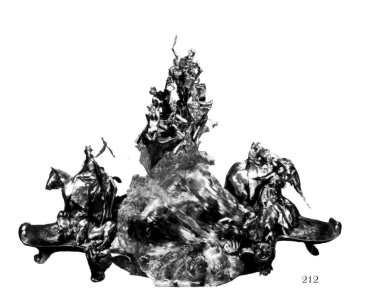

212

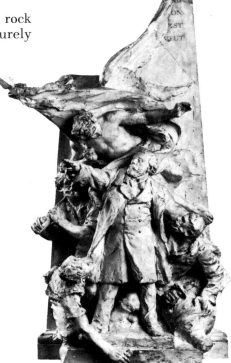

213

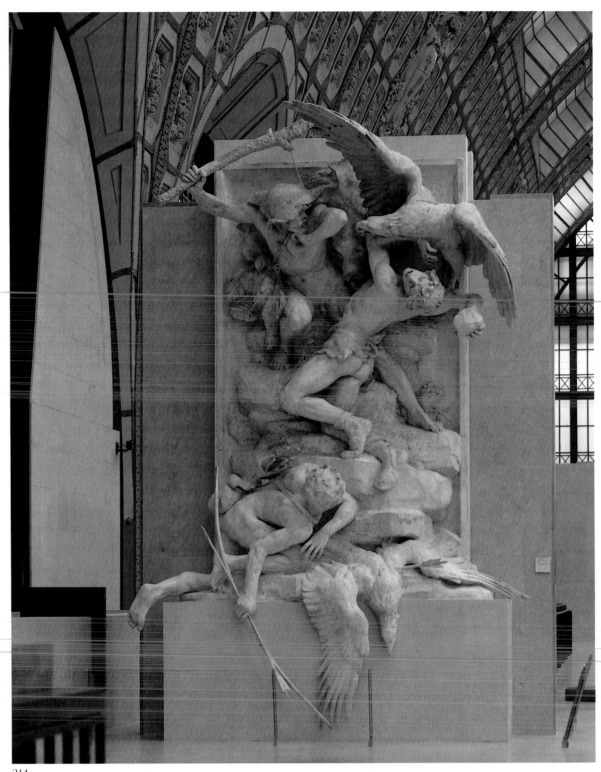

214

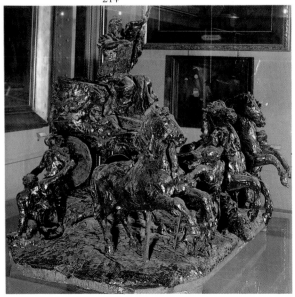

215

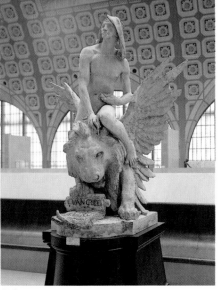

216

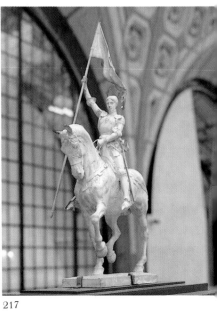

217

Science was one of the cornerstones of the Republic, and Ernest Barrias's weighty allegory of *La Nature se dévoilant a la Science* (*Nature Unveiling Herself to Science*) was intended to reflect the positivist certainties of the times. The beauty of the onyx, malachite and lapis lazuli in itself provides a potent – if unintended· – metaphor of the understanding of the material world.

The Third Republic relied heavily on popular celebrations to inspire and unite its citizens. The 14th of July was decreed a national holiday in 1880, and the World Fairs of 1878, 1889 and 1900 were accompanied by festivities on a massive scale. Just as the Counter-Reformation favoured the rise of the Baroque, so the Republic engendered a sculptural style that was exuberant and full of animation. Alexandre Falguière (1831–1900) produced just such a design for a sculptural group to crown the Arc de Triomphe. The wax model was displayed at the exhibition of decorative arts held in 1882, and a commission was extended for a full-scale plaster cast – the quadriga seen in photographs of Victor Hugo's funeral. However, the final commission was never issued, and the model remains virtually the only record of the many projects that were considered during the nineteenth century to crown the Arc de Triomphe.

Gustave Deloye (1838–99), who had travelled in Central Europe, made use of a similarly theatrical style for his group of *Saint Marc sur le lion* (*St Mark on the Lion*). Emanuel Fremiet (1824–1910) aligned himself with this vigorous trend when he created the Pegasuses which take wing on the north pylons of the Pont Alexandre-III – although his true vocation was for historical Realism. The replica of his *Saint Michel* (*St Michael*), on the Mont-Saint-Michel, is a massive work in beaten copper by the firm of Monduit, over 20 feet high; in spite of the scale, the armour is faithfully reproduced in every detail, as is that of his famous *Jeanne d'Arc* (*Joan of Arc*) in the place des Pyramides in Paris, commissioned in 1872. In response to criticisms that the horse was wrongly proportioned for its rider, the sculptor actually replaced the original statue with a new one in 1899, at his own expense.

214 *J. Coutan:* Les chasseurs d'aigles (The Eagle Hunters), *1900*
Plaster. 535 (210.6). Model for bronze commissioned 1893 for the palaeontology gallery of the Muséum d'histoire naturelle by the architect Detert

215 *A. Falguière:* Triomphe de la révolution (Triumph of the Revolution), *1882*
Wax. 97 (38.2). Design for a sculptural group to crown the Arc de Triomphe. Gift of Général de Beylie, 1902; loaned by Musée de Grenoble, 1982

216 *G. Deloye:* Saint Marc (St Mark), *1878*
Plaster. 205 (80.7). Acquired 1878

217 *E. Fremiet:* Jeanne d'Arc (Joan of Arc), *1872–74*
Plaster reduction of the first equestrian statue in the place des Pyramides, Paris. 75 (29.5). Given subject to a life interest by Madame Fauré-Fremiet, 1979; entered national collection 1984

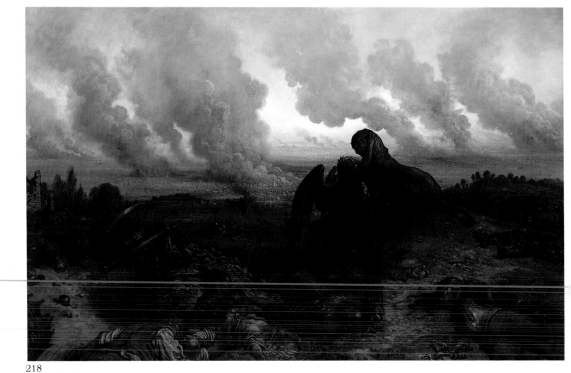

218 *G. Doré:* L'énigme (The Enigma), *1871* (*after two lines from Victor Hugo's* Les Voix intérieures, *1837*)
130 × 195.5 (51.2 × 77).
Acquired 1982

219 *J. P. Laurens:* L'excommunication de Robert le Pieux (The Excommunication of Robert the Pious)
130 × 218 (51.2 × 85.8). Salon of 1875. Acquired 1875

218

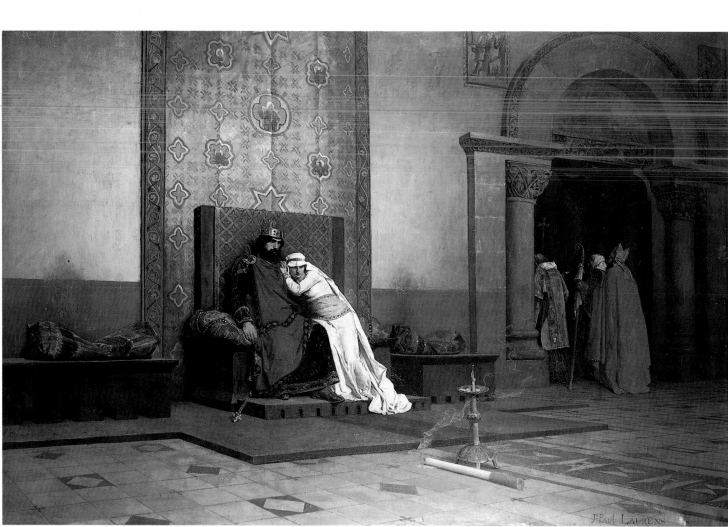

219

The political upheavals of 1870–71 – the Franco-Prussian War, the Commune, the installation of the Third Republic – could hardly fail to find some reflection in the artistic sphere. Works directly inspired by political events were, however, slow to emerge. Even *L'énigme* (*The Enigma*) by Gustave Doré (1832–83), painted in 1871 (as were two other compositions explicitly citing the German eagle), was in fact a response to some lines written long before by Victor Hugo:

> *O Spectacle. Ainsi meurt ce que les peuples font!*
> *Qu'un tel passé pour l'âme est un gouffre profond.*

> O spectacle. Thus do the deeds of peoples die!
> How deep an abyss, for the soul, is such a past!

These particular pictures remained in the artist's studio, and were not seen in public until the posthumous auction of Doré's work.

The old styles of painting suffered scarcely a setback. Jules Lefebvre (1836–1911) was a painter in the full academic tradition, and winner of the Prix de Rome in 1861. His *Vérité* (*Truth*) was exhibited at the Salon of 1870, purchased for the nation and installed in the Musée du Luxembourg in 1874, the year of the Impressionists' first exhibition.

A few years later the state severed its links with the official Salon, handing over responsibility for the selection process to the Société des Artistes Français in 1880. And yet official art continued to flourish. The reason is not hard to seek. Lefebvre and Bouguereau, for example, were teachers at the Académie Julian. It was they, and others of the same persuasion, who formed and modelled the younger generation of artists.

The history painter Jean-Paul Laurens (1838–1921) experienced his hour of glory in the early years of the Third Republic, specializing in patriotic themes which – like *L'excommunication de Robert le Pieux* (*The Excommunication of Robert the Pious*) of 1875 – were reproduced in school textbooks.

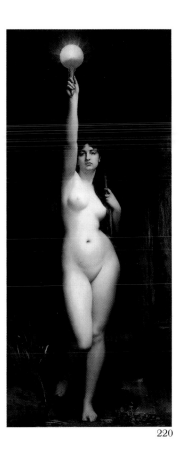

220

220 *J. Lefebvre:* La Vérité (Truth)
265 × 112 (104.3 × 44.1). Salon of 1870. Acquired 1871

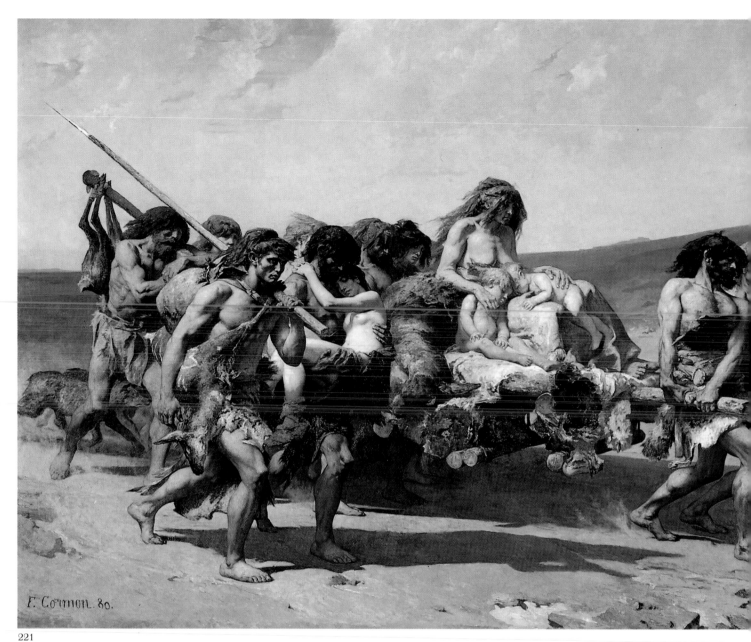

221

The younger artists were not entirely oblivious of the new Naturalism. One of the big successes of the Salon of 1880 was *Caïn* (*Cain*), an ambitious composition by Fernand Cormon (1845–1924) that dispensed entirely with the smooth-surfaced academic manner, while still being based on preparatory life drawings done in the studio in the conventional fashion. Jules Bastien-Lepage (1848–84) adopted the light palette and impulsive brushwork of Manet's young friends the Impressionists, and became the champion of the strain of 'official Naturalism' that was to take over the Salon in the years 1880–1900; much imitated outside France, this was the style that provoked vehement opposition from the Idealists and Symbolists.

221 *F. Cormon:* Caïn (Cain), *1880 (after the opening lines of 'La conscience', from* La Légende des siècles *by Victor Hugo, 1859)* *384 × 700 (115.2 × 275.6).* *Salon of 1880. Acquired 1880*

222 *J. Bastien-Lepage:* Les foins (Haymaking), *1877* *180 × 195 (70.9 × 76.8). Salon of 1878. Acquired 1885*

223 *E. Fremiet:* Saint Michel terrassant le dragon (St Michael Slaying the Dragon), *1879–96* *Hammered copper by the firm of Monduit, replica of the statue surmounting the spire of Mont Saint-Michel, Brittany.* *617 (243). Gift of Madame G. Pasquier to Monuments historiques. Loan from Direction du patrimoine, 1980*

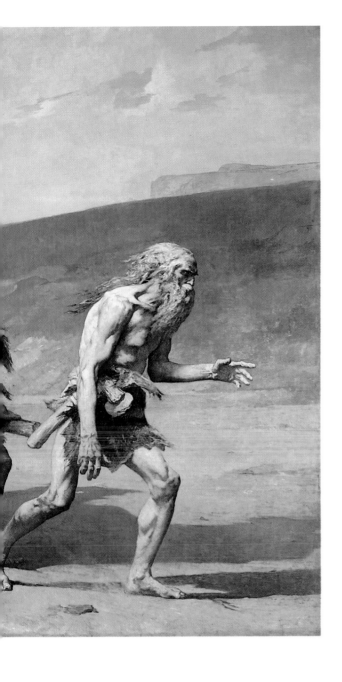

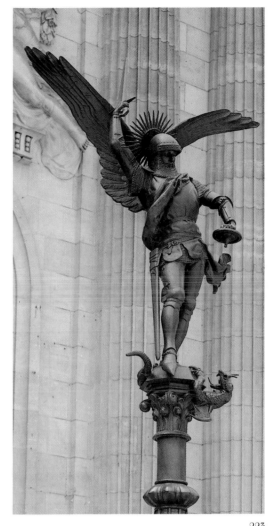

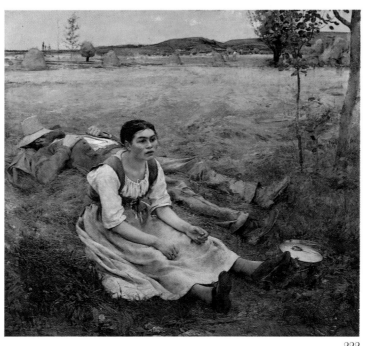

223

222

155

Dalou

Following the example of Courbet, Daumier and Zola, French sculpture determinedly reverted to the principles of 'Realism' – although in truth it had barely deviated from that course except under the influence of the academics. Vincenzo Vela (1820–91) in Italy and Constantin Meunier (1831–1905) in Belgium were among the innovators. They turned to their fellow men and women to find their subject matter, and dispensed with the window-dressing of historical, mythological or religious themes.

Jules Dalou (1838–1902) had played an active part in the 1870 Paris Commune and afterwards escaped to England with his family. It was from London that he submitted his design for the *Triomphe de la République* (*Triumph of the Republic*) in 1879, the year of the amnesty. *Le forgeron* (*The Blacksmith*) wears clogs and an apron as he rolls his cartwheel, and carries his hammer slung over his shoulder; no one could mistake him for Vulcan. Indeed, he was destined to be the central figure in a *Monument au travail* (*Monument to Labour*) that was never constructed.

Dalou's terracotta studies are rooted in the observation of life. His nude study for the *Republic* shows a body with weaknesses as well as strengths; it is clear that it represents a real woman and only secondarily an allegorical figure.

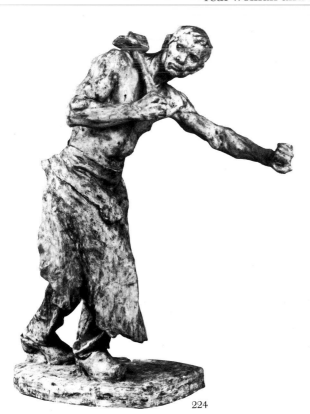

224

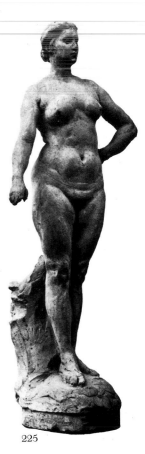

225

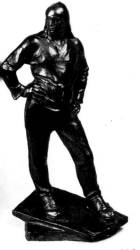

226

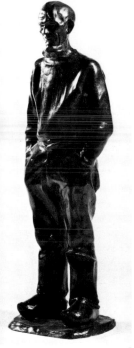

227

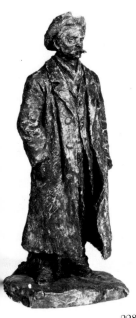

228

Sculpture: aspects of Naturalism

Naturalism tended to focus on a highly specific category of subjects: life underground in the mines, dockers in the ports, peasants and the hardships of peasant life, and industry – the crucible of suffering, but also the foundation of the economic growth that was transforming the face of Europe. Manual work, reserved in the ancient societies for slaves, was now recognized as the nation's life-blood. In recognition of his new importance, the working man was given the vote. Suddenly it was acceptable to study the distortions of his workworn body, his clothes and his way of life. The ideal of perfection embodied in Greek and Roman sculpture ceased to have any relevance: it was necessary to start afresh. The stylistic repertoire that had been developed over the years had become an obstacle to perception and free interpretation. Yet, within a relatively short time, these innovations in turn ossified into a system, became facile. The experimental was absorbed once more into 'official' art. The success enjoyed by the style, now respectable and accessible to all, is apparent in the proliferation of memorials that accompanied the expansion of urban development. Fame itself was democratized, and vast numbers of statues were erected of the great men of the day and of significant figures from the past (for example Dalou's *Lavoisier*, a belated tribute now that the Republic needed scientists). These furnish an incomparable source of material for historians – and in some ways it is not inappropriate that they have themselves in some instances been the victims of history. The bronzes, for example, were melted down during the Occupation. Thus the sketches displayed in the hall reserved for commemorative statues are of particular interest, because they are frequently the sole record of vanished works.

226 *C. Meunier:* Débardeur du port d'Anvers (Stevedore from Antwerp Harbour), *1890 Bronze. 48.3 (19). Acquired 1890*

227 *G. Devreese:* Pêcheur de la Panne (Fisherman from La Panne), *before 1900 Bronze. 39.5 (15.6). Entered national collection 1900*

228 *J. A. Injalbert:* Le fondeur (The Foundryman) *Terracotta. 33.5 (13.2). Gift of Mme Injalbert, the artist's widow, 1933*

229 *B. Hoetger:* La machine humaine (The Human Machine), *1902 Bronze. 44 (17.3). Gift of Mme Marcel Duchamp, 1977*

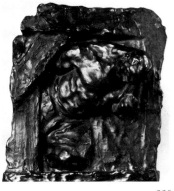

229

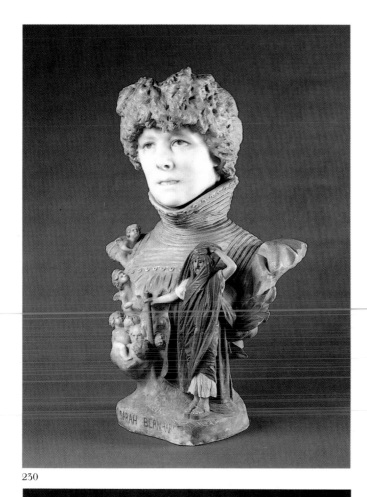

230

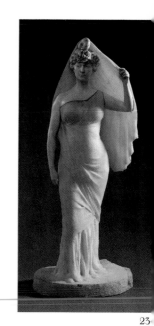

23

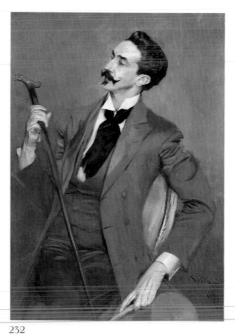

232

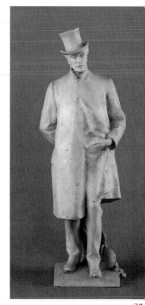

23

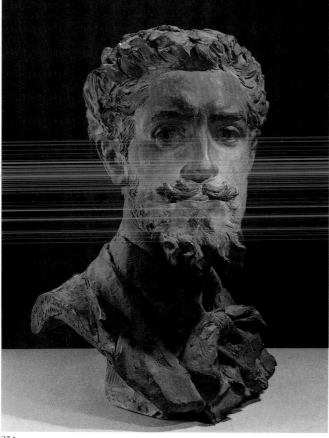

231

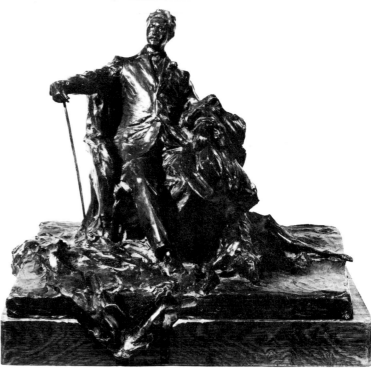

233

La vie parisienne

The collections of the Musée d'Orsay reflect many facets of life in Parisian high society during the period 1890–1900. It was a sparkling international scene, colourful and elegant, symbolized by the *Parisienne* of Louis Dejean (1872–1954) and before him by Paul Moreau-Vauthier (1871–1936), whose colossal *Parisienne* stood over the entrance to the World Fair of 1900. Alongside the genre scenes of Jean Béraud (1849–1936), Giuseppe De Nittis (1846–84) and others, the most fascinating record of all is provided by the various portraits and busts of individual figures. In an age when photography was not yet a serious rival, sculpture still served its primary function of recording a likeness for posterity, and there was a profusion of busts, medallions and statuettes. The small figures by Henri Gréber (1854–1941), for example, provide us with excellent portraits of such fellow artists as Gérôme and Fremiet.

Two personalities stand out: Robert de Montesquiou (1855–1921) and Sarah Bernhardt (1844–1923). The portrait by Jean (Giovanni) Boldini (1842–1931) of the former – 'sovereign of transient things', aesthete, Symbolist writer, collector, and above all man of the world – is matched ten years later by the marvellously vivid and expressive likeness of him by Prince Paul Troubetzkoy (1866–1938). The images of Sarah Bernhardt are more various, and provide in themselves almost a history of portrait sculpture at the turn of the century. Jean-Léon Gérôme (1824–1904) attempts to suggest her powerful talents as a tragedienne while observing the conventions of the bland official tribute. A more intimate aspect of the actress's personality is revealed – together with a talent for sculpture – in the mutual portrait-studies she exchanged with her close friend Louise Abbéma (1858–1927). Finally, one of Bernhardt's most devoted and loyal admirers was Georges Clairin, who executed the famous portrait of the actress now in the Petit Palais; he is represented here in the bust of him by Ernest Barrias (1841–1905), which is in the finest traditions of the French character-portrait.

230 *J. L. Gérôme:* Sarah Bernhardt *(1844–1923),* c. *1895* Polychrome marble. 69 (27.2). Gérôme bequest, 1904

231 *E. Barrias:* Georges Clairin *(1843–1919), painter,* 1875 *Terracotta. 43 (16.9). Gift of M. Petit de Villeneuve, 1922*

232 *G. Boldini:* Le comte Robert de Montesquiou *(1855–1921), writer, 1897* *116 × 82.5 (45.7 × 32.5). Gift of Henri Pinard, on the sitter's behalf, 1922*

233 *Prince P. Troubetzkoy:* Le comte Robert de Montesquiou *(1855–1921), writer* *Bronze. 56 (22). Acquired 1980*

234 *T. Rivière:* Madame Paul Jamot, *before 1913* *Marble, alabaster. 41 (16.2). Bequest of Paul Jamot, 1943*

235 *H. Gréber:* J. L. Gérôme *(1824–1904), painter and sculptor, 1904* *Marble. 46.8 (18.4). Acquired 1904*

236 *L. Dejean:* La Parisienne, *1904* *Bronze. 45.3 (17.8). Acquired 1904*

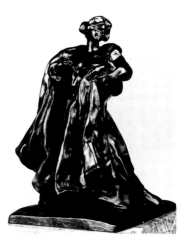

236

Symbolism

Symbolism was born of a reaction against official art 'effete and devoid of ideas', coupled with a desire to create a stylistic identity distinct from Impressionism. It was also the culmination of an urge to express abstractions by transposing them from one medium to another, in the Baudelairian sense of 'correspondences' ('the symbol is the metaphor, it is poetry itself,' wrote Verlaine), and, too, of an urge to appeal to the imagination ('My drawings inspire, they do not define,' wrote Redon).

From about 1890 the Symbolists exhibited regularly at the Salons of the Société nationale des Beaux-Arts, where their dominant figures were Rodin, Puvis de Chavannes and Eugène Carrière (1849–1906), whose subtle brown monochromes are particularly well represented in the Musée d'Orsay. Symbolist works are typically composed of forms in movement, deliberately blurred or left incomplete; the subjects are many and various, with a decided leaning towards expression of the artist's inner turmoil. Rodin and Camille Claudel made devouring human passion their major concern; by contrast Jean Carriès (1855–94) chose to dwell on death and the peace that it brings. Eschewing all attempt at realism, his head of *Charles I of England*, with its flowing locks, conveys a powerful impression of elegance and sweetness.

Sharing Carriès's sensitivity to materials, and attracted equally by sculpture and the creation of objets d'art, Pierre Roche (1855–1922), Jean Dampt (1854–1945) and Pierre Fix-Masseau (1869–1937) sought out unexpected subjects in medieval or Breton legend and used startling materials that shimmered like precious stones, creating effects reminiscent of Redon, of Moreau or of pastels by Lucien Lévy-Dhurmer (1865–1953).

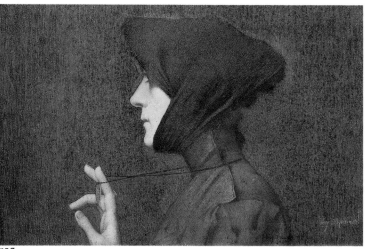

237

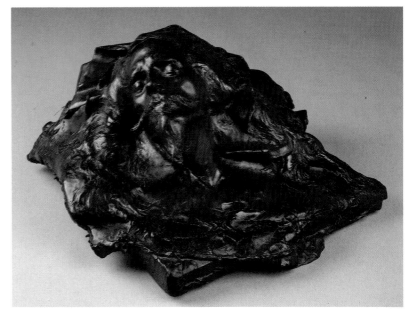

239

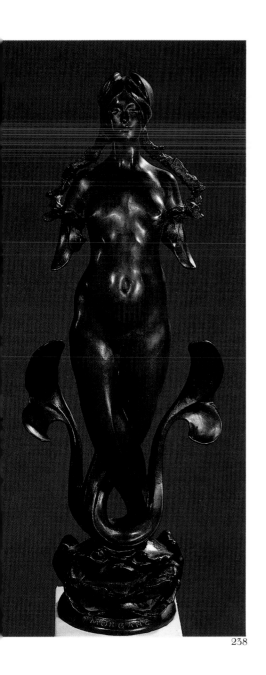

238

240

Aspects of painting outside France

Painting outside France in the 1880s and 1890s was largely dominated by different schools of Realism, often variants and extensions of movements in French painting such as Impressionism and Neo-Impressionism (Divisionism). In the last ten years of the century there was a trend towards Symbolism, variously interpreted in the different countries.

La dame en détresse (*The Lady in Distress*) of 1882 belongs to the early period of the Belgian painter James Ensor (1860–1949). He was influenced initially by Impressionism, but in the 1880s moved on to more domestic themes, following the *intimiste* paintings of artists like Bonnard and Vuillard. Later still, his canvases reflected an interest in the unconscious, becoming increasingly Symbolist in character, representing masks and grotesque figures that are in a direct line of descent from Hieronymus Bosch.

In Italy around 1892–95, Giuseppe Pellizza da Volpedo (1868–1907) adopted a technique derived from French Neo-Impressionism, as did Vittore Grubicy di Drago, Angelo Morbelli and – outstandingly – Giovanni Segantini. Pellizza drew extensively on social and humanitarian themes, but a work such as *Fleur brisée* (*Broken Blossom*), *c.*1896–1902, demonstrates that he also understood the vocabulary of Symbolism.

Of a different order altogether is the Symbolism of the Belgian painter Léon Frédéric (1896–1940). His great triptych *Les âges de l'ouvrier* (*The Ages of the Working Man*) is a celebration of manual labour in a style verging almost on Hyper-Realism, belonging to the same vein of social Symbolism as the contemporary works of his compatriots Constantin Meunier and Eugène Laermans.

One of the dominant figures in American painting was the Bostonian Winslow Homer (1836–1910), who discovered Impressionism when he visited Paris. His love of the sea is reflected in his *Summer Night*, a mysterious and resonant painting of great evocative power.

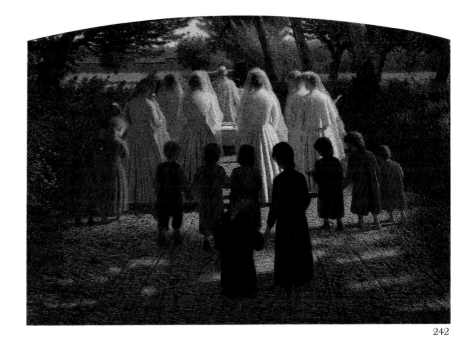

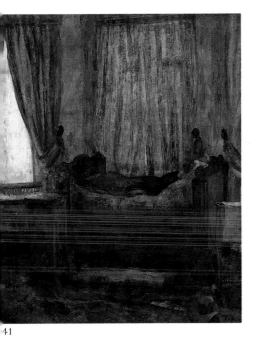

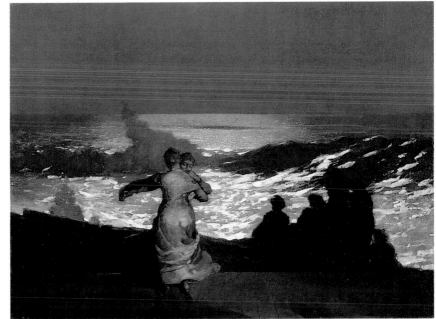

242

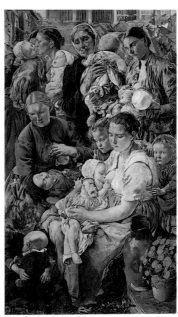

243

41

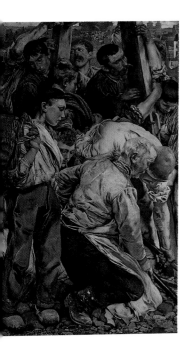

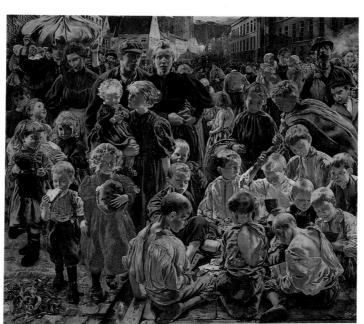

244

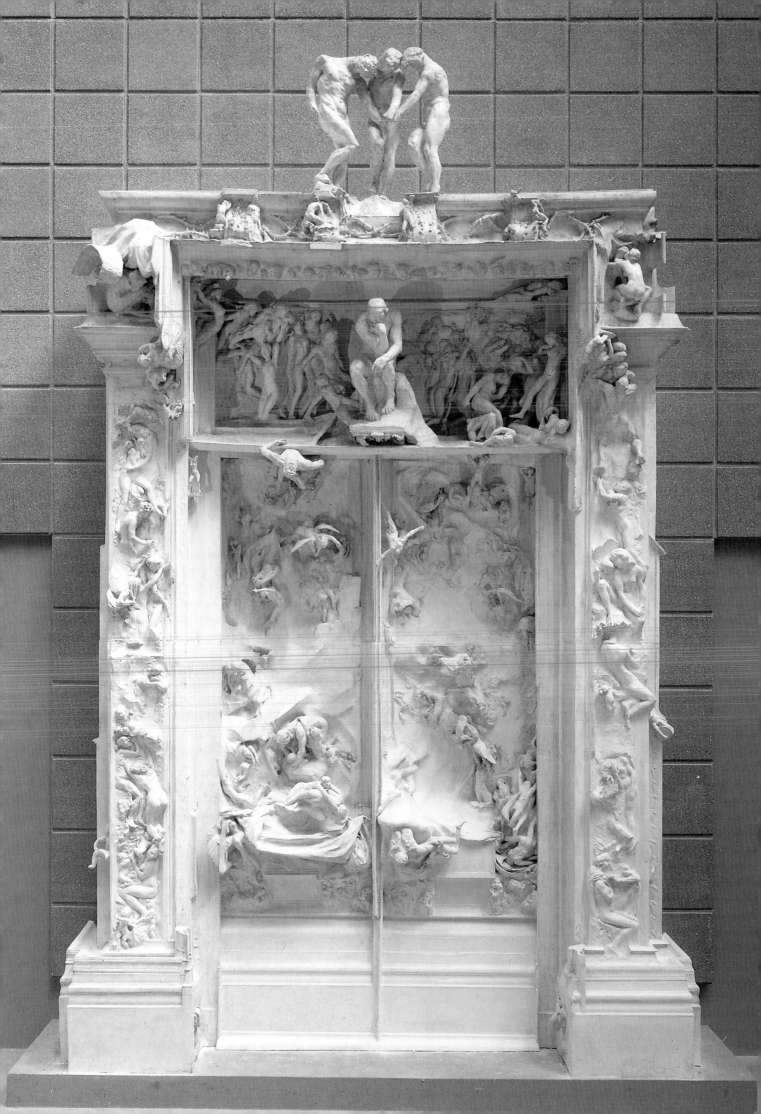

Rodin

A large area of the terraces on the first floor is given up to Auguste Rodin (1840–1917) and the group of young sculptors who worked with him as assistants: Jules Desbois (1851–1935), Lucien Schnegg (1864–1909), Antoine Bourdelle (1861–1929), and Camille Claudel (1864–1943), whose masterpiece *L'âge mûr* (*Maturity*), inspired by the ending of her relationship with Rodin, is shown together with the latter's sculptures.

The Musée d'Orsay is particularly fortunate in having in its possession four large plaster casts on permanent loan from the Musée Rodin. It is thus possible to trace Rodin's development from *L'âge d'airain* (*The Bronze Age*), with its naturalistic modelling, right through to the *Muse Whistler* (*Muse or Monument to Whistler*), handled with such freedom that it amounts to little more than a number of loosely related elements, linked together by a piece of draped cloth dipped in plaster.

During the 1880s Rodin's major project was *La porte de l'Enfer* (*The Gate of Hell*) commissioned for the nation in 1880 and changed only in minor details after 1890, and also to

245 *A. Rodin:* La Porte de l'enfer (The Gate of Hell), *1880–1917*
Plaster. 635 (245). Loan from Musée Rodin, 1986

246 *C. Claudel:* L'âge mur (The Age of Maturity), *1894–1903*
Bronze. 114 (44.9). 1982

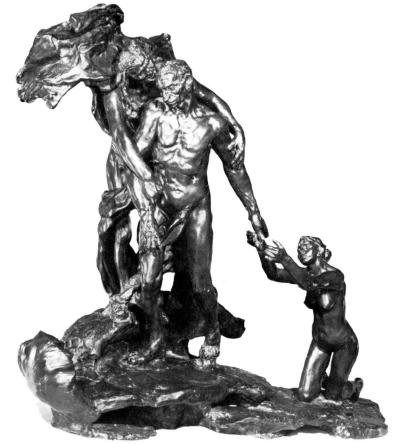

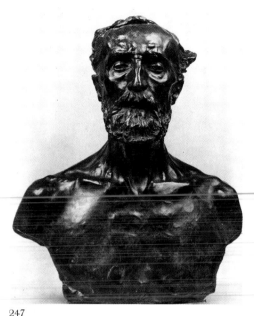

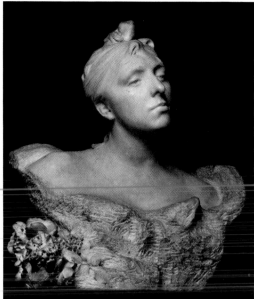

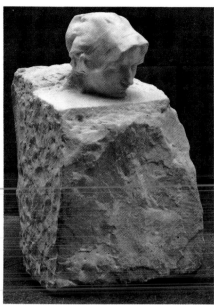

247

248

249

a series of portrait busts. Both the *Gate of Hell* and the bust of *Dalou* reveal Rodin's admiration for the Italian Renaissance, the former being inspired by Dante's *Divine Comedy*. Amid the tangle of bodies condemned by passion to the abyss, two principal episodes are represented: on the left, Paolo and Francesca locked in embrace (the origin of the famous *Baiser, The Kiss*), and on the right, the figures of Ugolino and his children (of which the exhibit in the Musée d'Orsay is a larger-scale copy). The *Gate of Hell* was too large to be worked in one piece of clay and was therefore modelled in sections, each of which exists as a separate sculpture: *Le Penseur* (*The Thinker*), *Fugit Amor*, *Ombres* (*The Shades*), etc.

Ultimately Rodin was to move increasingly in the direction of abstraction, as in *La pensée* (*Thought*) – which echoes another powerful image of human creativity, the bust of *Goethe* by Pierre Jean David d'Angers, situated in the entrance-hall of the museum – and, to outstanding effect, in his statue of *Balzac*. The change in his style can be measured by the progress from those early nude studies of visionary Realism, which become increasingly more simplified and distorted ('in my view, modern sculpture should exaggerate the forms to express mental attributes'), arriving finally at this pyramidal silhouette, the emphasis all on the large head. This almost abstract symbol of the novelist's powers aroused such a furore when it was shown to the public in 1898 that the commission was withdrawn. Today it is recognized as Rodin's most innovatory sculpture.

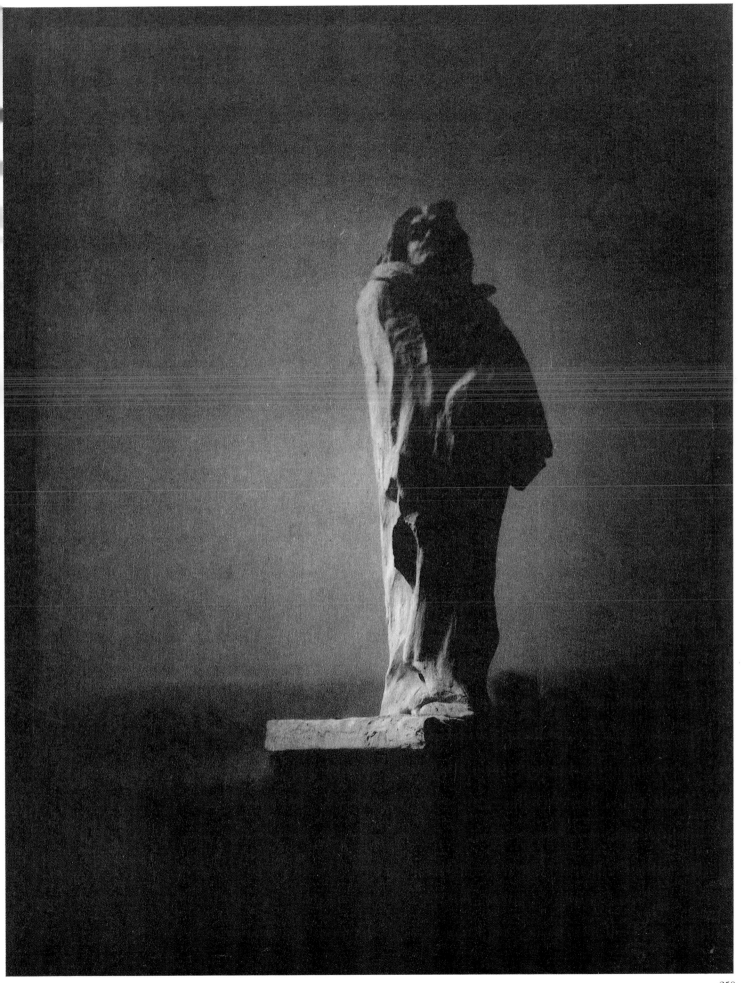

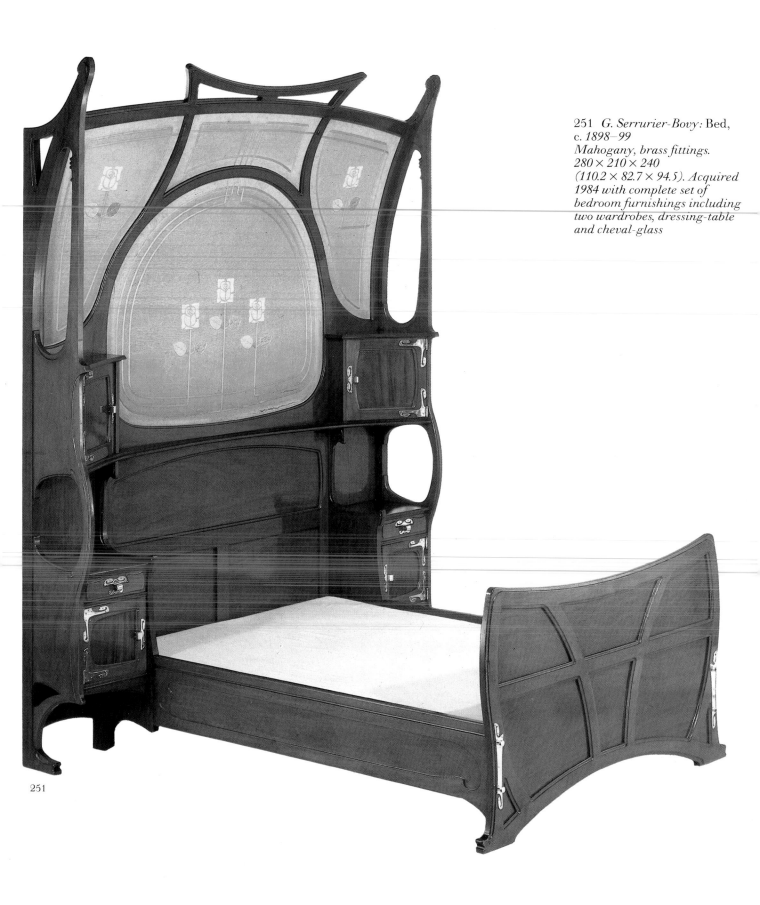

251 *G. Serrurier-Bovy:* Bed,
c. *1898–99*
Mahogany, brass fittings.
280 × 210 × 240
(110.2 × 82.7 × 94.5). Acquired
1984 with complete set of
bedroom furnishings including
two wardrobes, dressing-table
and cheval-glass

251

Art Nouveau

The last third of the nineteenth century saw a revival in architecture and the decorative arts. Art Nouveau was born out of a determination to reject the conventional and create an entirely new stylistic vocabulary. It was initially referred to as 'modern art' or 'the modern style'; only in 1890 did the term 'Art Nouveau' come into use, capitalized to mark its status as a distinctive style.

The movement achieved its major successes between 1890 and about 1905, although this varied a little from one art to another, as they reacted to external influences at different times. Thus the lessons of Japan and the Far East were absorbed first by the ceramicists, whose work perhaps reached its peak in the period between the two World Fairs of 1878 and 1889; certainly that was the first real intimation of the blossoming of Art Nouveau yet to come. Powerful and vigorous ceramics were produced at that time by Ernest Chaplet (1835–1909), Auguste Delaherche (1857–1940) and the great Jean Carriès (1855–94), who abandoned sculpture in favour of pottery. After 1905 Art Nouveau became derivative, although it continued as a force up to the outbreak of the First World War: its themes and motifs dwindled into mediocre repetitions of once-original designs, and were overtaken by an emergent rationalism that rejected the exuberance of its flowing decorative curves.

Although a short-lived phenomenon, Art Nouveau is not easy to pin down and describe, as it was by no means a homogeneous entity. There are, however, a number of fundamental principles that draw the different threads together.

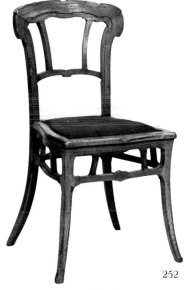

252

252 *V. Horta:* Dining-room Chair
Ash. 92 (36.2). From the dining-room of the house built by Horta in the avenue Louise, Brussels, for the industrialist Octave Aubecq in 1903–4. Acquired 1980 with other furniture and panelling from the same room

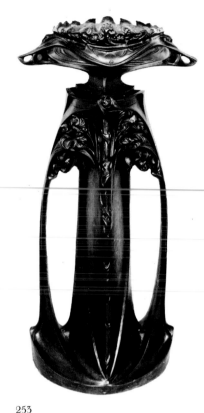

253

253 *H. Guimard:* Garden
vase and pedestal, c. *1905–7
Cast iron. 135 × 59 × 45
(53.1 × 23.2 × 17.7). One of the
castings designed by Guimard
for Fonderies Saint-Dizier
(Haute-Marne); among 56
castings given by Mme de
Menil in 1981*

254 *H. Guimard:* Wall
feature in the form of a
fireplace, *1897–98
Palisander. 302 × 179 × 29
(119 × 70.5 × 11.4). From a
house renovated by Guimard
at Les Gévrils (Loiret), when
he was working on the Castel
Béranger. Acquired 1979*

First of these is the belief in the Unity of Art – the notion
that art is one, even in its many and various manifestations –
one notable consequence of which, in France, was the
abolition of the distinction between the 'major' and the
'minor' arts, so that in 1891 the annual Salon of the Société
nationale des Beaux-Arts included examples from the
applied arts as well as painting and sculpture. In fact the part
played by sculptors in the evolution of Art Nouveau design
was quite significant, and a number of them turned their
attention to domestic items. The pewter vessels produced by
Jean Baffier (1851–1920) are robust, powerful pieces; Jules
Desbois (1851–1935) made silver and pewter plates and
flasks with incised designs of female nudes with flowing
tresses. Jean Dampt (1854–1945), Alexandre Charpentier
(1856–1909) – for a time members of an association called,
significantly, 'Art dans Tout' ('Art in Everything') – and
Robert Carabin (1862–1932) went beyond the production of
everyday objects to produce complete domestic interiors. The
role the painters played was perhaps less decisive, although in
1894 Victor Prouvé (1858–1943) provided the glassmaker
Emile Gallé with a number of designs based on the human
figure to be used as motifs in glass engravings; and in 1895
the dealer Siegfried Bing (1838–1905) exhibited in his newly
opened gallery, itself called 'L'Art Nouveau', a famous series
of stained-glass windows by L. C. Tiffany (1848–1933) based
on sketches by Toulouse-Lautrec and the Nabis.

Another principle of Art Nouveau, constantly reiterated,
relates to the form of objects: this held that construction must
always be related to use, and form and decoration must arise
out of the material used. As a theory this was functional in the
extreme, but the results in practice were often the reverse of
what was intended.

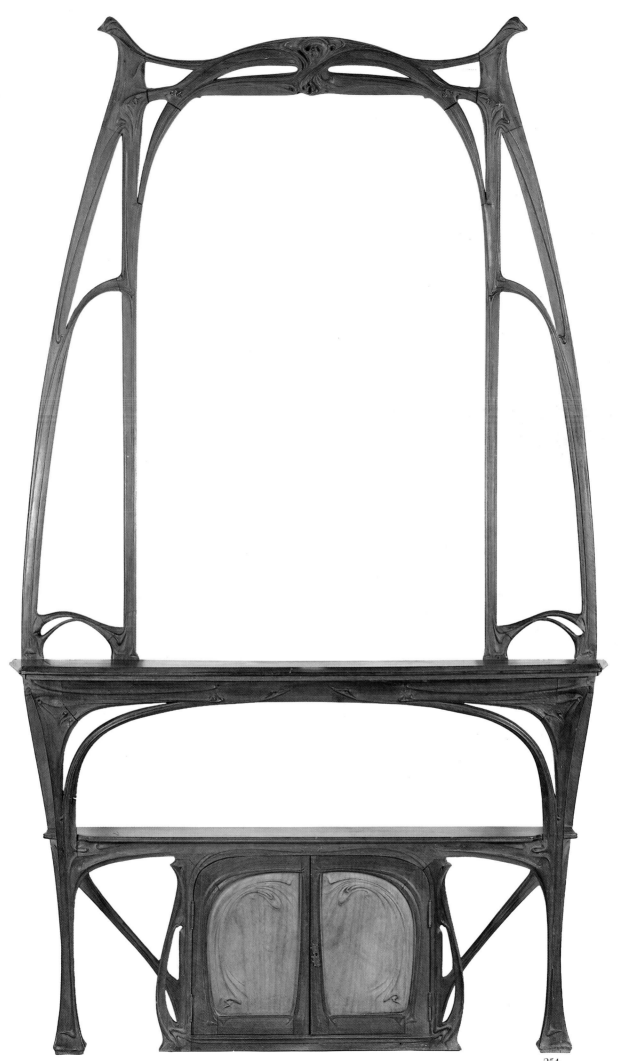

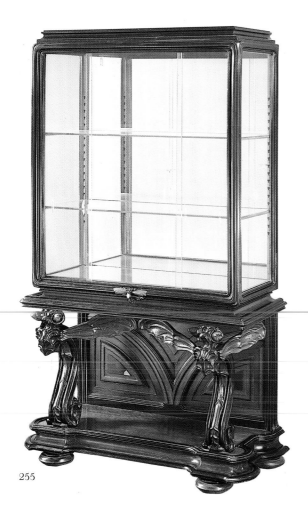

255

It remains a fact that, in spite of their common ideals, in
spite of a shared desire to reject models from the past, to free
themselves from what Gallé called the 'archaeological
poison' – although here once again the vociferous verbal
protestations against official art were often tempered in the
actual work produced – in spite of a universally held belief in
the possibility of creating new forms and decorations for a
modern age, vocabularies adopted by individual artists were
widely divergent. Indeed, even their artistic philosophies
differed, depending on their personal inclination or on the
historical or cultural influences that affected the places where
they lived and worked (Brussels, Paris, Nancy, Vienna,
Glasgow, etc.). Looked at in this light, it is hardly surprising
that the work produced in these various centres was so
diverse.

One of the Art Nouveau ideals was to unite form and
decoration in an organic unity. The theoretical basis for this
idea rested largely on the Naturalistic principles put forward
by Viollet-le-Duc, which were based on his studies of
medieval architecture: that line should be free and untram-
melled, that structure and decoration should be one and the
same, the major function of ornamentation being to illustrate
structure. In Brussels and Paris, the architects Victor Horta

(1861–1947) and Hector Guimard (1867–1942) developed their own distinctive interpretations, and they eliminated anything that might disrupt the unity of the concept, designing even the door-knobs and handles, the espagnolettes for the windows and the bathroom tiles. Guimard referred with some pride to the 'Guimard style', and indeed it is impressive how the vocabulary is carried through over the whole range of materials, wood, cast and wrought iron, copper, glass, etc.: evidence of a desire for artistic integrity. After the turn of the century, the fashion for the characteristic features of Art Nouveau, asymmetry and 'whiplash' curves, was on the wane: the decoration and furnishings of the Hôtel Aubecq (1902–24) are more restrained and severe than those of the Hôtel Solvay, and the patterns designed by Guimard and cast by the Saint-Dizier foundry (1903–7) are more harmonious and regular than those used in the Castel Béranger. In the work of Gustave Serrurier-Bovy (1858–1910), who regarded himself as operating in the populist traditions of the Arts and Crafts Movement, curves

256 *E. Gallé:* Liseron d'octobre (Autumn Convolvulus), *1891 Crystal in two layers, inlays, incised decoration. 18.8, d. 9.8 (7.4, d. 3.9). Base in cut and incised crystal. On the piece is engraved Verlaine's line: 'Vous vous êtes penché sur ma mélancolie' ('You have stooped over my melancholy'). Acquired 1892*

257 *E. Gallé:* La limnée des étangs (Pond Snail) *Vase in the shape of a freshwater snail* (Lymnaea). *Clear glass, partly burnished, inlays, intaglios, opaque enamels. 31.6, d. 12.4 (12.4, d. 4.9). The motif of Cupids playing with pond snails was supplied by V. Prouvé. Designed 1884. Acquired 1985*

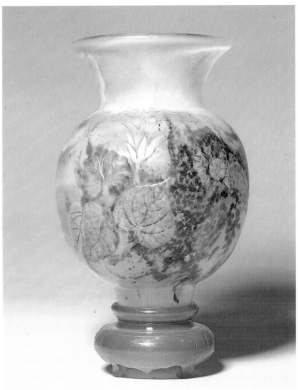

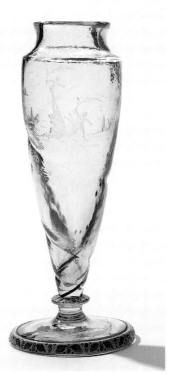

256   257

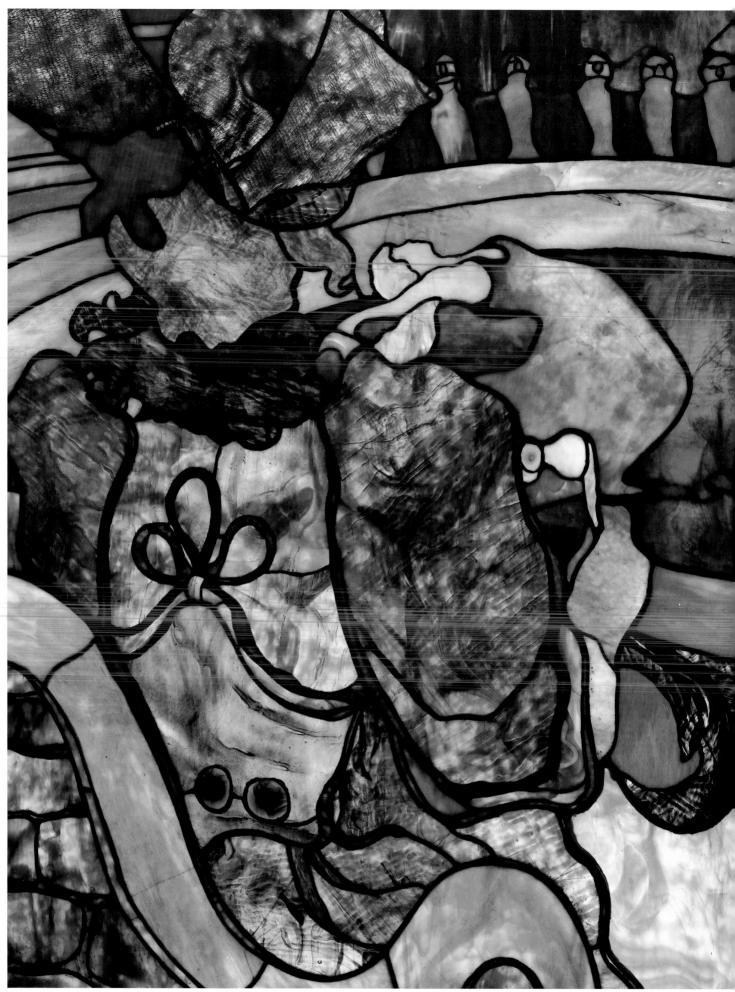

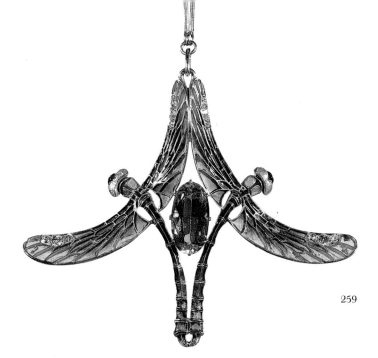

259

are used purely as linking elements and not to emphasize structure. Unlike Horta and Guimard, he used metal decoration as surface relief on his items of furniture.

To the members of the School of Nancy, in eastern France, nature itself was the only admissible source of inspiration. Although the School was formally constituted only in 1901, it had in effect been active over the previous thirty years, dominated by the figure of Emile Gallé (1846–1904). Roger Marx (1859–1913), another citizen of Nancy, described him as '*homo triplex*', referring to his prowess as a ceramicist, glassmaker and cabinet-maker. Always experimenting and looking for new ideas, Gallé was responsible for numerous technical advances and decorative innovations, interpreting models from nature with seemingly inexhaustible imagin-

258 *H. de Toulouse-Lautrec and L. C. Tiffany:* Au nouveau cirque, Papa Chrysanthème (At the New Circus, Papa Chrysanthemum, detail), 1894–95
Stained glass, jasper, sandwich and cabochon glass. 120 × 85 (47.2 × 33.5). Given by Henry Dauberville in honour of his children, Béatrice and Guy-Patrice Dauberville, 1979

259 *R. Lalique:* Neck pendant, c. 1903–5
Gold, enamel, brilliants and aquamarine. 6.9 × 5.7 × 0.08 (2.7 × 2.2 × 0.03). Acquired 1983

260 *E. Chaplet:* Vase *Hard porcelain, high-fired decoration. 45, d. 20 (17.7, d. 7.9). World Fair, Paris 1900. Acquired 1900*

261 *J. Carriès:* Cache-pot *Glazed stoneware heightened with gold. 16, d. 16.8 (6.3, d. 6.6). Salon de la Sociéte nationale des Beaux-Arts, Paris 1892. Acquired 1892.*

262 *E. Feuillâtre:* Bonbonnière
Crystal, enamels and silver. 8.3, d. 14.5 (3.3, d. 5.7). Salon des artistes français, Paris 1904. Acquired 1904

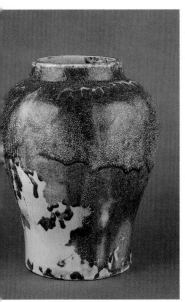

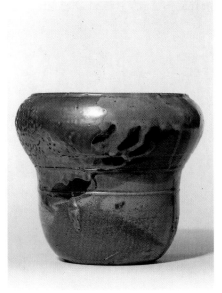

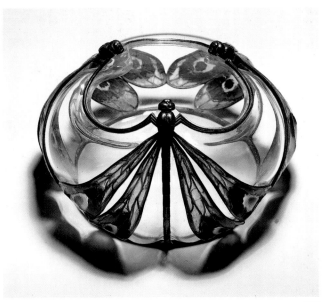

260

261

262

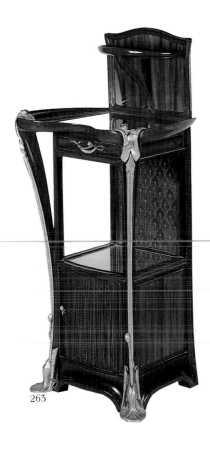

263

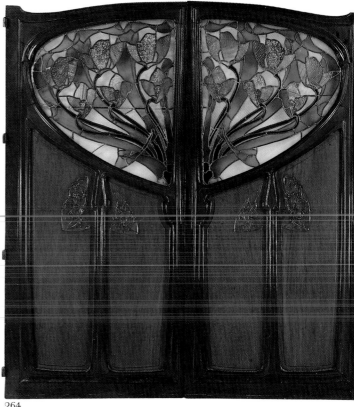

264

ation and an unfailing aesthetic sense. He never deployed his prodigious technique gratuitously: it is always subordinated to a superb creative intelligence, uniting form and content in a harmonious whole. His emphasis on nature influenced other artists from the same region, such as Eugène Vallin (1856–1922) and Louis Majorelle (1859–1926), the two great cabinet-makers of the School of Nancy. Encouraged by him, they developed a distinctive style of their own, abandoning their earlier pastiches of the medieval or eighteenth-century manner. The furniture they produced is outstanding in its finish and the quality of materials employed, and demonstrates a remarkable ability to use decoration as an integral element of an overall design.

263 *L. Majorelle:* Chevet 'nénuphars' (Waterlily pattern bedside table), c. *1905*
Mahogany, acacia wood, marquetry of various woods, gilt bronze. 110 × 55 × 45 (43.3 × 21.7 × 17.7). Acquired 1980

264 *E. André, architect; E. Vallin, joiner and cabinet-maker; J. Gruber, master glazier:* Double doors *Hardwood. 198 × 182 × 65 (78 × 71.7 × 25.6). From the fitting room of the François Vaxelaire store built in Nancy in 1901. Acquired 1983*

265 *R. Carabin:* Bookcase, *1890*
Walnut and wrought iron. 290 × 215 × 83 (114.2 × 84.7 × 32.7). Salon de la Société nationale des Beaux-Arts, Paris 1891. The earliest of the twenty pieces of furniture designed by Carabin

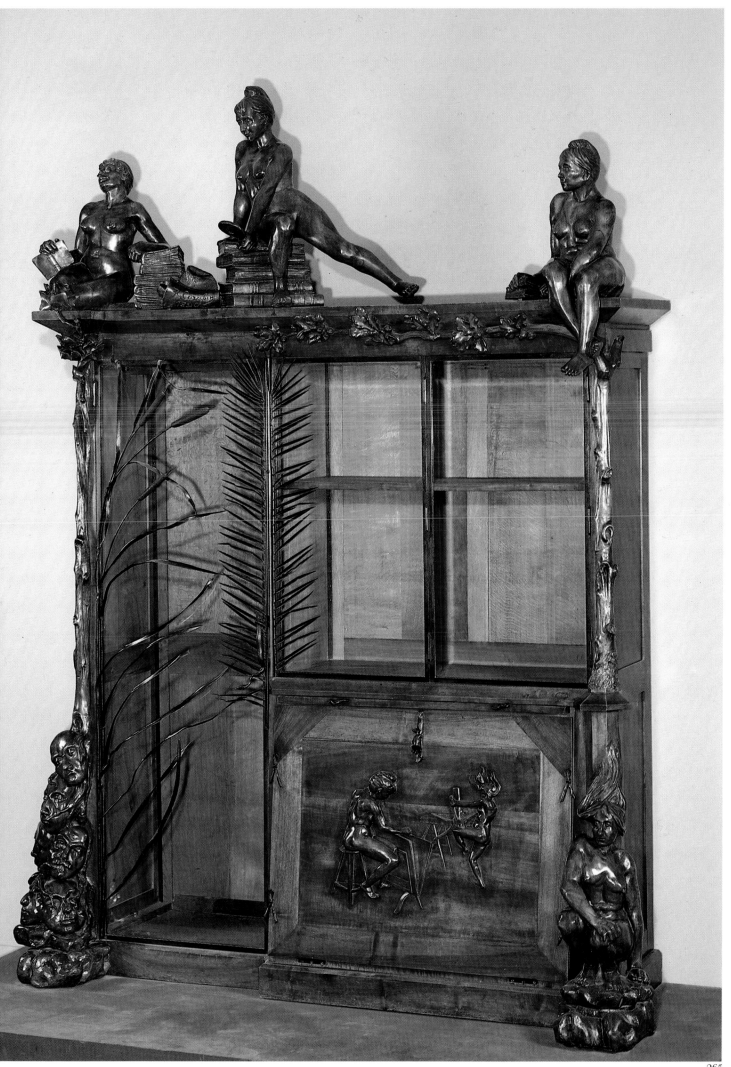

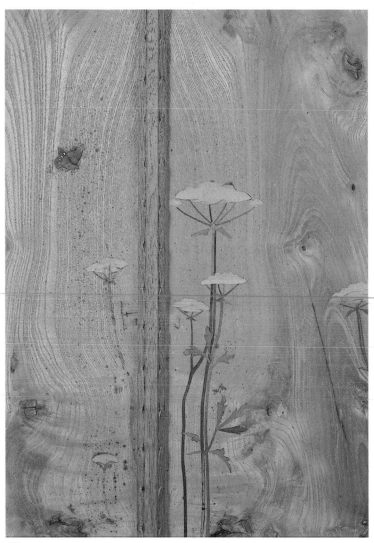

266

266 *J. Dampt:* Detail of
panelling, *1900–06*
From the 'Salle du Chevalier'
designed and built for
Comtesse René de Béarn. Elm,
ash and oak with mother-of-
pearl inlay. 100 × 66
(39.4 × 26). Lent by Musée des
Arts décoratifs, to which the
whole ensemble was given in
1927

267 *A. Charpentier:* Dining-
room, *1901*
For the villa of the banker
Adrien Bénard at
Champrosay. Panelling in
mahogany; fountain and tiling
in glazed stoneware by
A. Bigot; metalwork on doors,
windows and furniture in gilt
bronze. 346 × 1055 × 621
(136.2 × 415.4 × 244.5) overall.
Acquired 1977

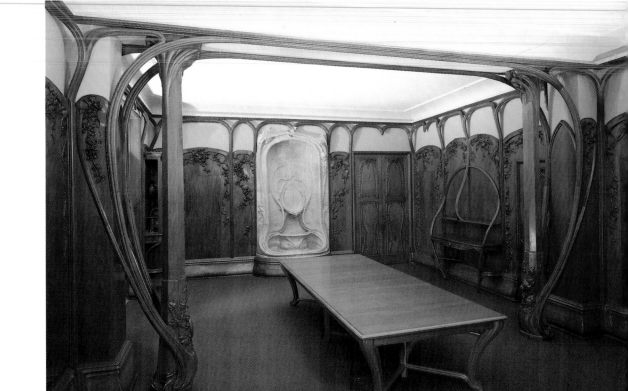

267

Glasgow, Vienna, Chicago

In the early 1890s Art Nouveau spread throughout Europe and the United States. In 1894, Otto Wagner (1841–1918) designed Vienna's first example of 'modern' architecture, the Karlsplatz metropolitan railway station. In the same year, in Chicago, Louis Sullivan (1856–1924) completed the Stock Exchange building, its strongly stated decorative theme emerging naturally from the structure.

The World Fairs provided an international forum for artists, and various publications were started in the wake of the exhibitions – the most important of which were held in Chicago in 1893, Brussels in 1897, Paris in 1900, Turin in 1902, and Saint Louis in 1904. The annual exhibitions of the avant-garde (such as the 'Libre Esthétique' in Brussels and the 'Secession' in Vienna) provided another meeting-place for artists and encouraged the exchange of ideas. Lavishly illustrated art periodicals ensured that news of recent developments reached a wide audience. Thus Charles Rennie Mackintosh (1868-1928) was better known for his decorative work, which was given publicity in the art magazines and exhibited abroad (notably in Vienna in 1900), than for his major buildings in Glasgow.

268 *Gebrüder Thonet, Vienna, manufacturers of bentwood furniture:* Number 4 chair
Dyed ash, cane seat. 90 (35.4). Acquired 1984

269 *Gebrüder Thonet, Vienna, manufacturers of bentwood furniture:* Number 51 chair
Black-dyed ash, cane seat. 90 (35.4). Probably designed by August Thonet for Astoria Hotel, New York, 1888. Acquired 1984.

270 *A. Loos, architect; J. & J. Kohn, Vienna, manufacturers of bentwood furniture:* Café chair
Varnished beech, cane seat. 87 (34.3). Designed by Loos in 1898 for the Café Museum, Vienna. Acquired 1981

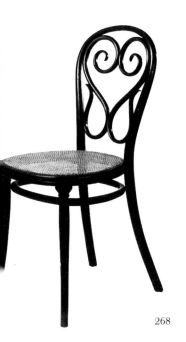

268

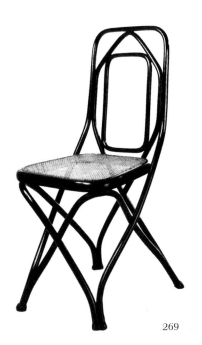

269

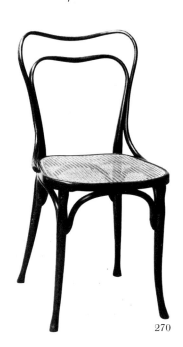

270

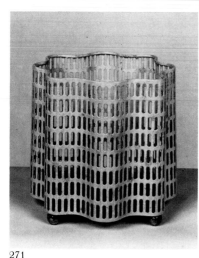

271

Yet the success of the international 'modern style' of Art Nouveau was shortlived. The interchange of ideas between the architects of Glasgow and Vienna led in turn to a more radical reappraisal of form, and a move in the direction of geometrical abstraction. When, in 1903, Josef Hoffmann (1870–1956) and Kolo Moser (1868–1918) founded the Wiener Werkstätte – a complex of studios for industrial artists, modelled on the contemporary English craft guilds – they were far more concerned to appeal to an élite of aesthetes than to produce articles at a modest price aimed at the mass market.

It was not until the turn of the century that the Viennese architects began to take an interest in bentwood furniture, although it had in fact been pioneered in Vienna by Michael Thonet and mass-produced there for thirty years. The prototypes of furniture devised at this period by Adolf Loos, Siegel, Josef Hoffmann and Otto Wagner are among the finest the twentieth century has produced.

Loos (1870–1933) worked outside the Secession, whose doctrinaire attitudes he criticized in polemical articles. An admirer of the New World, he believed passionately in the need for a functionalism that corresponded to the requirements of modern life.

Over the same period, in the United States, Frank Lloyd Wright (1869–1959) designed his Prairie Houses, superb examples of the integration of architecture with its Environment. Anticipating the European avant-garde by several years, he successfully developed a style of pure abstraction, exemplified by his use of coloured glass in the Coonley house (1908).

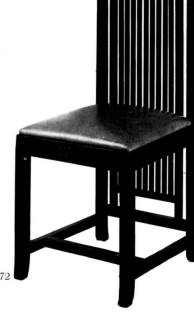

272

271 *Wiener Werkstätte, craft workshops founded in Vienna in 1903; K. Moser, painter and designer:* Wastepaper basket, c. *1903–04*
Enameled and nickel-plated sheet-metal. 29.5 × 21 (11.6 × 8.3). Acquired 1986

272 *F. L. Wright, architect:* Chair
Oak and leather. 125 (49.2). From the house of Isabel Roberts, River Forest, Ill., built by Wright in 1908. Acquired 1982

273 *C. R. Mackintosh, architect:* Dressing-table and mirror
Painted wood, ebony and mother-of-pearl, silver-plated bronze, glass. 79.6 × 101.6 × 45.7 (31.3 × 40 × 18). From the house of Catherine Cranston, Hous'hill, Glasgow, renovated by Mackintosh in 1904. Acquired 1985

274 *J. Hoffmann, architect; J. & J. Kohn, Vienna, manufacturers of bentwood furniture:* Armchair with adjustable back, c. *1905*
Beech and cut-out plywood, mahogany stain and varnish, iron. 110 (43.3). Acquired 1986

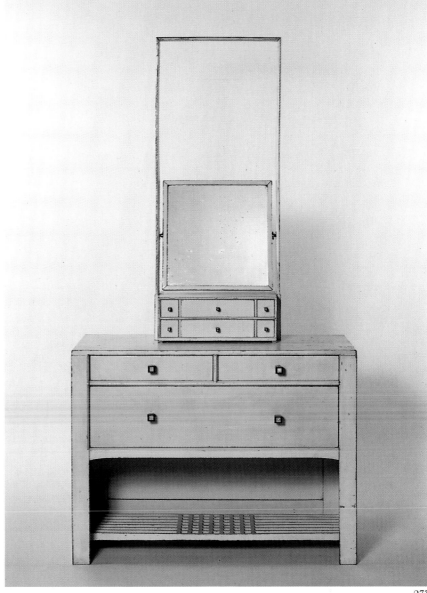

273

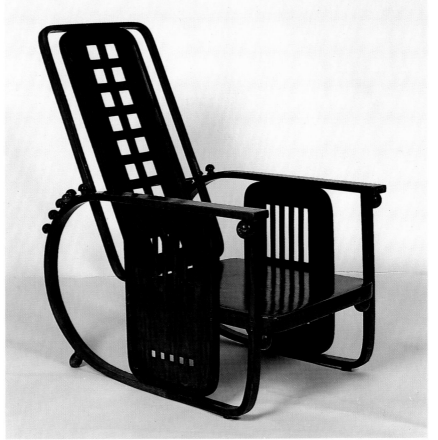

274

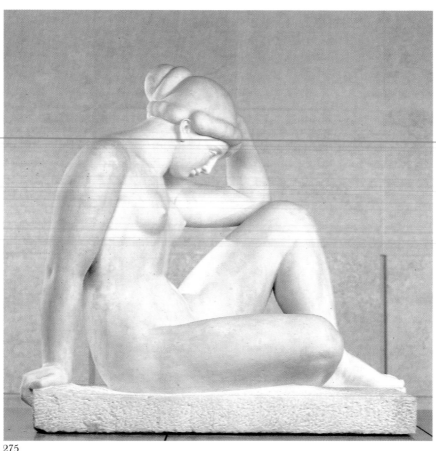

275

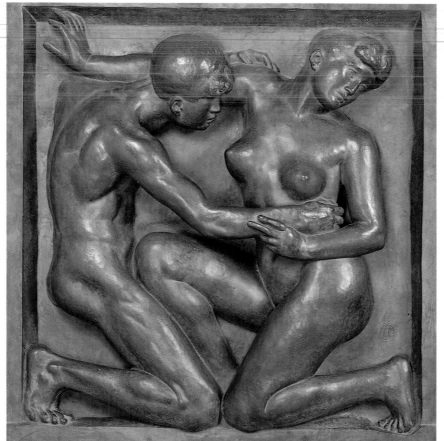

276

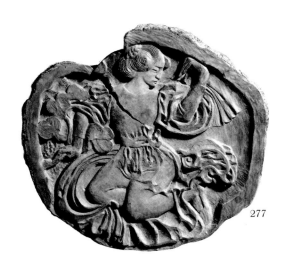

277

Maillol, Bourdelle, Bernard

'The complete work of art will be that ... in which the most contrary, the most apparently contradictory qualities – strength and gentleness, discipline and grace, logic and abandon, precision and poetry – will sit together with such ease that they seem natural and not in the least surprising. Which means that the first thing that must be renounced is the pleasure of amazing one's contemporaries.' This new aesthetic doctrine was formulated by the writer André Gide, as a reaction both against Rodin and against academic art.

Although the undulating lines of the *Danseuse* (*Dancer*) by Aristide Maillol (1861–1944) still bore some resemblance to those beloved of Symbolism and later Art Nouveau, it was nevertheless Maillol who produced the first and most brilliant manifestation of what has come to be known as the Stylistic Renewal (*retour au style*): the sculpture *La Méditerranée* (*The Mediterranean*), exhibited at the Salon of 1905. Static and uncommunicative, it must have stood out against Rodin's figures, described by Gide as 'quivering, anxious, gesticulating, full of noisy pathos'. Gide went on: 'Monsieur Maillol's large seated woman ... is beautiful, she means nothing ... I think we have to go back a long way to find such a complete disregard for any other concern except beauty.'

Maillol chooses a single viewpoint and simplifies his composition: there are no tensed limbs, no symmetries, but strictly defined and distinct elements that fill up their allotted space. If the frame were removed from one of his reliefs, the spectator would mentally replace it, obedient to the dictates of the composition. This same desire for simplification is apparent in the treatment of the surface, which is of untroubled regularity and smoothness.

In 1900, putting behind him the Romantic indulgences of his youth, Antoine Bourdelle (1861–1929) turned to Greek models for inspiration. He then executed *Tête d'Apollon* (*Head of Apollo*), in 1900–9, *Pénélope* (*Penelope*), in 1905–8, and *Héraklès archer* (*Heracles the Bowman*), a superb example of his compositional skill and ability to produce rhythmic variations of stillness and tension. Charles Morice

275 *A. Maillol:* La Méditerranée (The Mediterranean), *1923–29 Marble. 110 (43.3). The model for this was shown at the Salon d'Automne, Paris 1905. Marble commissioned by state, 1923*

276 *A. Maillol:* Le désir (Desire), *1905–07 Lead. 120 (47.2). Assigned by Office des biens privés, 1951*

277 *A. Maillol:* Danseuse (Dancer), *1895 Wood. 22 (8.7). Bequest of Mme Thadée Natanson, 1953*

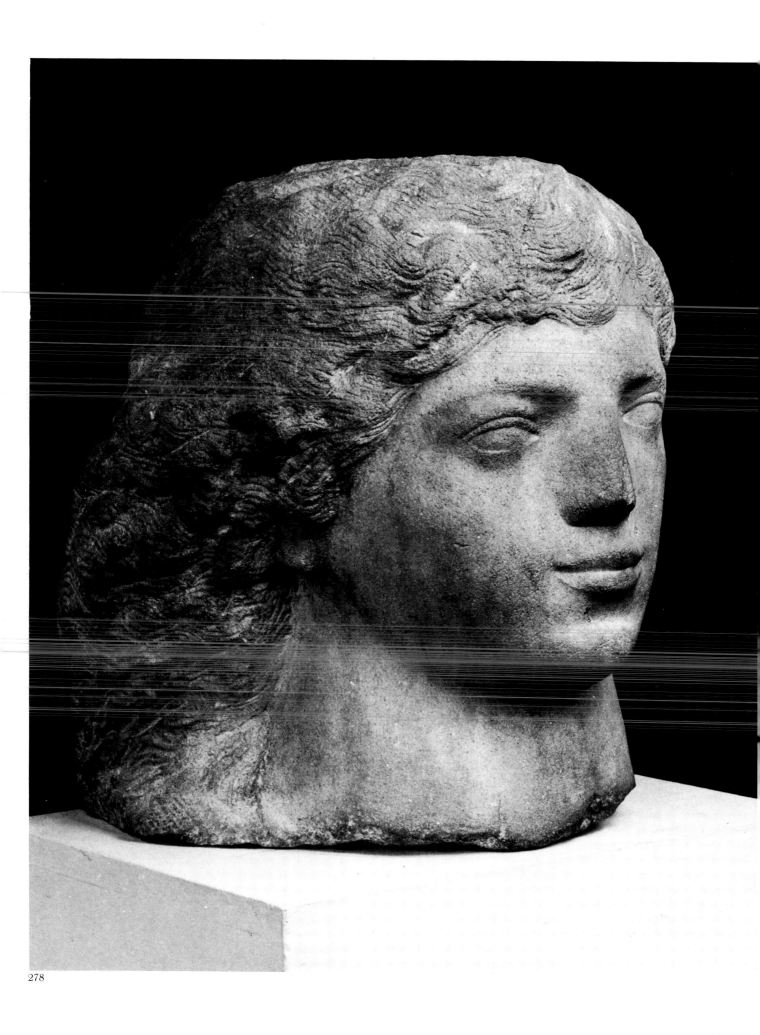

278

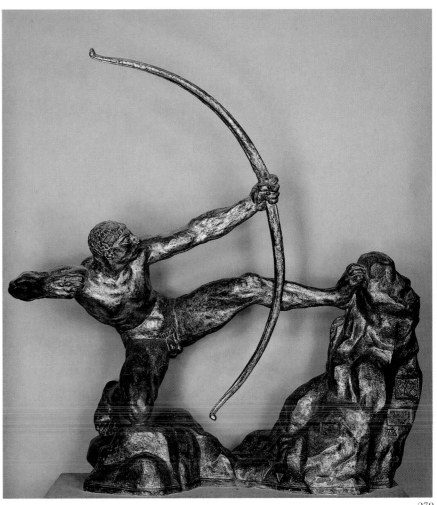

279

wrote of it: 'The extraordinary exaggerated stance of the archer poised in space ... that human form which seems to surge forward even in immobility, that incisive and accurate modelling, so full and vibrant; it is one of the most prodigious efforts of contemporary art.'

Whereas Gauguin and Lacombe – and Maillol in his early years – had carved almost exclusively in wood, Joseph Bernard (1866–1931) adopted the practice of direct carving in stone. His *Effort vers la nature* (*Towards Nature*) suggests, both by its title and its massive, primitive appearance, a desire for close harmony between form and matter; it was the prelude to works carved directly out of huge blocks of stone, in the manner that was to be adopted by Henry Moore, Amedeo Modigliani, Jacob Epstein and Constantin Brancusi. Bernard's figures are more supple and rhythmic than Maillol's, with a spirituality reflecting the artist's own mysticism. A particularly fine example is the *Porteuse d'eau* (*Water Carrier*) of 1912.

278 *J. Bernard:* Effort vers la nature (Towards Nature), c. *1906–07*
Stone, directly carved. 32 (12.6). Gift of Jean Bernard, 1980

279 *E. A. Bourdelle:* Heraklès archer (Heracles the Bowman), *1909*
Bronze. 248 (97.6). Acquired 1924

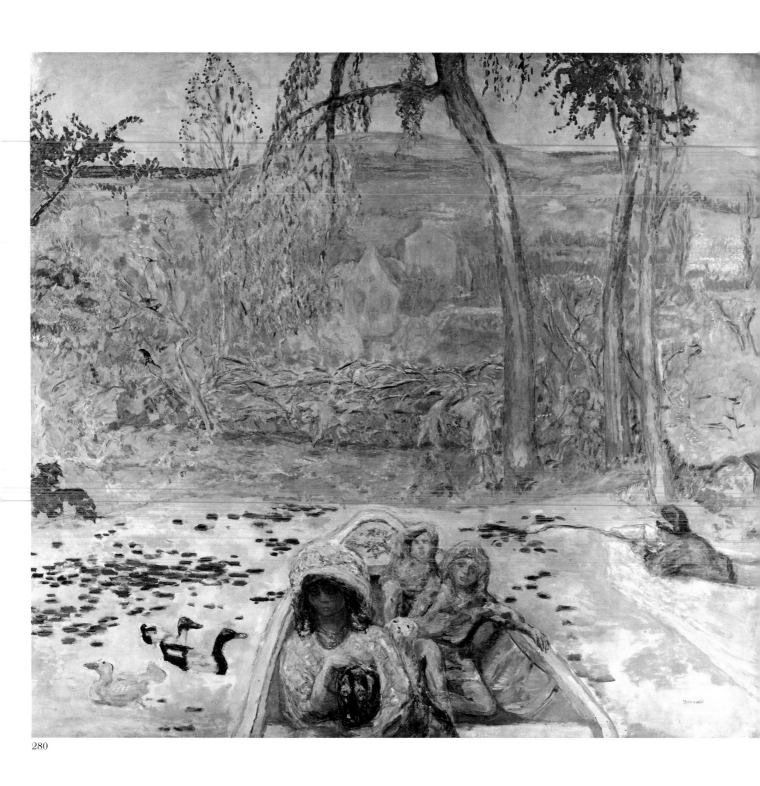

280

After 1900

The Nabis did not hold together as a coherent group much beyond 1900, when the individual members began to develop in their distinctive ways, while still maintaining their friendship. Bonnard, after reverting to a more realistic manner, notably in his portraits, then became absorbed in exploring the possibilities of colour in a series of magnificent nudes and still-lifes. Remaining largely outside the major movements of the early twentieth century – Fauvism, Cubism and Abstraction – he continued his investigations of the pictorial space, as in *En barque* (*In the Boat*), which looks down over its subject and makes use of the widest possible visual field. This vast composition was the prelude to sumptuous panoramas of landscapes at Vernon and Le Cannet.

Bonnard, Vuillard, Denis and Roussel never lost the taste for decoration acquired in their early Nabi years. Vuillard produced decorative ensembles for Claude Anet and Henri Bernstein, and decorated the villa at Villers-sur-Mer owned by the Bernheims, Paris picture dealers. Otherwise he continued to paint domestic subjects and also numerous portraits: those in the Musée d'Orsay collection include likenesses of many of the notable personalities of the day, the Comtesse Jean de Polignac and Jeanne Lanvin among them.

In vast dynamic compositions in brilliant colours, Roussel explored mythological themes such as *L'enlèvement des filles de Leucippe* (*The Abduction of the Daughters of Leucippus*). His pastels too are peopled with nymphs and fauns.

A number of the former Nabis were reunited in 1912–13 when they worked together on the decoration of the Théâtre des Champs-Elysées, built by the Perret brothers. The cupola was painted by Maurice Denis, while Vuillard and Roussel respectively undertook the decoration of the foyer and drop-curtain of the adjoining Comédie des Champs-Elysées.

With Symbolism and Art Nouveau at their peak, the World Fair held in Paris in 1900 demonstrated a poverty of creative inspiration in Western painting as a whole – and that in spite of the continued presence of masters of the Impressionist generation such as Monet, Cézanne and Renoir, and also Gauguin and Bonnard.

280 *P. Bonnard:* En barque (In the Boat), *1907*
278 × 301 (109.4 × 118.5).
Acquired 1946

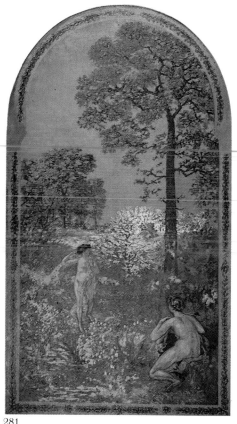

281

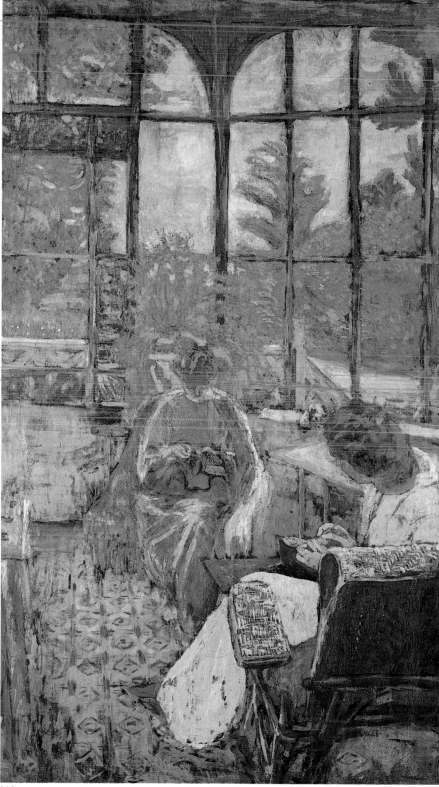

282

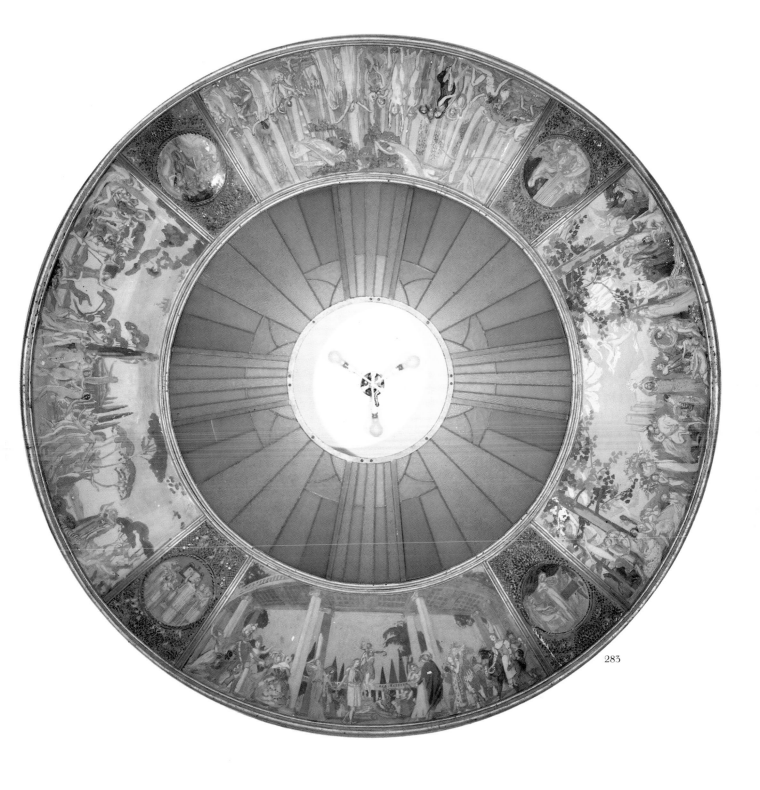

283

281 *K. X. Roussel:*
L'enlèvement des filles de
Leucippe (Abduction of the
Daughters of Leucippus), *1911*
430 × 240 (169.3 × 94.5).
Acquired 1935

282 *E. Vuillard:* Les dames
Natanson brodant sous la
véranda (The Natanson
Ladies Embroidering on the
Veranda), *1913*
201 × 113 (79.1 × 44.5). One of

seven decorative panels
executed for the Bernheims'
villa, Bois-Lurette, at Villiers-
sur-Mer. Gift of Henry
Dauberville in honour of his
children Béatrice and Guy-
Patrice Dauberville, 1979

283 *M. Denis:* Maquette for
the cupola of the Théâtre des
Champs-Elysées, *1912*
Tempera on plaster. D. 240
(94.5). Acquired 1983

The transition between the centuries was not to be a smooth progression but a brutal wrench, the banner of modernity being taken up by a largely new generation of younger artists. Yet, clearly, twentieth-century art had roots in the past: Gustav Klimt (1862–1918), Ferdinand Hodler (1853–1918) and Edvard Munch (1863–1944), for example, were the direct precursors of German Expressionism, but at the same time they had close links with Symbolism.

In France, new departures in architecture by Perret and Sauvage, and by Maillol in sculpture, were matched by two new movements in painting: these were Fauvism, which burst onto the scene at the Salon d'Automne of 1905, and Cubism, which may be said to have begun with Picasso's *Demoiselles d'Avignon* (1907; The Museum of Modern Art, New York). Cubism, its indebtedness to Cézanne notwithstanding, was a movement that reached out to the future, very much a twentieth-century phenomenon. Fauvism, on the other hand, lasted barely a few years and was really no more than the exploration of one facet of the Post-Impressionist aesthetic, the exploitation of colour. It is for this reason that the Musée d'Orsay shows a number of Fauve paintings, among them *Luxe, calme et volupté* by Matisse, which shows a direct link with Divisionism. Henri Matisse (1869–1954), together with his friends from student days in Gustave Moreau's studio, Georges Rouault (1871–1958) and Albert Marquet (1875–1947), was one of the leaders of the Fauve movement, with which Georges Braque (1882–1963) was for a time associated. Their colleagues André Derain (1880–1954) and Maurice de Vlaminck (1876–1958) – the so-called School of Chatou – were, like the German Expressionists, the inheritors of the tradition of Van Gogh.

190

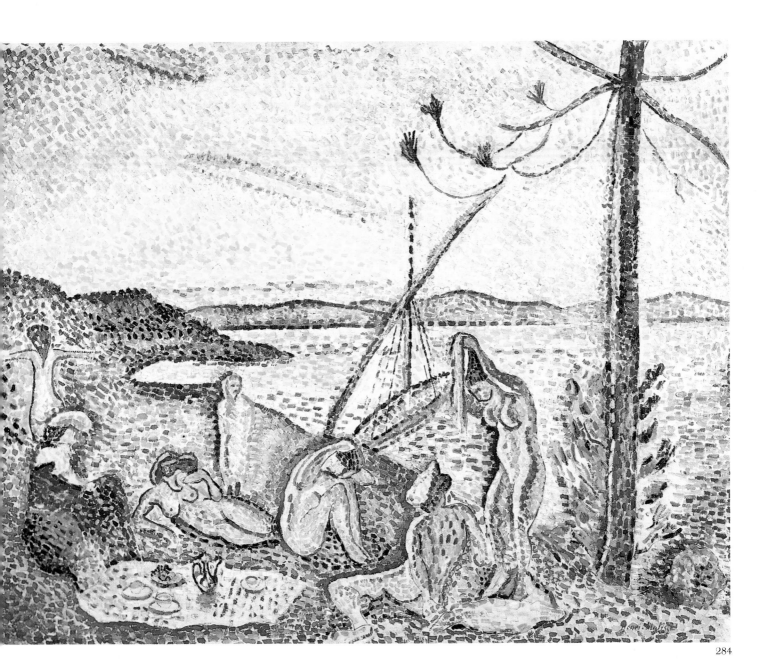

284

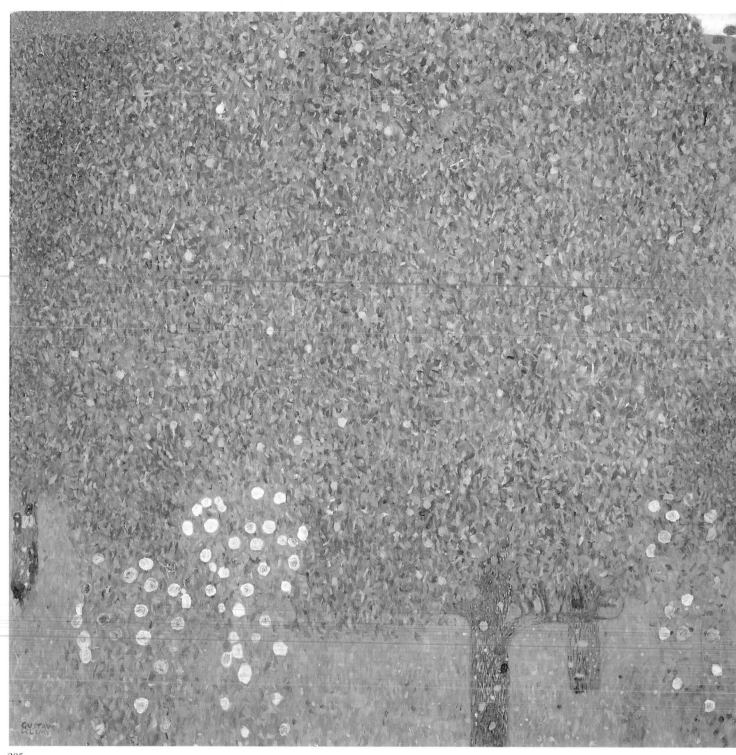

285

285 *G. Klimt:* Rosiers sous les
arbres (Roses under Trees),
c. *1905*
110 × 115 (43.3 × 45.3).
Acquired 1980

286 *E. Munch:* Nuit d'été à
Aasgaarstrand (Summer
Night, Aasgaarstrand), c. *1904*
99 × 103.5 (39 × 40.7).
Acquired 1986

287 *A. Derain:* Westminster
Bridge, c. *1906*
*81 × 100 (31.9 × 39.4). Gift of
Max and Rosy Kaganovitch,
1973*

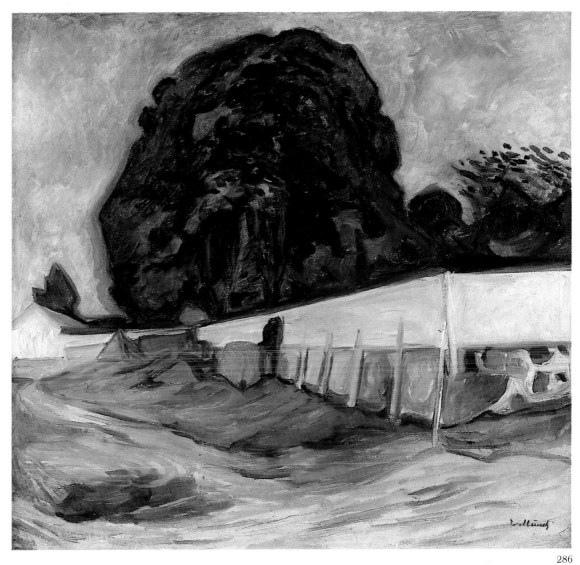

286

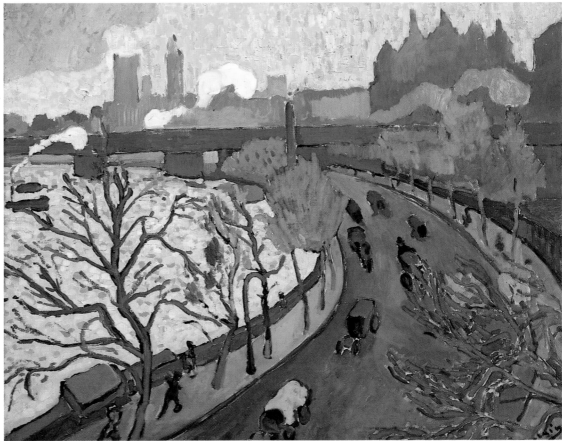

287

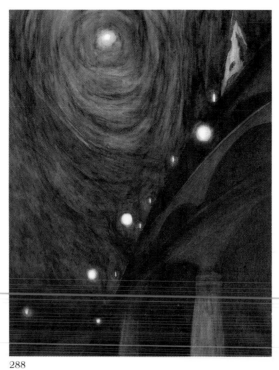

288

288 *L. Spilliaert:* Clair de
lune et lumières (Moonlight
and Lamps), c. *1909*
Indian ink wash and pastel.
65 × 50 (25.6 × 19.7). Gift of
Mme Madeleine Spilliaert, the
artist's daughter, 1981

289 *J. Toorop:* Le Désir et
l'Assouvissement (Desire and
Fulfilment), *1893*
Pastel on beige paper. 76 × 90
(29.9 × 35.4). Acquired 1976

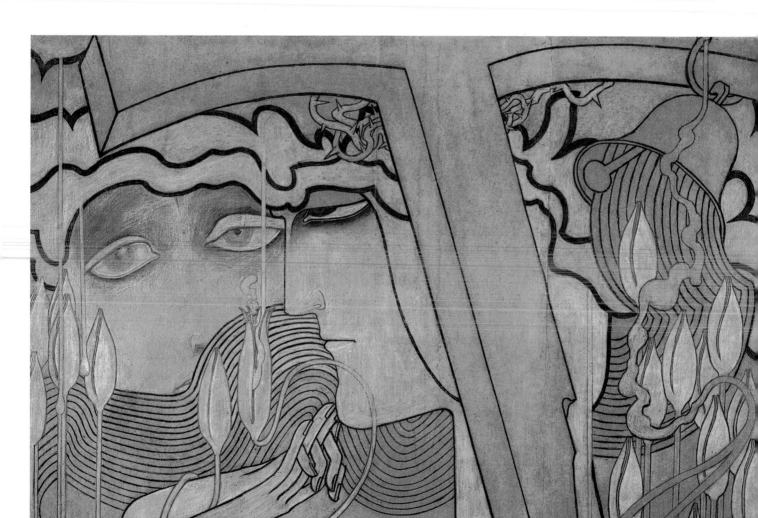

289

Drawing and watercolour

The Nabis were enthusiastic practitioners of all the graphic arts – prints, posters, book illustrations, etc. – and between them produced a vast quantity of drawings, those by Bonnard being probably the finest and most attractive. His wide-ranging imagination is evident both in rapid sketches and more finished pastels and watercolours. Théophile Steinlen (1859–1923), in a more down-to-earth spirit, presents us with a vivid picture of his times. The major collection of works by Cappiello reflects the revival of poster art, also represented by Jules Chéret (1836-1932) and Toulouse-Lautrec. The Symbolists too, like Gustave Moreau, were prolific draughtsmen: the drawings of Lévy-Dhurmer or Carlos Schwabe, for example, are of particular appeal to contemporary taste. As in a similar vein, although different in mood, are the works of the Italian Segantini, the Belgian Léon Spilliaert (1881–1946), and the Dutchman Jan Toorop (1858–1928), which – like the major series by Alfons Mucha (1860–1939), linked to Art Nouveau – are recent additions to the collections.

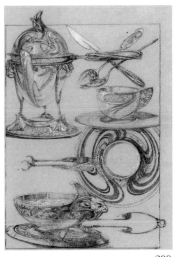

290

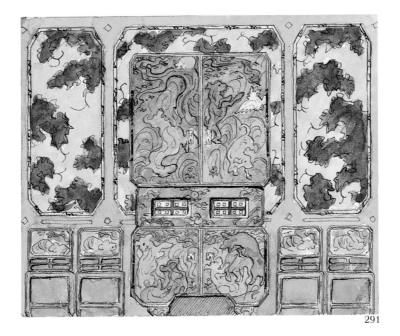

291

290 *A. Mucha:* Plate for 'Documents décoratifs' *Crayon and white gouache on beige card. 54.4 × 40.5 (21.4 × 15.9). Gift of Jiři Mucha, 1979*

291 *P. Bonnard:* Project for an Interior (detail) *Pen and watercolour. 50.2 × 35.6 (19.8 × 14) overall. Gift of Mlles Alice and Marguerite Bowers, 1984*

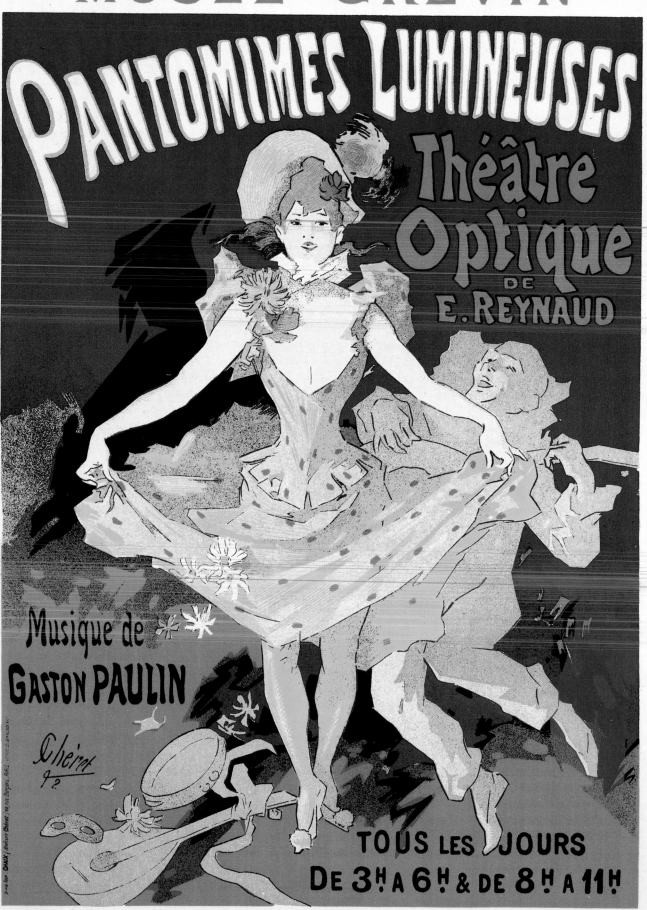

Moving pictures

To the positivists of the nineteenth century, committed to conquering and controlling the natural world, the invention of cinematography represented the achievement of an ambition to capture reality, pin it down and make it permanent and accessible.

The dream of creating a moving image was not a new one. Optical and mechanical devices had been evolving for centuries: the camera obscura, shadow pictures, the magic lantern. Yet the history of moving pictures proper does not go back beyond 1829, when the Belgian physicist Joseph Plateau (1801–83) formulated the law of retinal persistence: 'The sensations produced in us by light have a certain duration.... The impressions diminish gradually, so that it is impossible to capture precisely the instant in which they disappear.... The total duration of the impression is approximately one third of a second.'

The fundamental scientific principle was thus established, and was soon applied to a variety of optical gadgets: Dr Paris's Thaumatrope, Plateau's Phenakistiscope, the Praxinoscope invented by Emile Reynaud (1844–1918). This last was adapted successively as the Praxinoscope Theatre, the Projection Praxinoscope (1882) and the Optical Theatre; and if anyone can be said to be the precursor of the movies it was Reynaud. All that was needed was for someone to apply Plateau's theories to photography, a step taken by the American Eadweard Muybridge (1830–1904) and the French physiologist Jules Marey (1830–1904), both of whom independently developed the process of chronophotography, 'the photographic production of images in succession, taken at precisely measured time-intervals'. Once movement had been analysed into its constituent parts, the only substantial problem was the discovery of a method of synthesis.

292 *J. Chéret:* Pantomimes lumineuses, *1898*
Poster. 190 × 80 (74.8 × 31.5).
Emile Reynaud, whose invention the Théâtre optique *was patented in 1888, displayed it at the Musée Grévin in Paris, 1892–1900*

293 Praxinoscope theatre, *end of 19th century*
Acquired 1983

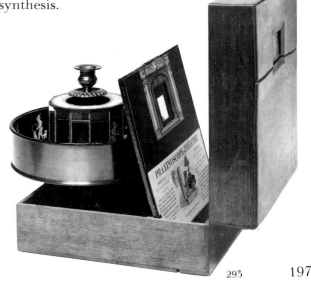

293

LE CINÉMATOGRAPHE

SALON INDIEN

GRAND CAFÉ

14, Boulevard des Capucines, 14

PARIS

*Cet appareil, inventé par MM. Auguste et
Louis Lumière, permet de recueillir, par des séries
d'épreuves instantanées, tous les mouvements qui,
pendant un temps donné, se sont succédé devant
l'objectif, et, de reproduire ensuite ces mouvements
en projetant, grandeur naturelle, devant une salle
entière, leurs images sur un écran.*

SUJETS ACTUELS

1. La Sortie de l'Usine LUMIÈRE à Lyon.	5. Les Forgerons.
2. La Voltige.	6. Le Jardinier.
3. La Pêche aux Poissons Rouges.	7. Le Repas.
4. Le Débarquement du Congrès de Photographie à Lyon.	8. Le Saut à la Couverture.
	9. La Place des Cordeliers à Lyon.
	10. La Mer.

294   295

294 Bill announcing the first
public showing of moving
pictures, *28 December 1895
Lyon, collection Institut
Lumière. These first 'vues',
brief sequences of film, are
now classics of cinematic
history*

295 Train Entering the
Station at La Ciotat, *1895
A frame from the film by the
Lumière brothers*

It is to the Lumière brothers (Auguste, b. 1862, and Louis, 1864–1948) that the credit must be awarded for drawing together the conclusions of earlier experiments and producing the cinematograph, the first movie projector. The cinema was truly born on 28 December 1895 at the Grand Café in Paris, when an astonished audience was presented with a programme consisting of *L'entrée du train en gare de La Ciotat, La sortie des usines Lumière, Le déjeuner de Bébé*: trains, crowds, babies, and all in motion. The ancient dream had come true.

From these small beginnings the modern film industry grew. The first years of the twentieth century saw the foundation of two great film companies, Pathé and Gaumont. Films became popular entertainment, enjoyed in cafés, music halls, fair booths, cabarets, department stores, schools and even church halls. The early film-makers included Lumière, Meliès, Zecca, Linder, Edison, Williamson. There were realist films, novelties, comedies, documentary reconstructions and religious epics. For a long time the cinema was the victim of its own success, looked down on by the cultural élite. Laffitte tried to remedy that situation in 1908 by making the first 'art film', *L'assassinat du duc de Guise*. No more than a filmed stage play, it was a complete failure. Yet it was a decisive moment in the development of the cinema, marking the realization that this was a separate medium from the theatre. It was the beginning of film as a major twentieth-century art form.

History at the Musée d'Orsay

Specializing as it does in the creative arts of the latter half of the nineteenth century, the Musée d'Orsay also provides some of the historical background. The first display, 'Ouverture sur l'Histoire' ('Introduction to History'), is in the entrance hall. Made up of a variety of objects, pictures, sculptures such as *L'Alsace et la Lorraine* (*Alsace and Lorraine*) by Dubois, busts of presidents of the Republic and paintings such as *L'incendie des Tuileries* (*The Burning of the Tuileries*) by Clairin, and *Jules Ferry recevant les délégués des colonies* (*Jules Ferry Welcoming the Colonial Delegates*) by Frédéric Régamey, which are either owned by the Musée d'Orsay or loaned by other museums, it provides a rapid sketch of political, social and economic history between 1848 and 1914. The presentation is for the most part chronological and restricted to events in France. Essentially no more than a brief historical survey, it acts as an introduction both to a general tour of the museum and to the reference section, the Galerie des Dates, which is far more comprehensive and scholarly in its scope.

Installed in the Galerie des Dates are a number of computer consoles linked to audio-visual displays. These are available for visitors' use and can call up information about any date from 1848 to 1914. It is possible, for example, to list the events of any one year — not only political, economic and social but also artistic, cultural and scientific. Equally, if an enquirer wishes to pursue a particular topic, he or she has access to information on a range of themes spanning the whole of the period: the development of education, the relationship of Church and State, radicalism, the condition of women, mining, the World Fairs, Impressionism, the vogue for statuary, improvements in health and hygiene, the development of modern mathematics. There are also biographies of leading figures of the day: Lamartine, Thiers, Gambetta, Carpeaux, Rodin, Manet, Darwin, Claude Bernard, Pasteur, Hugo, Flaubert, Offenbach, Gounod, Apollinaire, Jarry, Dickens, etc. In all, the information covers a total of 600 events, 200 topics and 200 biographies, illustrated by 15,000 different images and accompanied by 20 hours of narration.

Finally there is a third section of the museum which is devoted specifically to the history of the press, that great disseminator of words and images which, if not themselves always aspiring to the level of art, nevertheless reflects developments in the broader artistic sphere.

The basic consideration in providing a historical dimension to the museum displays was to provide the visitor with a simple frame of reference to the major events of the period, and to give him or her a flavour of the atmosphere in which the works to be seen in the course of a visit were created. The information is aimed primarily at the visitor who wants a general idea of what was happening on the political or cultural front at the time when, say, Flaubert was writing *Madame Bovary*, or Manet painting his *Olympia*, or Maillol sculpting his *La Méditerranée*. The historical emphasis also serves to bring out certain relationships or parallels that tend to be obscured by the grouping of works according to stylistic principles – few would guess, for example, that Bouguereau's *Naissance de Vénus* (*Birth of Venus*) dates from the same year as Redon's *Le rêve* (*The Dream*). This, in turn, may give rise to more general speculations about the financing of works of art, the status of the artist in society – whether painter, sculptor, photographer, writer or musician – and about the relationship between art and society. But the intention is not to impose ideas, merely to suggest areas for further exploration. Historical references have deliberately been excluded from the main galleries in order to cater equally for the visitor who wants to approach the works of art directly, on a purely aesthetic level.

Music at the Musée d'Orsay

The museum's coverage of the arts from 1848 to 1914 would be incomplete without reference to the music of the period, which is represented in a number of exhibitions and in an ambitious programme of concerts.

Musical activities are catered for in a number of attractive settings. The main auditorium, with seating for 385, will be the venue for evenings of chamber music, covering the major European works of the period and also less well-known works that merit revival. The seasons are planned in such a way that it will, over a period, be possible to hear the entire repertoire of chamber and piano works by, for example, Brahms, Schumann, Debussy, Fauré or Ravel.

The *Salle des Fêtes* of the Palais d'Orsay has been restored and now houses sculptures of the Third Republic. It provides a perfect setting for recreating the atmosphere of turn-of-the-century-bourgeois salon-life, and will be used for shorter recitals in a lighter vein, held in the late afternoon. Some of these programmes will be repeated in the auditorium, at lunch-times, aimed primarily at the many people who work in the area. Music also plays a part in the activities provided for the young; the history of music is one of the themes of the programme of lectures and seminars. Selections of light music will be a regular feature in the renovated restaurant, and it is intended to revive the tradition of café music at tea-time on Sunday afternoons.

On special occasions the great nave of the museum will house large-scale concert performances of the major symphonic and choral works of the latter half of the nineteenth century.

Finally, it is intended to make available to the public a selection of recordings, both reissues of historic performances and live recordings of concerts of rarely performed works. Many of the concerts are to be broadcast by Radio-France, enabling the musical activities of the Musée d'Orsay to reach a wider public in France and abroad.

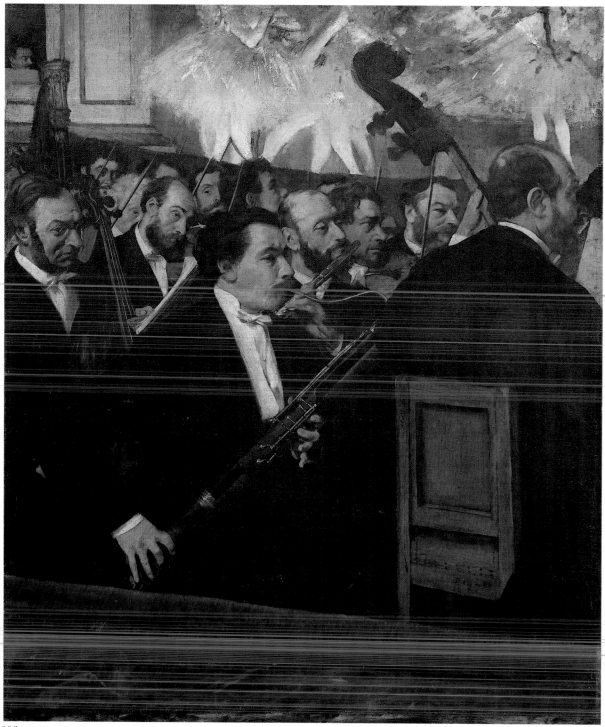

296

296 *E. Degas:* L'orchestre de
l'Opéra (The Opéra
Orchestra), *c. 1868–69*
56.5 × 46 (22.2 × 18.1). In the
foreground is Désiré Dihau,
bassoonist and friend of
Degas; in the box is the
composer Emanuel Chabrier
who was a great collector of
Manet and the Impressionists.
Acquired from Marie Dihau,
the sitter's sister, subject to a
life interest, 1924; entered
national collection 1935

Literature at the Musée d'Orsay

The year 1848 saw the publication of the first volume of François-René de Chateaubriand's *Mémoires d'Outre-Tombe*; 1913 that of the first volume of Marcel Proust's *A la Recherche du temps perdu*. A world separates them. Chateaubriand records the history of the first half of the century, from Revolution to Romanticism, while Proust's great fictional sequence looks ahead to the modern novel, as exemplified by Joyce, Musil or Faulkner. It is impossible to outline in a few words the literary history of a period of such upheaval, full of trends and counter-trends, schools and factions, and individual acts of iconoclasm – a period, too, in which new links were forged between literature and the press. If one were to attempt to sum up the spirit of the age – that drive towards modernity exhibited in so much of the writing of the time – it would be necessary to look beyond France itself. For this was a European impulse, manifested as much in London, Vienna or Prague as in Paris. Inevitably, however, our principal concern here must be with French writers.

With the benefit of hindsight, it is possible to establish a progression from Baudelaire to Arthur Rimbaud (1854–91), who wrote in 'Le bateau ivre', 'I regret the passing of Europe with its ancient parapets'; or, equally, from Stéphane Mallarmé (1842–98) through to Guillaume Apollinaire (1880–1918), who began his poem 'Zone', the first in the sequence *Alcools* (1913), with these words: 'In the end you tire of this ancient world'. 'Zone' is both a poetic manifesto and an exhortation to start afresh – appallingly ironic in view of the long and bloody war that followed.

One undeniable feature of literature in the period 1848–1914 was its pessimism, particularly marked in the novels of the period. Gustave Flaubert (1821–80) acidly dispels any last shreds of romantic illusion; Victor Hugo (1802–85) tears apart the classical narrative tradition, left untouched by Stendhal (1783–1842) and Honoré de Balzac (1799–1850), and attacks conformity with a bitterness born of despair. *Germinal* by Emile Zola (1840–1902) is a chronicle of disaster, despite its author's belief in work and progress; the Naturalism of J.K. Huysmans (1848–1907) dwindles into decadent aestheticism, taking refuge finally in mysticism. Ultimately it was Proust who painted on a vast canvas the picture of a society whose foundations were crumbling, a pathetic ruin standing on the brink of a new century. It is ironic that these years, from 1830 to 1914, saw the finest flowering of the French novel. It is almost as though the writers sensed a new era in the making, as though their creative powers were stimulated by the discontent and unease provoked in them by the awareness that their society was in crisis.

The period was also characterized by the close relationship that developed between art and literature – a phenomenon recorded in the press, in books and later in films. Great writers were also painters, great painters published books. Victor Hugo was one of the best graphic artists the century produced; Eugène Fromentin (1820–76) was as much a writer as he was a painter; Théophile Gautier (1811–72) and Baudelaire both sketched; and we turn to Delacroix's *Journal*, or the writings of Gauguin or Van Gogh, with a pleasure that derives as much from their value as literature as from their relevance as art-historical documents.

Following in the tradition of Diderot and Stendhal, writers such as Baudelaire, Octave Mirbeau (1850–1917), Zola and Mallarmé were also self-appointed art critics, often publishing their reviews of the Salons and other articles alongside the writings of professional journalists, in reviews such as *L'Artiste* or *La Revue Blanche* – to which the painters and engravers themselves also contributed.

The movements of Romanticism, Realism and Symbolism were common to painting and literature. Inter-relationships between the practitioners bore unexpected fruits: Baudelaire's passion for Delacroix and for Wagner, for example, had a profound influence on his poetry. The brief period of Symbolist dominance brought together all the arts in an unprecedented unity.

Art became one of the principal topics discussed in literature. Novels were full of painters and paintings: Gustave Moreau lives again through the pages of Huysmans' *A Rebours*, and Cézanne haunts Zola's *L'Oeuvre*. In Proust's *A la Recherche du temps perdu*, Elstir, Vinteuil and La Berma are the synthesis of all the painters, musicians and artists of the turn of the century.

Thus literature, too, has its place in the Musée d'Orsay. It will be discussed in debates and lectures, in terms of its relationship to art and history; it will even feature – somewhat paradoxically one might think – in exhibitions, displayed on the walls together with the paintings (though that will seem less strange if one refers to Pierre Larousse's *Grand Dictionnaire Universel du XIXème siècle* and reads its astonishing definition of a museum: '... *fig:* Collection, assembly for the purposes of study. A dictionary, with its many examples, is a *Museum*').

Hugo once likened 'cathedrals of paper' to cathedrals of stone: both are monuments, both endure.

297 *E. Manet:* Stéphane Mallarmé *(1842–98), poet, 1876.*
27.5 × 36 (10.8 × 14.2).
Acquired 1928 with the assistance of the Société des Amis du Louvre and D. David-Weill.

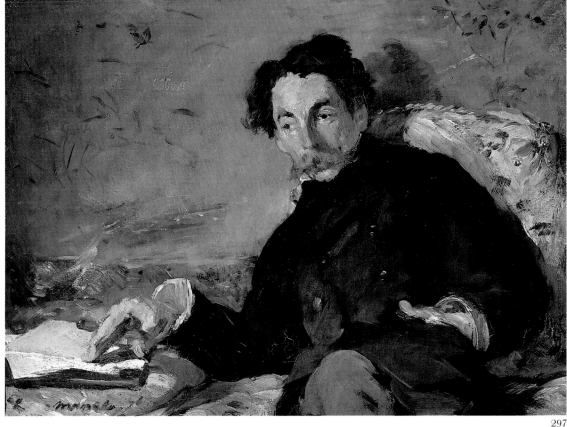

Index

Numbers in *italic* refer to the illustrations.

Photo credits

Réunion des musées nationaux (D. Arnaudet, G. Blot, C. Jean, J. Schormans)
and Musée d'Orsay (Jim Purcell)
with the exception of the following:
Fonds Urphot (pp 10, 11)
Bibliothèque nationale (195, 196, 198, 199)
Cliché musée de Roubaix (215)
Cinémathèque française (295)
Lyon, coll. Institut Lumière (294)

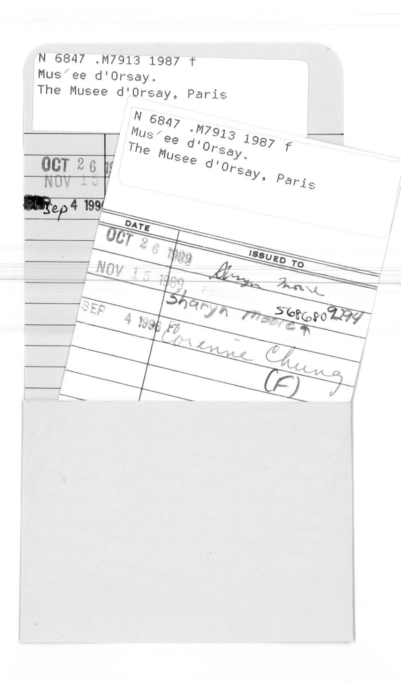